IMAGES
of America

HILO

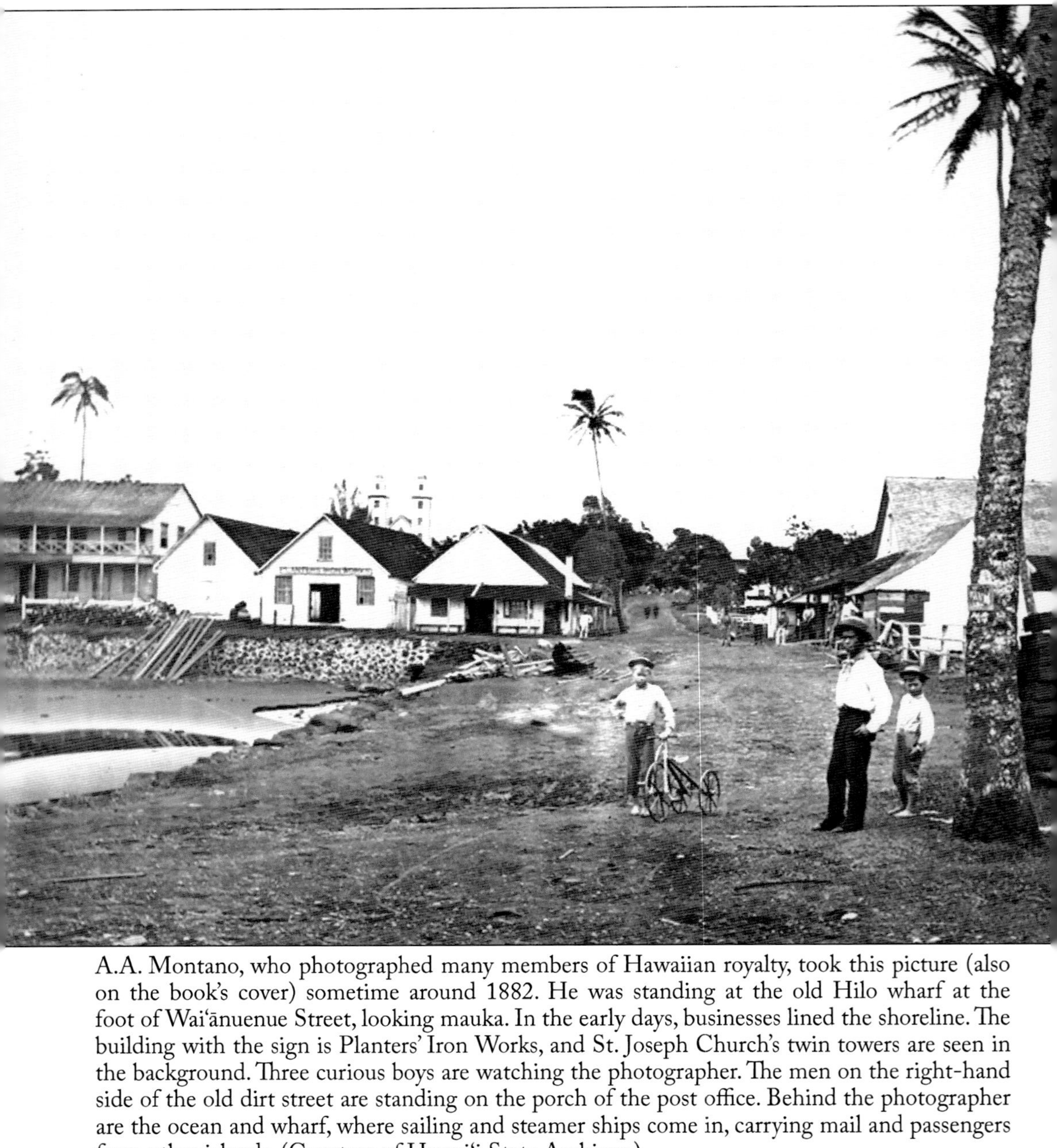

A.A. Montano, who photographed many members of Hawaiian royalty, took this picture (also on the book's cover) sometime around 1882. He was standing at the old Hilo wharf at the foot of Wai'ānuenue Street, looking mauka. In the early days, businesses lined the shoreline. The building with the sign is Planters' Iron Works, and St. Joseph Church's twin towers are seen in the background. Three curious boys are watching the photographer. The men on the right-hand side of the old dirt street are standing on the porch of the post office. Behind the photographer are the ocean and wharf, where sailing and steamer ships come in, carrying mail and passengers from other islands. (Courtesy of Hawai'i State Archives.)

IMAGES
of America

HILO

K.M. Valentine

ARCADIA
PUBLISHING

ISBN 978-1-4671-3126-1

Published by Arcadia Publishing
Charleston, South Carolina

Printed in the United States of America

Library of Congress Control Number: 2014932225

For all general information, please contact Arcadia Publishing:
Telephone 843-853-2070
Fax 843-853-0044
E-mail sales@arcadiapublishing.com
For customer service and orders:
Toll-Free 1-888-313-2665

Visit us on the Internet at www.arcadiapublishing.com

This book is dedicated to those intrepid chroniclers who explored Hawai'i Island in the 1800s and left their legacy in pictures and words, without which these stories could not be told today, and to the maka'ainana *of Hilo and their ancestors.*

CONTENTS

Acknowledgments

Cracked and fragile, the photographs sit in folders waiting to be carefully handled. Peering at handwritten notes several centuries old, I see that someone cared enough to leave a trace of history. These photographs lie in museums and archives, but thankfully today also on the Internet in sources such as Wikimedia, US National Archives and Records Administration, and the National Oceanic and Atmospheric Administration/National Geophysical Data Center (NOAA/NGDC) Natural Hazards Photo Archive. A unique and valuable resource for me was the Hawai'i State Archives. Established by statute in 1905 and located on the grounds of 'Iolani Palace in Honolulu, the archives collects, preserves, and makes available to the public Hawai'i government records and donated photographs dating from the monarchy to the present time. In Hilo, I am especially grateful to Miki Bulos, archivist for the Lyman Museum, and Barbara Shipman, descendent of the Shipman missionary-and-business family. Special gratitude goes to Wayne Subica, director of the Hawai'i Plantation Museum, for his generosity in sharing photographs and stories that he has collected over a period of nearly 50 years. Wayne is himself a plantation worker descendant and author of a number of books on Hawai'i Island history, which are included in the bibliography in the back of this book. The Hawai'i Plantation Museum opened its doors in Papaikou as a center for Hawai'i Island's rich sugar plantation history and cultural heritage. The purpose of the museum is to collect, preserve, and exhibit original artifacts and memorabilia from the plantation era for education and enjoyment. It has an all-volunteer staff. The Lyman Museum is a wonderful repository of not only missionary memorabilia and photographs, but also an amazing rock and mineral collection. The museum began when the descendants of New England missionaries David and Sarah Lyman chose to preserve their original home and family collections. Today, the restored Mission House is listed both as a historic property by the Historic Hawai'i Foundation and in the National Register of Historic Places. It is an invaluable source for anyone seeking to know more about Hilo's history and to attend museum events.

All unattributed images are included courtesy of the author.

Introduction

Hilo is a city today, but this was not always so. Hilo is also the name for two districts of the island of Hawai'i, and this was so before there was a city. Native Hawaiians had already divided their islands, or *moku*, into districts, as well as smaller divisions called *ahupua'a*. North Hilo and South Hilo once encompassed a series of small villages and agricultural settlements that dotted the densely foliated, multihued-green slopes that travel upward—just as rushing streams travel down—like spokes in a half-wheel whose hub is Hilo Bay. Among the villages were Waiākea, Wailuku, Ola'a, and Pana'ewa.

The sun rises over Hilo Bay and kisses the tops of the two great mountains, Mauna Kea and Mauna Loa, as it travels across the sky, creating rainbows that follow the waterfalls, constant mists, and heavy rains that frequent this eastern, and windward, side of the island. The sun then hides behind the vast mountains as it sets on the western, or leeward, side of the island, leaving behind rosy hues that color the sky and water of Hilo Bay as evening falls.

Nature rules in Hilo in a dramatic way. It provides for the people by way of the abundance of food products that can be grown here. It also commands respect when its more dramatic floods and waves loom large. Hilo is famous for being a city that has survived a series of one of the most destructive forces of nature—the tsunami—and yet has historic buildings still standing after it struck the downtown area. Ironically, the changed landscape left in the wake of the major waves of 1946 and 1960 is a series of scenic, oceanfront parks instead of buildings, a feature that residents and visitors alike enjoy today. Nature sometimes has a way of being the best of city planners.

Up until the early 18th century, all the Hawaiian Islands, including the Hilo area, were ruled by a polyglot mix of chiefs and kings whose entitlement came through a complicated system of relationships, not always directly aligned, as the practice of *hanai*, adopting offspring by different parents, was common and determined by politics or the perceived needs of the child. Wars and battles also determined which chief was going to rule which lands while he (or she) could hold onto them. The latter 18th century saw the consolidation of all the islands of Hawai'i into one kingdom for the first time; this was accomplished by the warrior who became King Kamehameha I. The Hilo districts were one of the centers of operations for the legendary king.

Just as the tsunami are a major force that has affected Hilo, other kinds of forces during the 19th century brought perhaps the most dramatic sociopolitical and cultural revolution the Hawaiian Islands has ever faced, and Hilo was impacted in a big way. It was during this time that Hawai'i was exposed to the world, forced to leave behind much of its native culture and become a globally recognized, sovereign country with diplomatic relations worldwide as well as a center of commerce for the entire Pacific region. Among those whose attention was caught by the sleepy islands was a cadre of missionaries who arrived and set up new Christian churches in order to bring enlightenment to the "heathens" of Hilo at the same time hundreds of whaling and trading ships unloaded sailors ready for fun and mayhem. The zealous and earnest missionaries had their hands full with the double duty of reforming natives and taming debauched sailors. As well-intentioned as the missionaries were, with admirable educational endeavors, there is much to say about Native Hawaiian spiritual beliefs and practices that were suppressed during this incursion of foreign religion, even though Christianity was endorsed by the ruling monarchs of the time. The repercussions remain today.

Descendants of missionaries soon became the leading business personalities in Hilo. After being educated on the mainland, they returned to participate in the great land grab made possible by the decisions of the monarchy to parcel out land to both foreigners and high-ranking Hawaiians in a move called the Great Mahele. Many foreigners married Hawaiian women, which also facilitated their accumulation of property.

With Hilo Bay providing a safe anchorage for ships, it became a center for transpacific and interisland shipping and commerce. Hawai'i was "discovered" by navigators from many foreign countries, and it became a target for potential colonial expansion as well as a center for the trading of goods, such as the valuable sandalwood and pulu that were native to the islands. As lands were denuded, the potential for agricultural products grew in the form of pineapples, coffee, and, finally, sugar. Travel increased between islands and also across the Pacific. More foreigners arrived during the late 19th and early 20th century in the form of Japanese, Chinese, and Filipino labor, brought in when the burgeoning Hawaiian sugar plantations were finding a local labor shortage. Sadly, the labor shortage had come in part as the result of foreigners' diseases that had decimated the indigenous population.

New communities or neighborhoods, called camps, were constructed to house each of the groups, divided up by individual cultures and languages. Efforts were made to continue their cultural practices, languages, religions, and social life. A brand-new language developed called Hawaiian Pidgin. In common use today, it evolved from a mixture of words and phrases in Hawaiian, English, Chinese, Portuguese, Japanese, and Filipino all jumbled together. Descendants of these immigrants became leaders of the community over the following decades as merchants, professionals, and politicians. Hilo is a rainbow of cultures and people living side by side. For example, even today there exists the Hawai'i Island Chamber of Commerce, Japanese Chamber of Commerce, Filipino Chamber of Commerce, and Portuguese Chamber of Commerce.

The east side of the island experienced a new prosperity thanks to its abundant water supply, rich soil, and favorable shipping and transportation systems. Sugar plantations flourished in neighboring districts as well, and Hilo became a major center of railroads to transport the crop, people, and supplies. The collection of small villages became a city with streets, roads, and bridges, as well as thriving businesses, a university, and the seat of government for the island.

Geopolitical influences all over the world impacted Hawai'i, not the least of which was the overthrow of the monarchy and annexation of Hawai'i by the United States in 1893. Hilo in the 20th century rode the wave of all of these developments up until World War II and the great tsunami of 1946, which ends the period of time covered by this book.

One

The Hilo Landscape and People in Ancient Hawaiʻi

The population of Hilo was in ancient times, as it is now, concentrated primarily surrounding Hilo Bay, but originally it was in scattered settlements.

The reason for this, as well as personal characteristics of the Native Hawaiians, are described in the highly respected guide to native Hawaiian life *Native Planters in Old Hawaii, Their Life, Lore, and Environment*:

> The nature of the terrain and the requirements of farming favored the dispersal of homesteads rather than the development of compact villages. . . . And it was because wars were rare that isolated homesteads were safe to live in. . . . There were villages only where the aggregation of houses around good fishing localities along the shore induced propinquity, or where the availability of fresh water was limited.

As a people, the Hawaiians were peaceful and friendly.

> The planter did not have a calculating mind. He was not a trader. There being no great density of population, and such as there was being dispersed rather than concentrated in villages, there was sharing and giving and receiving instead of trade. These stemmed from motives of practicality, sympathetic interest in the general welfare of the scattered *ʻohana* (family), and as a matter of self-respect. Generosity was admired, and it enhanced both self-respect and prestige. His relationship to *akua* (gods), *kāhuna* (priests), and *aliʻi* (chiefs) was less a matter of calculation or expectation than of affectionate dependence, mixed with reverence, awe, and sometimes fear . . . His was a temperament which by reason of comfort and the beauty and bountifulness of nature, luxuriated in a sense of well-being and expressed itself in exuberant cheerfulness; in a word, he enjoyed life wholly, and in consequence felt and spontaneously expressed aloha.

Foreigners who arrived in the Hilo area found the Hawaiians to be welcoming and willing to assist. Being comfortable with the landscape, they often carried luggage and even sedan chairs on foot, traveling over treacherous terrain, down steep gullies, and over mountains. They provided passage in outrigger canoes and also, as reported by missionary Titus Coan, carried men on their shoulders while crossing raging streams and rivers.

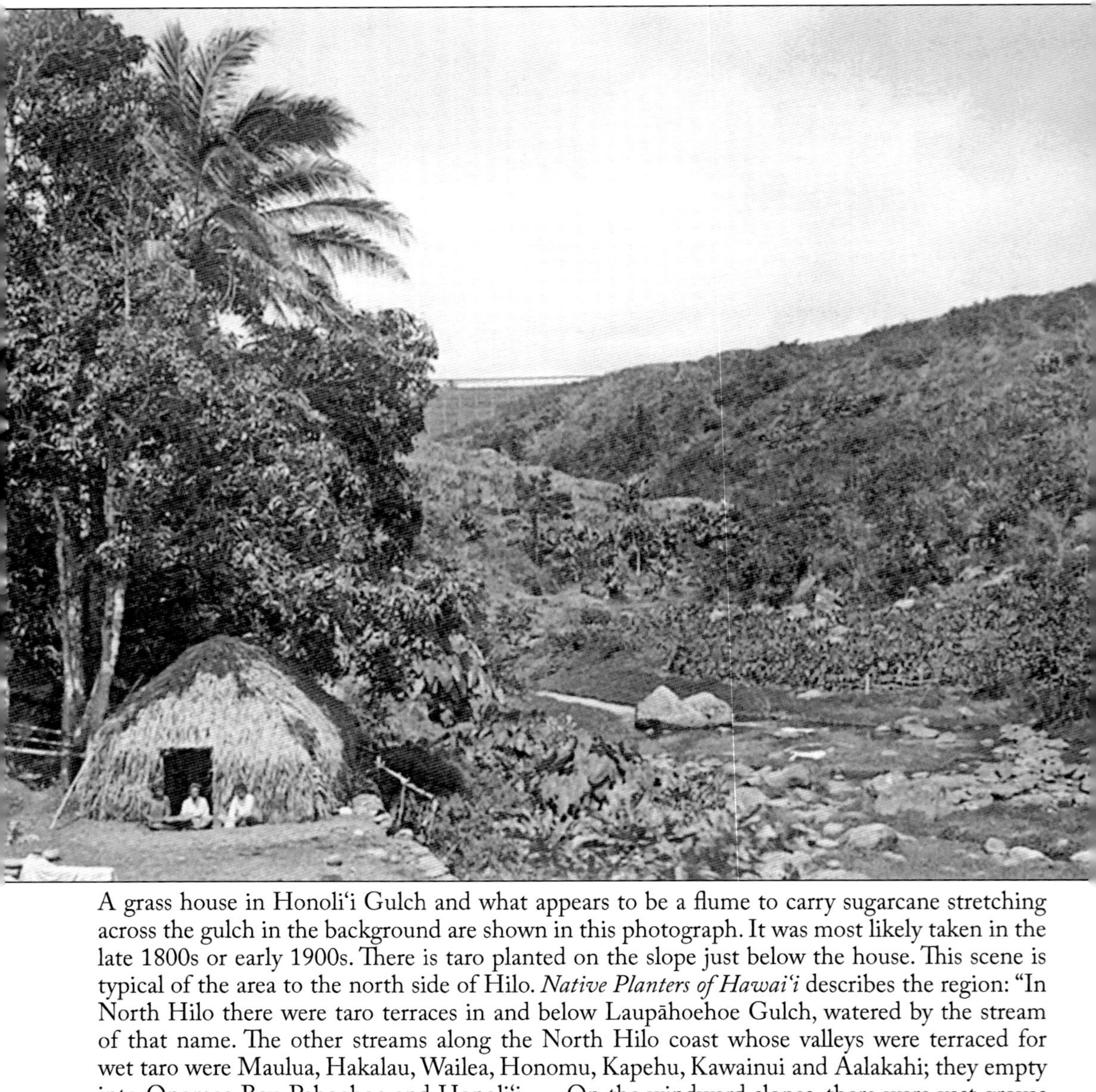

A grass house in Honoli'i Gulch and what appears to be a flume to carry sugarcane stretching across the gulch in the background are shown in this photograph. It was most likely taken in the late 1800s or early 1900s. There is taro planted on the slope just below the house. This scene is typical of the area to the north side of Hilo. *Native Planters of Hawai'i* describes the region: "In North Hilo there were taro terraces in and below Laupāhoehoe Gulch, watered by the stream of that name. The other streams along the North Hilo coast whose valleys were terraced for wet taro were Maulua, Hakalau, Wailea, Honomu, Kapehu, Kawainui and Aalakahi; they empty into Onomea Bay, Pahoehoe and Honoli'i . . . On the windward slopes, there were vast groves of candlenut trees before the forests were razed to make way for the sugar-cane [*sic*] fields that covered the slopes during the late 19th and 20th centuries. Within the candlenut groves were clearings where taro was cultivated in the old days. Taro flourished in these patches with great luxuriance, it is said, fertilized by the decaying leaves, trunks and branches of the felled trees."

This 1825 painting by artist Robert Dampier is titled *'Karaikapa, a Native of the Sandwich Islands.* Judging by his clothing, he is likely not a child of chiefly rank, although he is wearing a neck ornament. *Native Planters of Hawai'i* distinguishes between people of common rank and those in ali'i, or chiefly, families: "Only in the ali'i families was there any accumulation of wealth in the form of feather capes and garlands, whale-tooth neck pendants, feather helmets, and emblems of rank, carved utensils, handsomely decorated sheets of bark cloth, canoes, and, in post-discovery days, substantial trade goods of all sorts." This painting hangs at Washington Place, the former home of Queen Lili'uokalani, in Honolulu.

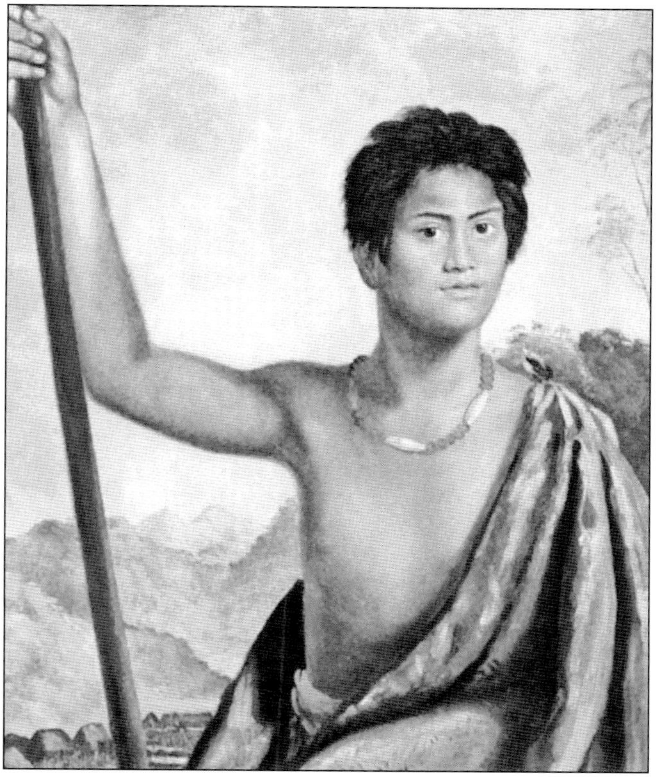

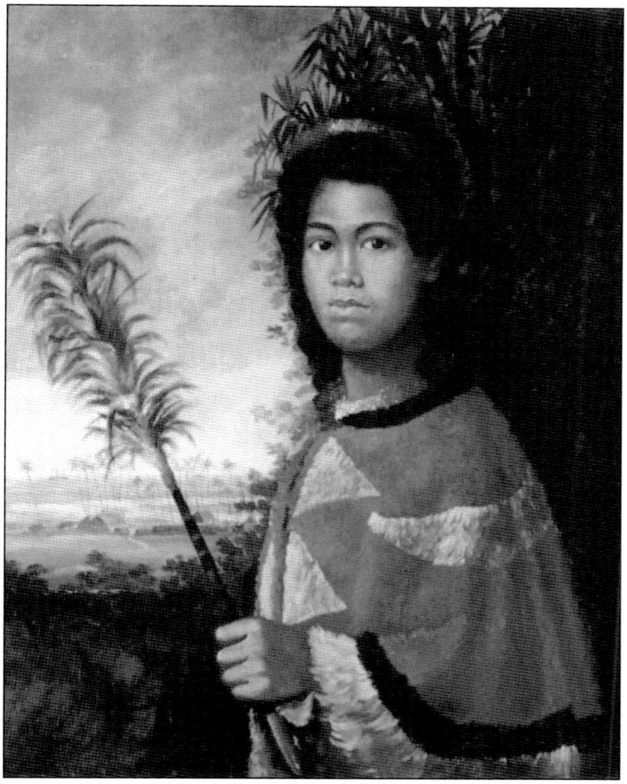

Dampier, an Englishman, was chosen to be the expedition artist on the ship HMS *Blonde* under the command of Capt. George Anson Byron. The ship was returning the bodies of King Kamehameha II and Queen Kamāmalu to the Hawaiian Islands (known by the British as the Sandwich Islands), after both died from measles during a visit to England. Dampier spent 11 weeks in Hawai'i painting portraits in oil and making pencil drawings of landscapes. Here is his 1825 portrait of Princess Nahi'ena'ena of Hawai'i, daughter of Kamehameha I and sister of Kamehameha III.

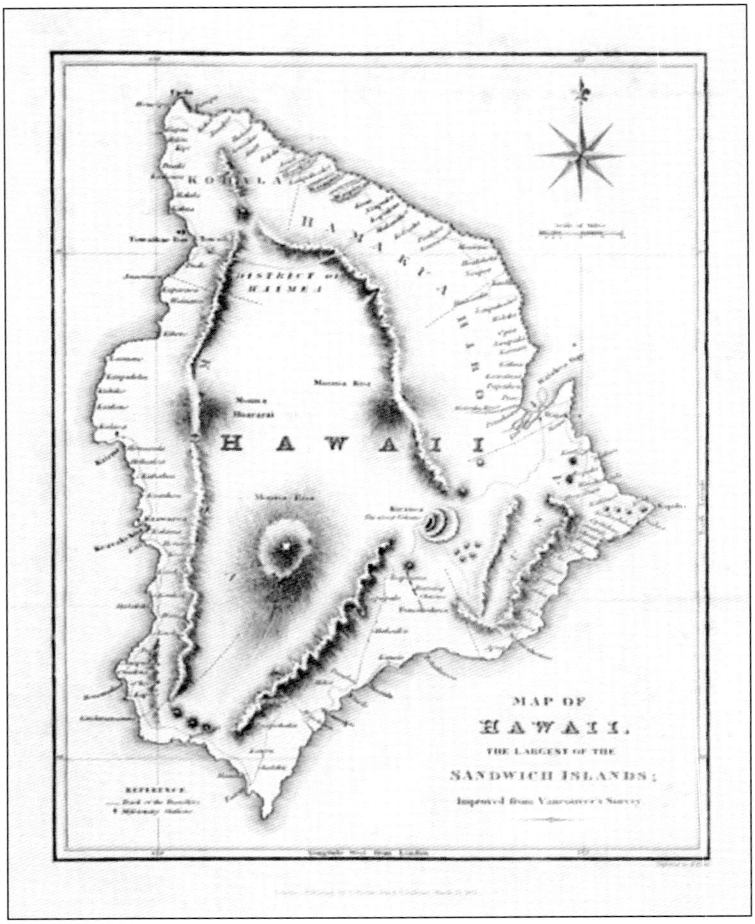

The missionary William Ellis toured Hawai'i Island in 1823 on a scouting expedition to locate missions. He traveled by canoe, on horseback, and by foot, describing in detail the terrain and people in his journals. This drawing was published in *Narrative of an 1823 Tour Through Hawai'i* by Ellis in 1826. It is extremely detailed, showing many towns, bays, anchor places, volcanoes, mountains, paths, roads, and missionary stations.

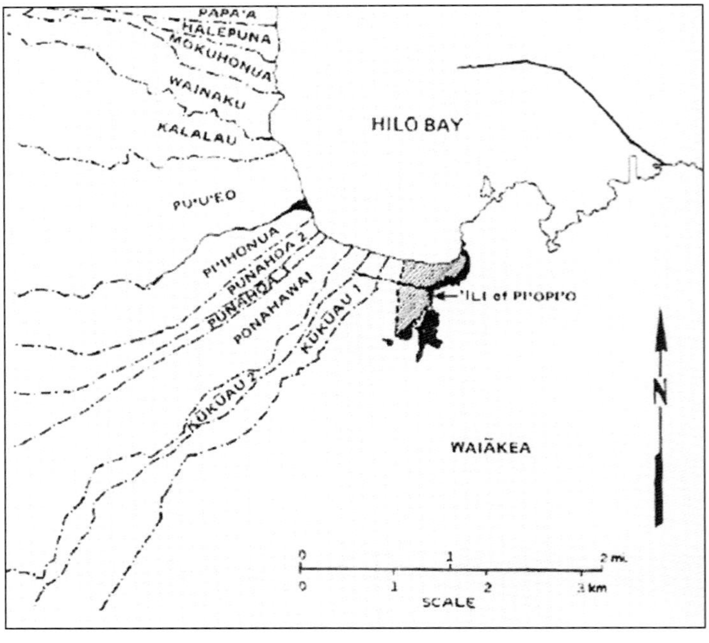

This map shows the ahupua'a of Hilo. It was the renowned High Chief Umi of the Island of Hawai'i, based in the Hilo area, who originated the practice of dividing the lands of the islands into districts and subdistricts. Other islands followed his example. Divisions that remain to this day are seen in the districts and ahupua'a of the area. In the early times, the ahupua'a was ruled by a chief, or ali'i, and was, in turn, divided into smaller sections that were allotted to families.

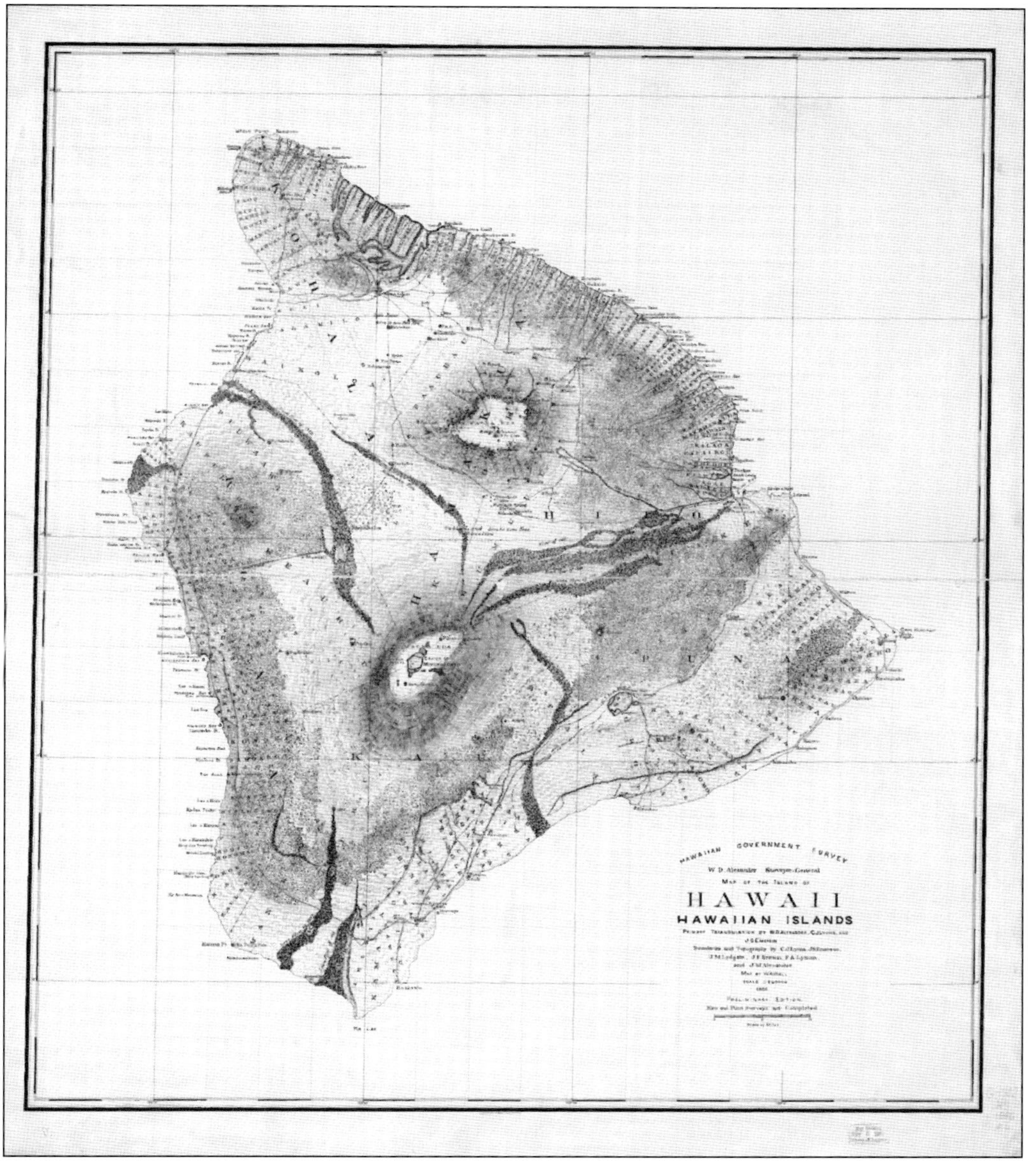

As William Ellis viewed the land from the sea, he wrote, "The face of the country by which we sailed was fertile and beautiful, and the population throughout considerable. The numerous plantations on the tops or sides of the deep ravines, or vallies [*sic*], by which they were frequently interspersed, with the meandering streams running down them into the sea, presented altogether a most agreeable prospect." The city of Hilo is centered within the two districts of South Hilo and North Hilo. An ahupua'a is a smaller division, originally designed as a section of land that has all the attributes to support a community, and is typically a long, pie-shaped section that stretches from the mountain to the sea. Within that area lie lands of different elevations, each of which favors the growing of different food crops. At the sea would be fishing and the making of salt, as well as the collection of seaweeds. At the higher elevations would be the forests that supply wood for making canoes and birds to be used for food or feather harvesting. This detailed Hawaiian Government Survey map from 1886 shows even greater detail of the island upon which Hilo sits. (Courtesy of Library of Congress.)

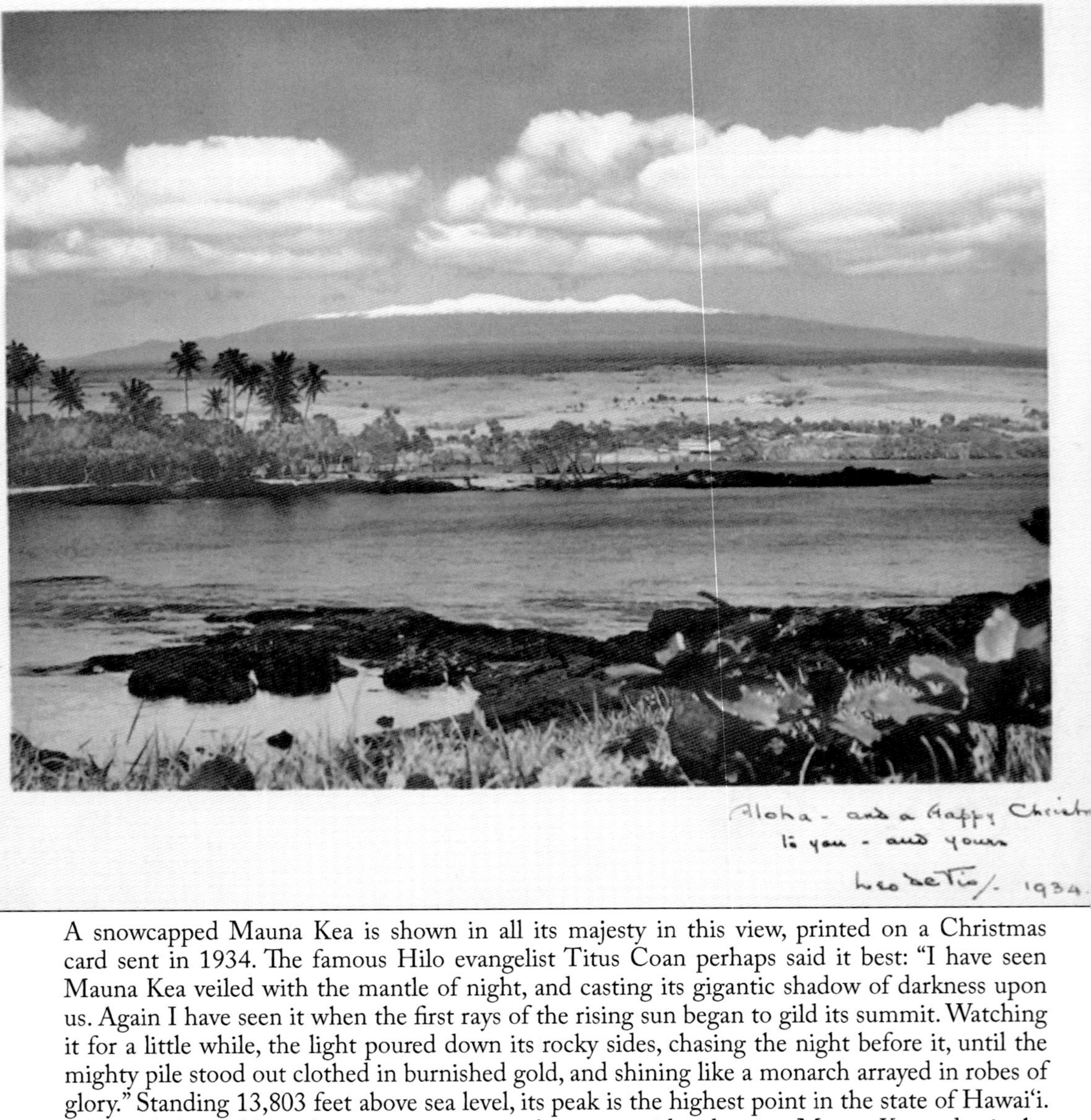

A snowcapped Mauna Kea is shown in all its majesty in this view, printed on a Christmas card sent in 1934. The famous Hilo evangelist Titus Coan perhaps said it best: "I have seen Mauna Kea veiled with the mantle of night, and casting its gigantic shadow of darkness upon us. Again I have seen it when the first rays of the rising sun began to gild its summit. Watching it for a little while, the light poured down its rocky sides, chasing the night before it, until the mighty pile stood out clothed in burnished gold, and shining like a monarch arrayed in robes of glory." Standing 13,803 feet above sea level, its peak is the highest point in the state of Hawai'i. Although formed by volcanic action, it is no longer considered active. Mauna Kea today is the site of numerous astronomical observatories owned by different nations. They have often been in conflict with the Native Hawaiian understandings of Mauna Kea as a sacred site and temple. With its high altitude, dry environment, and stable airflow, Mauna Kea's summit is one of the best sites in the world for astronomical observation, and one of the most controversial. Since the creation of an access road in 1964, a total of 13 telescopes funded by 11 countries have been constructed at the summit; more are planned to come.

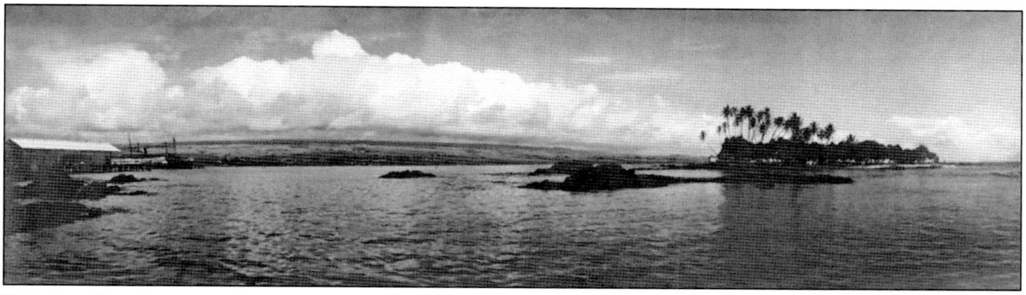

Panoramic photographs were popular beginning in the late 1880s, and the Hawai'i State Archives has a collection of them. One is this image from around 1910, with a view of Hilo and Coconut Island. The Big Island's other majestic mountain, Mauna Loa, is shown in the background. Appearing as a gentle, rounded-peaked, serene mountain, it is a still-active volcano that has surprised Hilo residents several times. Standing 13,679 feet above sea level, it is the most massive mountain on earth when measured from its base in the ocean. The photographer was R.W. Perkins. (Courtesy of Hawai'i State Archives.)

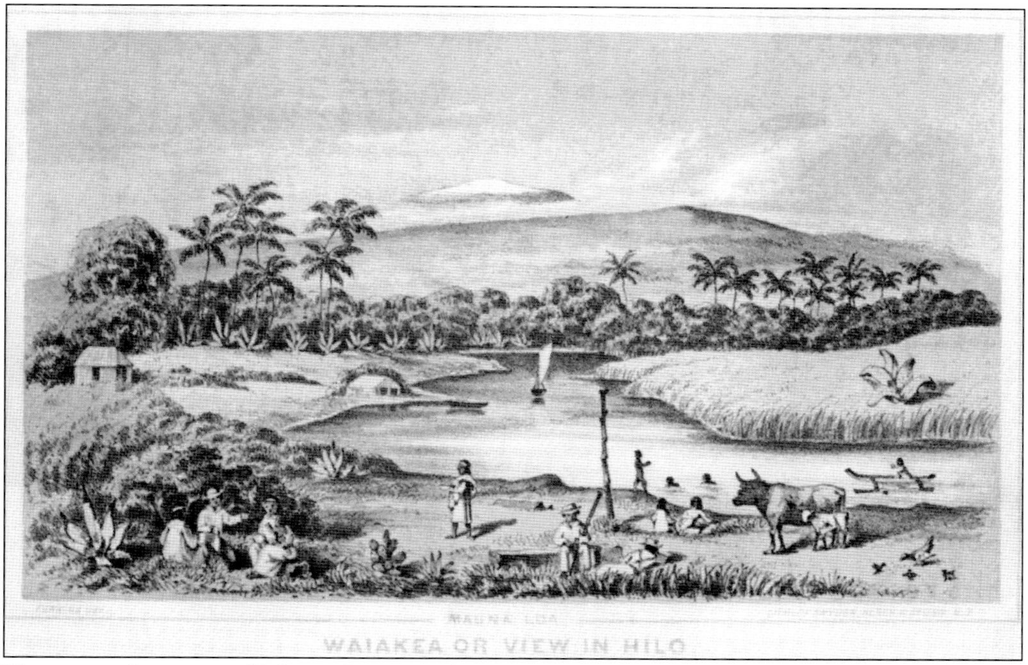

This is another view of Mauna Loa in a drawing by Edward T. Perkins, titled *Waiākea or View in Hilo*, dated 1854, from his book *Na Motu; or, Reef-Rovings in the South Seas*. It shows Native Hawaiian life along the Wailoa River.

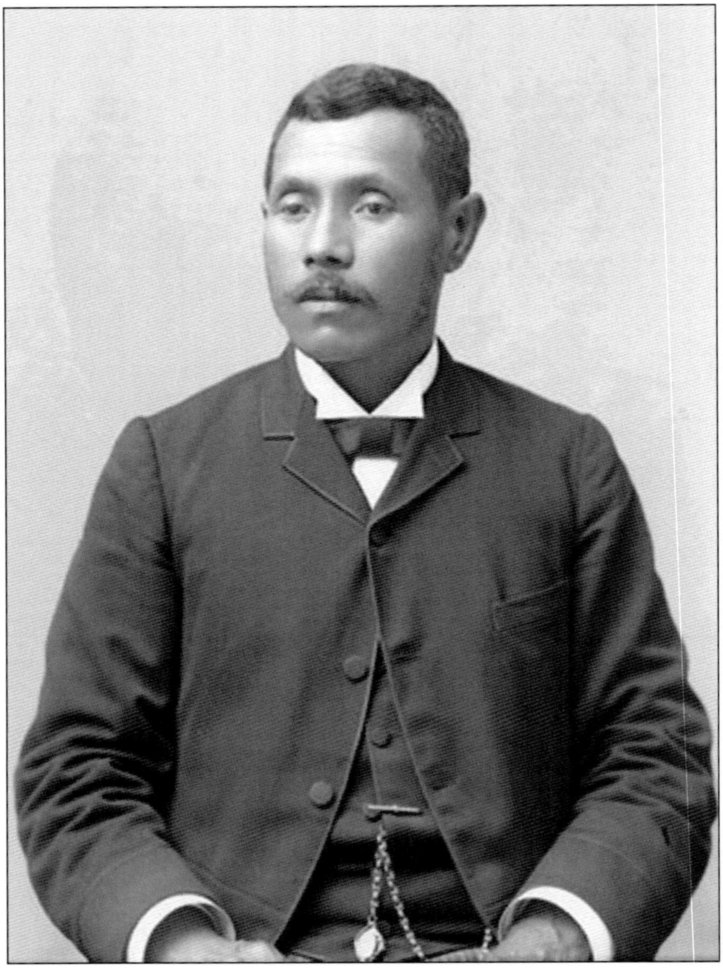

A famous artist from Hilo was Joseph Nāwahī. Nāwahī was not only a Native Hawaiian painter, but also a legislator, lawyer, activist, and newspaper publisher. As a young man, he was educated in Protestant mission schools such as the Hilo Boarding School, the Royal School, and Lahainaluna School on Maui. (Courtesy of Mission Houses Museum, Honolulu.)

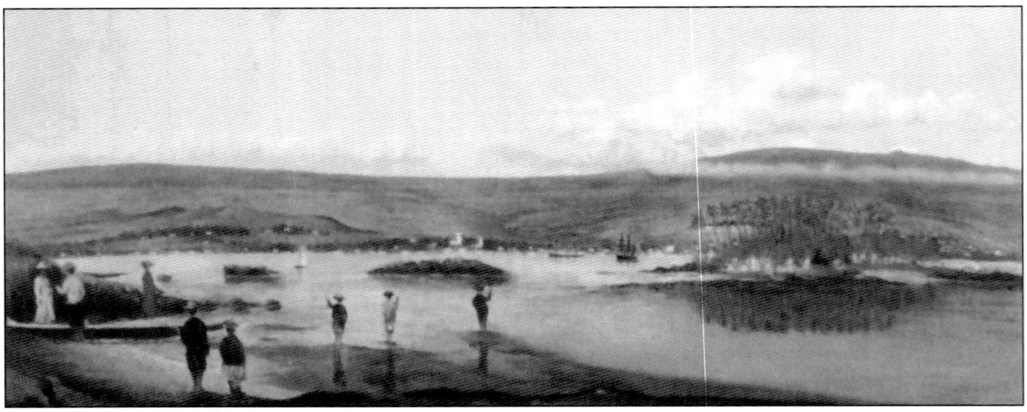

Nāwahī was born January 13, 1842, at Kaimū, in the Puna District. He served for 20 years in the Hawaiian Legislature and was a member of the cabinet of Queen Lili'uokalani, serving as her minister of foreign affairs, and was head of the Liberal Party. He was also the president of the Hawaiian Patriotic League and opposed the 1893 overthrow of the Kingdom of Hawai'i. Nāwahī operated *Ke Aloha Aina*, a Hawaiian-language newspaper. Shown here is one of his famous works, the c. 1888 *View of Hilo Bay*, owned by Kamehameha Schools of O'ahu.

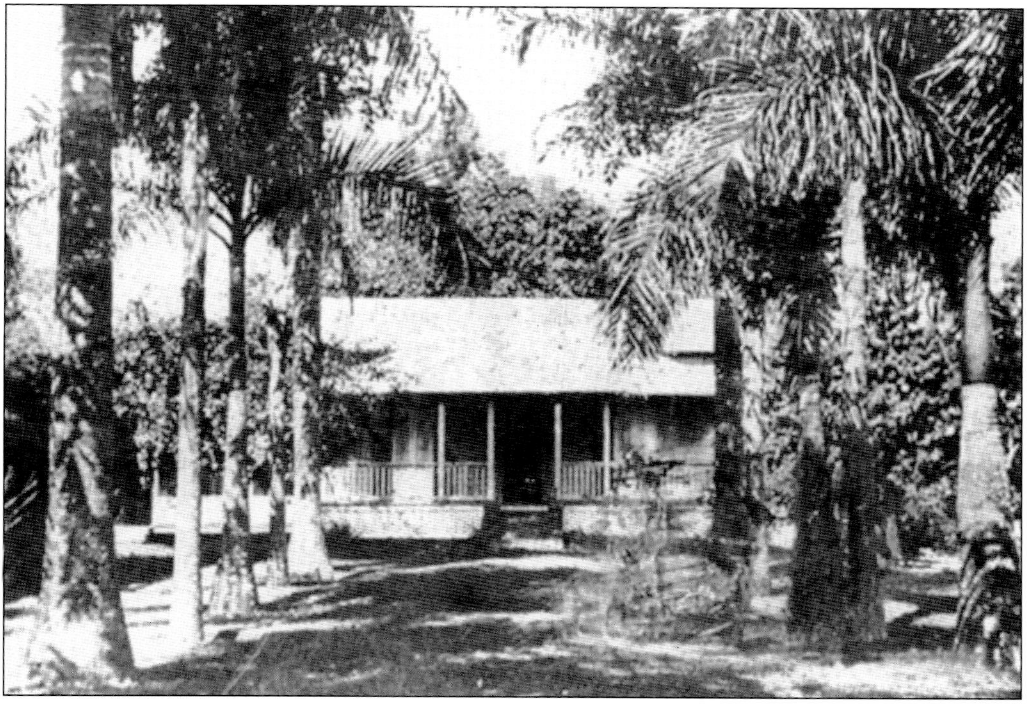

In December 1894, a search warrant was served on his Kapālama home looking for "sundry arms and ammunition." Although nothing was found, Nāwahī was arrested for treason and spent nearly three months in jail. It is believed that this is where he caught the tuberculosis that would later take his life. He was a self-taught artist and was the first Native Hawaiian to become an accomplished painter in the western style. Only five or six of his paintings are known to exist. Pictured above is Nāwahī's home in Hilo. Pictured below is his c. 1868 painting *Hilo Bay*. (Below, courtesy of Mission Houses Museum, Honolulu.)

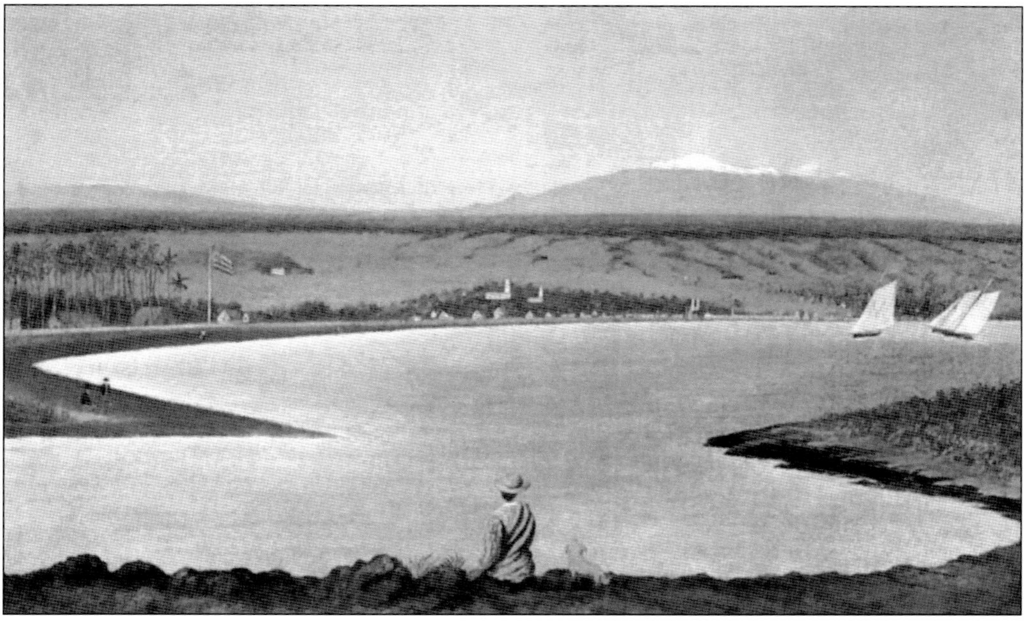

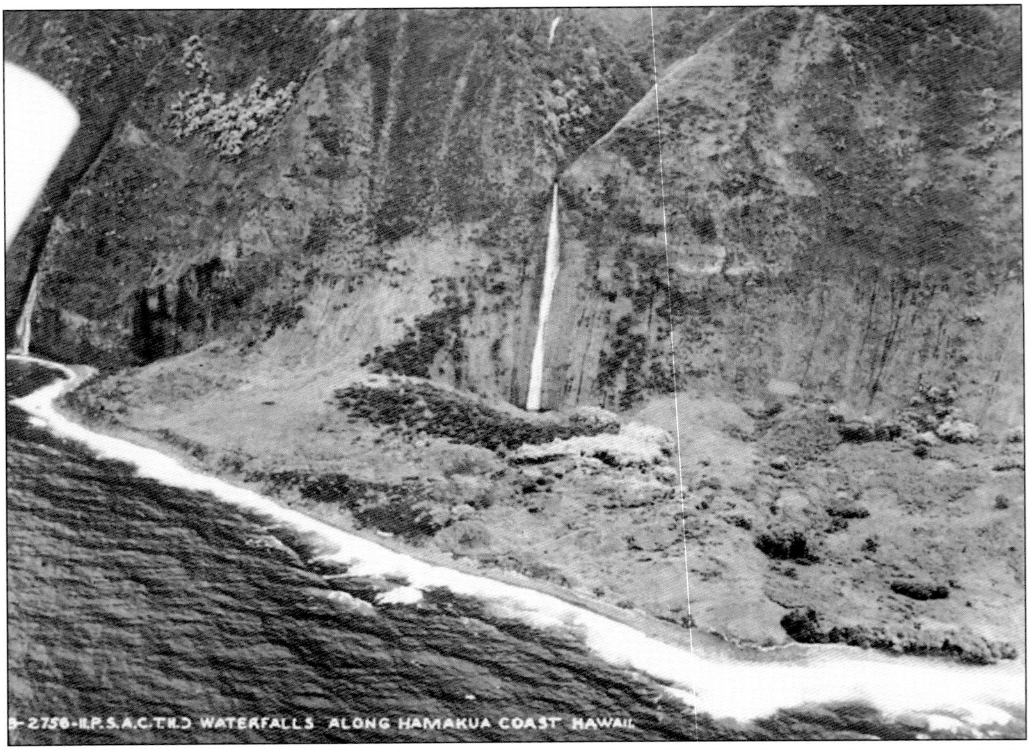

Many waterfalls grace the coastline north of Hilo town. This photograph was taken in the 1920s from a US Army Air Corps plane, yet this is still a typical scene today. (NOAA/NGDC Natural Hazards Photo Archive.)

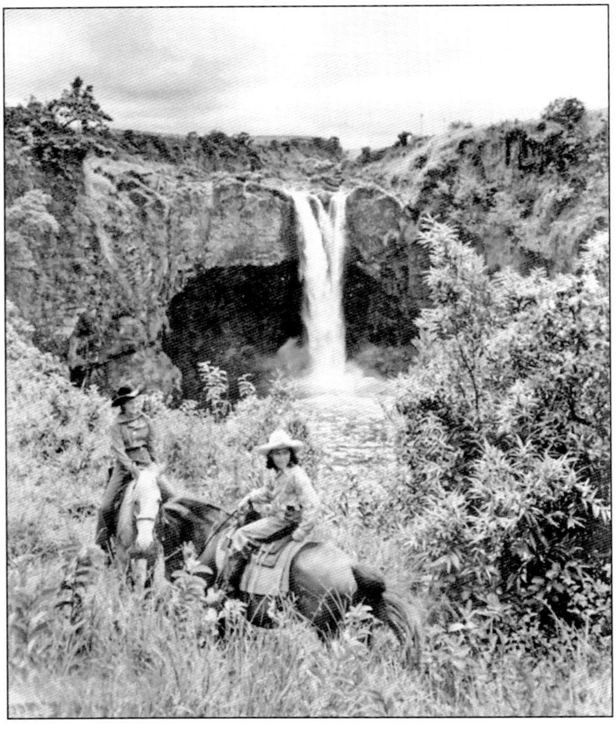

Two girls on horseback are at Rainbow Falls in Hilo. Today, it is part of Wailuku River State Park. The waterfall's name in the Hawaiian language is Wai'ānuenue (literally "rainbow water"); a street near the falls in Hilo also carries that name. Rainbow Falls derives its name from the fact that on sunny mornings around 10:00, rainbows can be seen in the mist thrown up by the waterfall. These falls on the Wailuku River flow over a natural lava cave that is the mythological home of Hina, an ancient Hawaiian goddess said to be the mother of the demigod Maui. In the Hawaiian language, the name of the river is translated from *wai*, meaning "fresh water," and *luku*, meaning "destruction," essentially making it "river of destruction." The date of the image is unknown. (Courtesy of Hawai'i State Archives.)

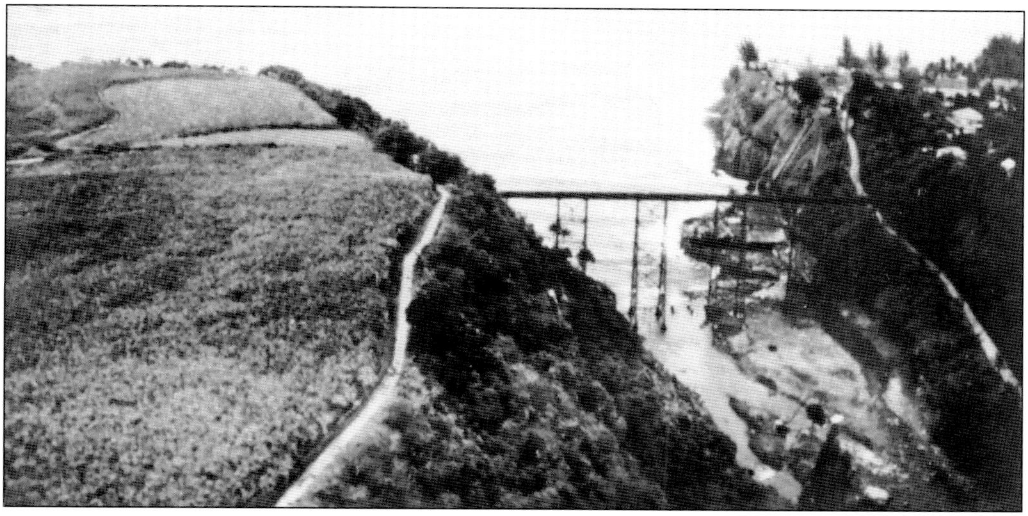

Another aerial view dramatically showing the depth of the gulches north of Hilo is this photograph of Hakalau Gulch, with the Hakalau Sugar Plantation on the opposite side and a flume constructed across the span. (Courtesy of NOAA/NGDC Natural Hazards Photo Archive.)

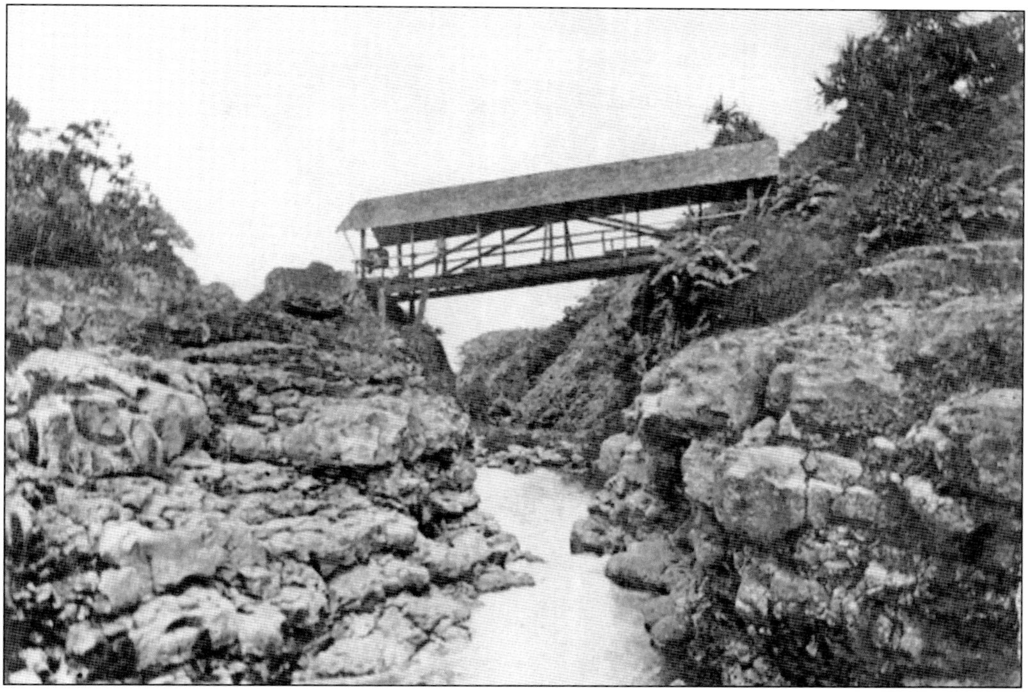

This photograph from around 1880 shows the earliest recorded bridge in Hawai'i—a crude footbridge across the Wailuku River at Hilo—as reported by missionary C.S. Stewart in 1825. Hilo's dangerous Wailuku River was finally spanned again in September 1859, this time by a 196-foot-long suspension bridge. Less than seven weeks after it was opened, this bridge collapsed while being crossed by a party of 8 or 10 persons and their horses; the group narrowly averted death from the falling timbers or by drowning. In 1923, the railroad bridge over this same river collapsed just after one loaded passenger train had crossed and as another was approaching. For a more extensive, illustrated treatment of island bridges, see "Early Hawaiian Bridges" in the *Hawaiian Journal of History* (1986). (Courtesy of Hawai'i State Archives.)

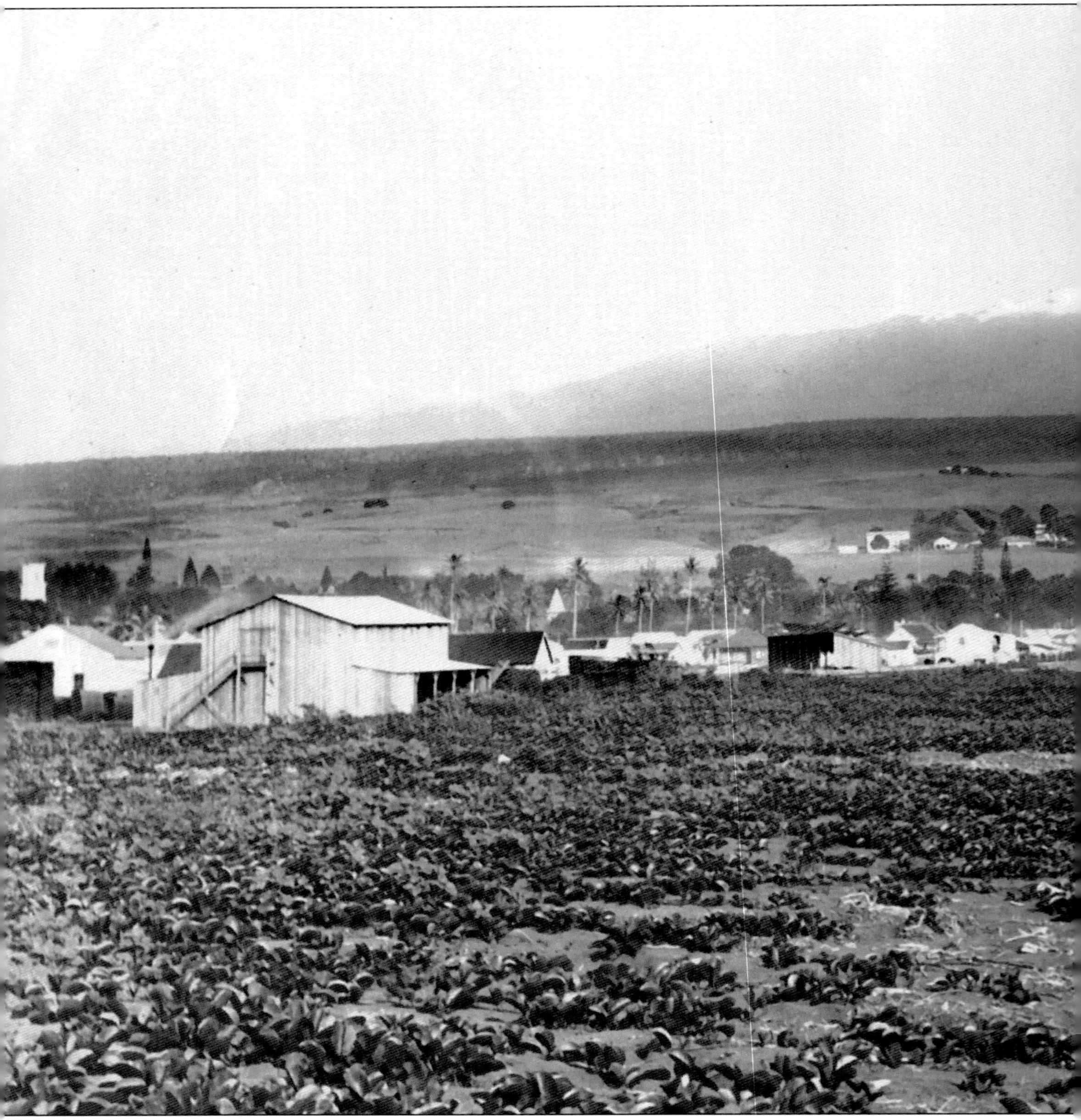

A c. 1895 photograph shows a broad view of Hilo and Hilo Bay, with Mauna Kea in the background. In the foreground is a marshy area near Waiākea Stream and Pond, where taro was once grown, that today is filled in. *Native Planters in Old Hawai'i* describes how "in the marshes surrounding Waiākea Bay, east of Hilo, taro was planted in a unique way, known as *kanu*

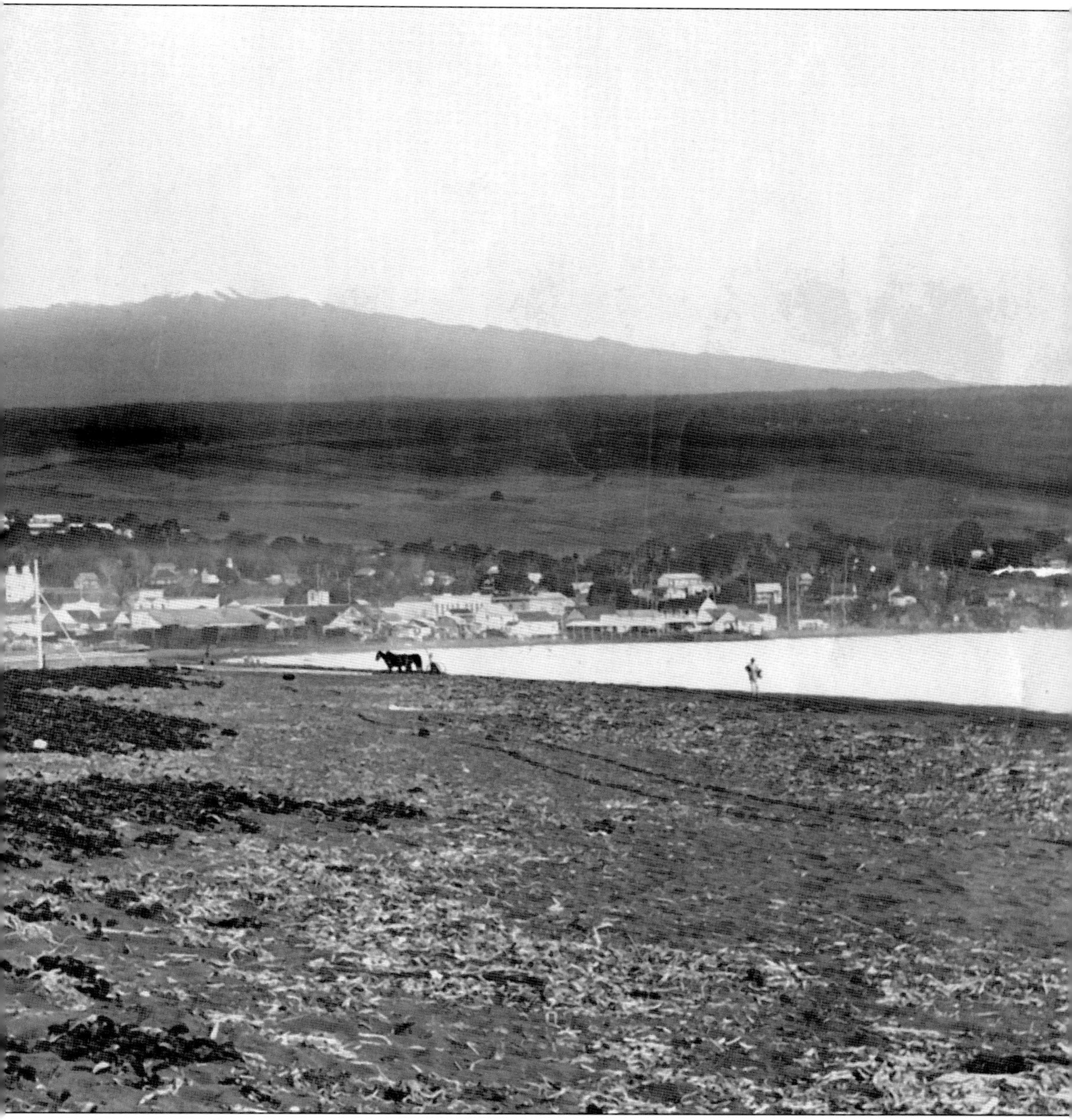

kipi. Long mounds were built on the marshy bottom with their surface two or three feet above water level. Upon the top and along the sides of these mounds taro was planted. Flood waters which occasionally submerged the entire mound are said to have done no harm, as the flow was imperceptible." (Courtesy of Hawai'i State Archives.)

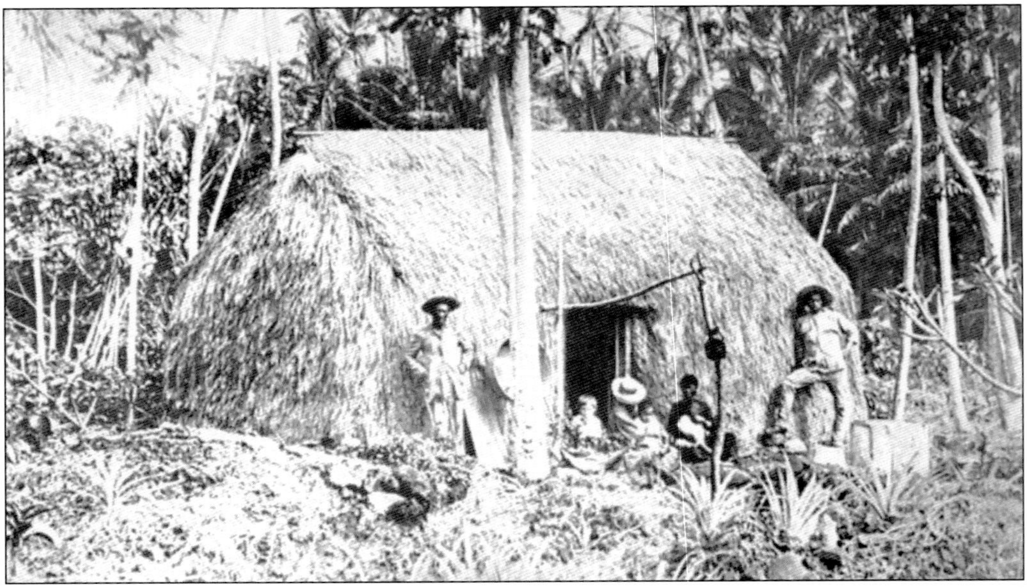

A Native Hawaiian grass house built among the trees is shown in this photograph from around 1901. Pineapple plants are in the front. The Great Mahele of 1848 made the term *kuleana* into a legal definition meaning that its tenant was granted fee simple title to the land that he or she had previously been managing under the former feudal system. Kuleana in old Hawaiian meant rights, responsibility, and stewardship. It was the first time that any kind of ownership was conferred in the kingdom. This photograph appears in *Report of the Governor of the Territory of Hawai'i, 1901.*

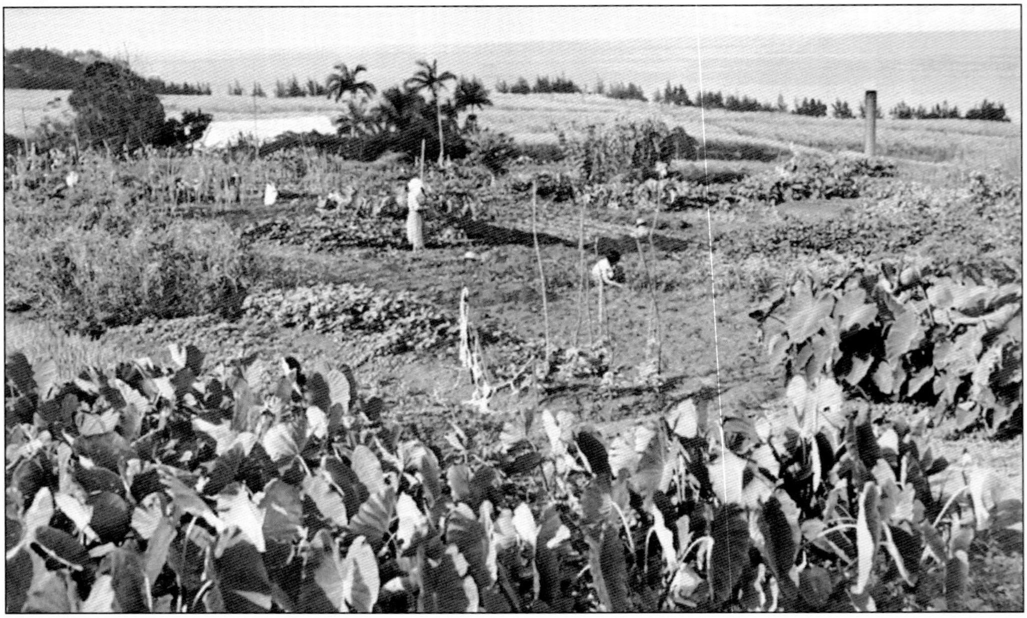

This family has a large taro and vegetable garden during the 1930s. The land supports the growing of many food crops. In the 1800s, William Ellis described the area: "The whole is covered with luxuriant vegetation, and the greater part of it formed into plantations, where plantains, bananas, sugarcane, taro, potatoes and melons come to the greatest perfection. Groves of coconut and breadfruit trees are seen in every direction, loaded with fruit, or clothed with luxuriant foliage." (Courtesy of Hawai'i State Archives.)

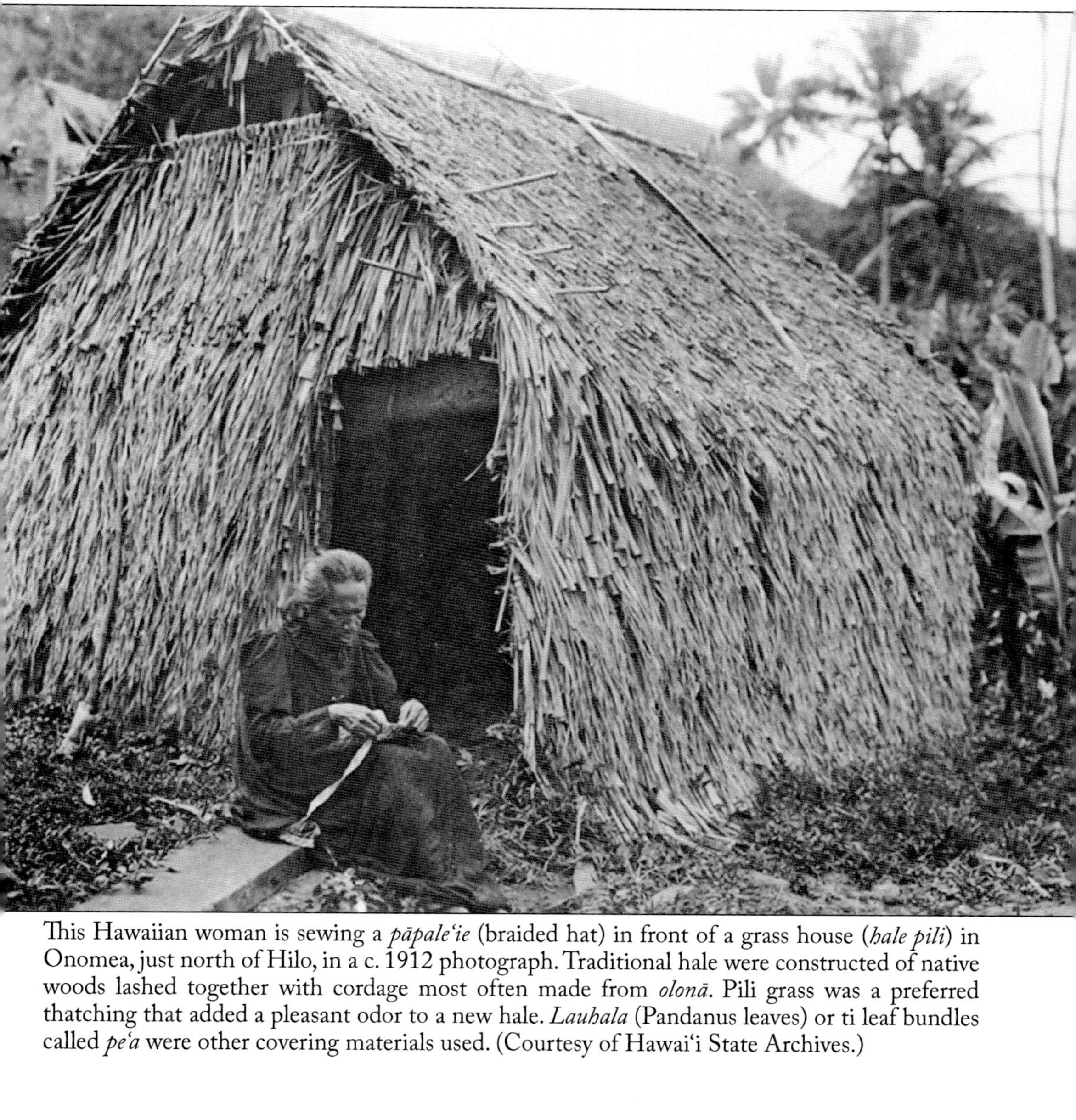

This Hawaiian woman is sewing a *pāpale'ie* (braided hat) in front of a grass house (*hale pili*) in Onomea, just north of Hilo, in a c. 1912 photograph. Traditional hale were constructed of native woods lashed together with cordage most often made from *olonā*. Pili grass was a preferred thatching that added a pleasant odor to a new hale. *Lauhala* (Pandanus leaves) or ti leaf bundles called *pe'a* were other covering materials used. (Courtesy of Hawai'i State Archives.)

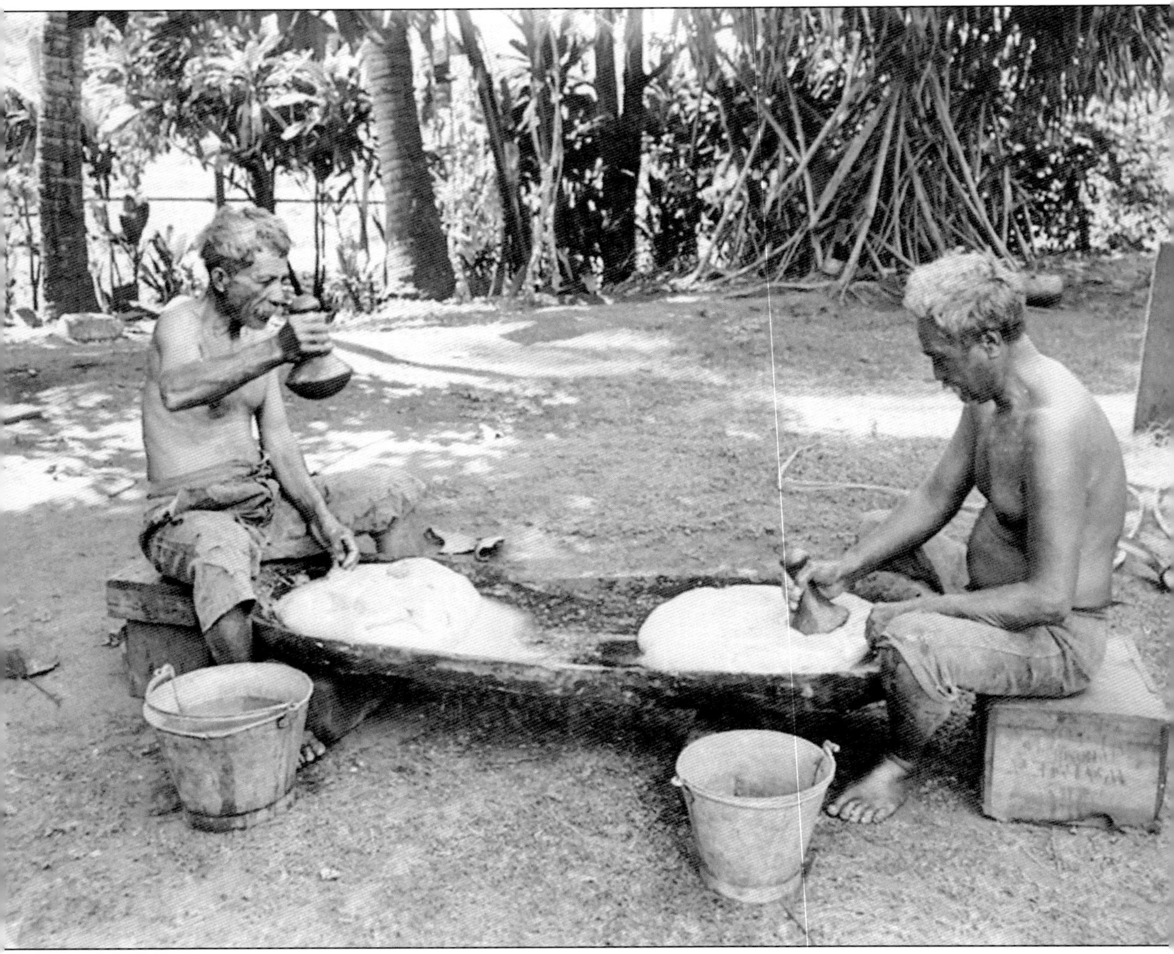

Taro, or *kalo,* a plant seen in many of these photographs, was the staple of the early Hawaiian diet, so much so that it was considered sacred. Poi is made from the root of the taro. Made by pounding the cooked root or corm, it is an extremely nourishing and easy to digest food that was fed to babies and adults alike. The poi bowl was a centerpiece of the Hawaiian table, with people helping themselves with their fingers. Poi comes in different consistencies, considered one-finger, two-finger, or three-finger depending on how many fingers it takes to scoop it out. These Hawaiian men are shown pounding poi, adding water to achieve the desired consistency. (Courtesy of Hawai'i State Archives.)

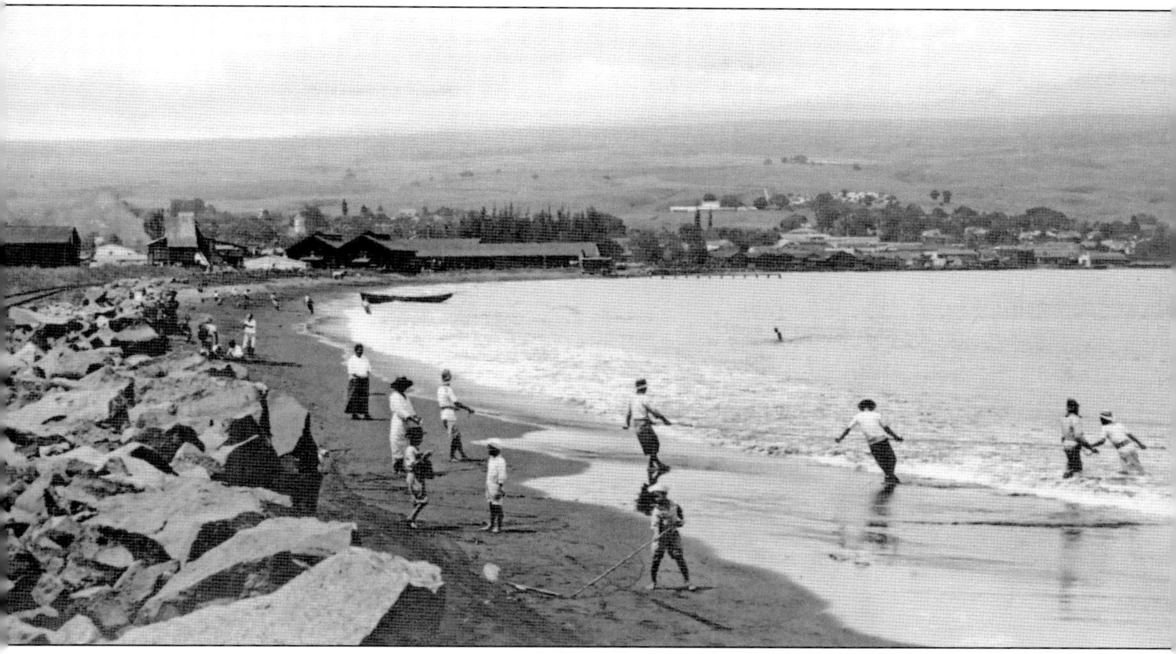

There was once an expansive black sand beach edging Hilo Bay, filled with people enjoying life while bathing, walking, canoeing, or fishing. The boys in this 1928 photograph are fishing with a net. A popular tradition was the *hukilau*, a party or festival during which a large community of people gathered around a big net to catch fish and celebrate afterwards. Today, all of this beautiful black sand is still there, but buried and anchored down by Kamehameha Avenue, parking lots, and the Bayfront Highway. At one time, this beach was the landing where sailing vessels that were anchored just offshore loaded passengers and cargo. It stretched for three miles all around Hilo Bay to the Wailoa River. Black sand is formed by fresh lava hitting the sea in an explosion that cools the lava into tiny shards that are over time rounded by the ocean, creating a soft walking surface. (Courtesy of Hawai'i State Archives.)

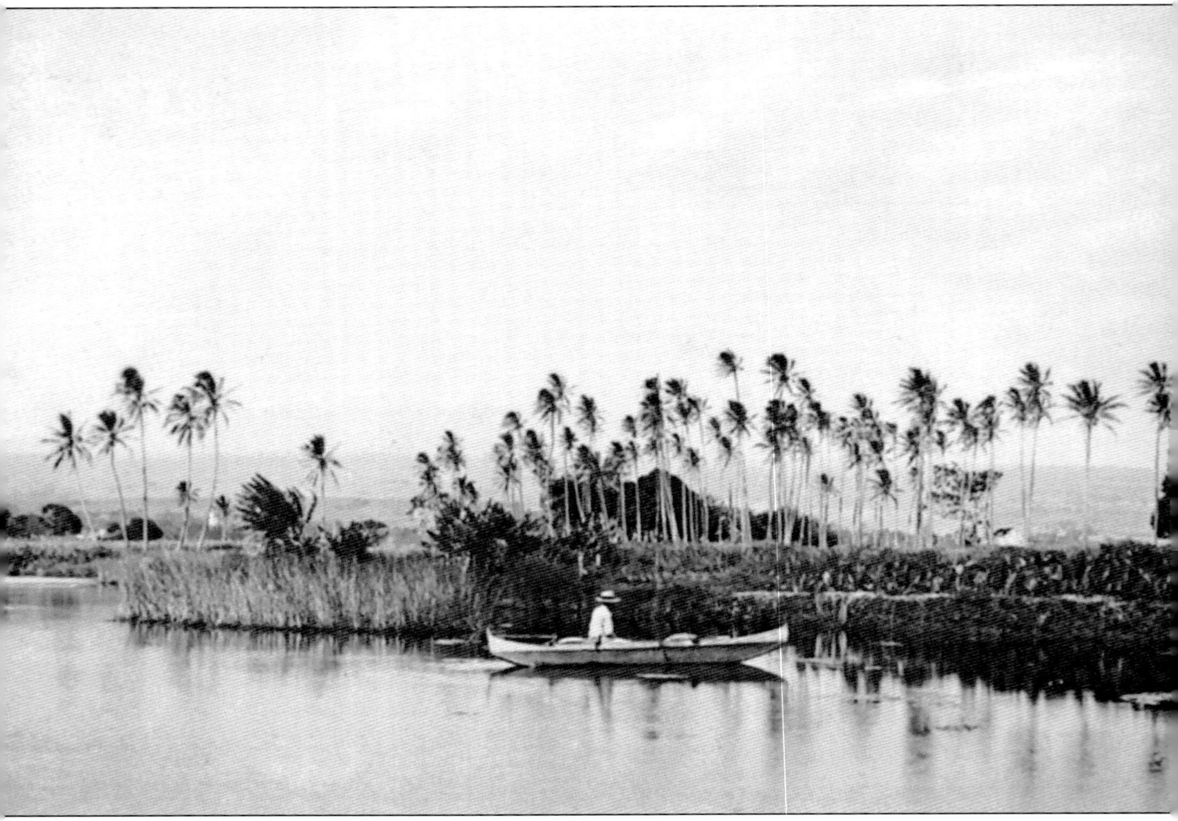

A man in a canoe is enjoying a day on the Wailoa River upstream. This photograph shows the peaceful and serene setting that is common in this area. According to Titus Coan, "Inland, from the shore to the bases of the mountains, the whole landscape is arrayed in living green, presenting a picture of inimitable beauty, so varied in tint, so grooved with water channels, and so sparkling with limpid streams and white foaming cascades, as to charm the eye, and cause the beholder to exclaim, 'This is a scene of surpassing loveliness.'" (Courtesy of Hawai'i State Archives.)

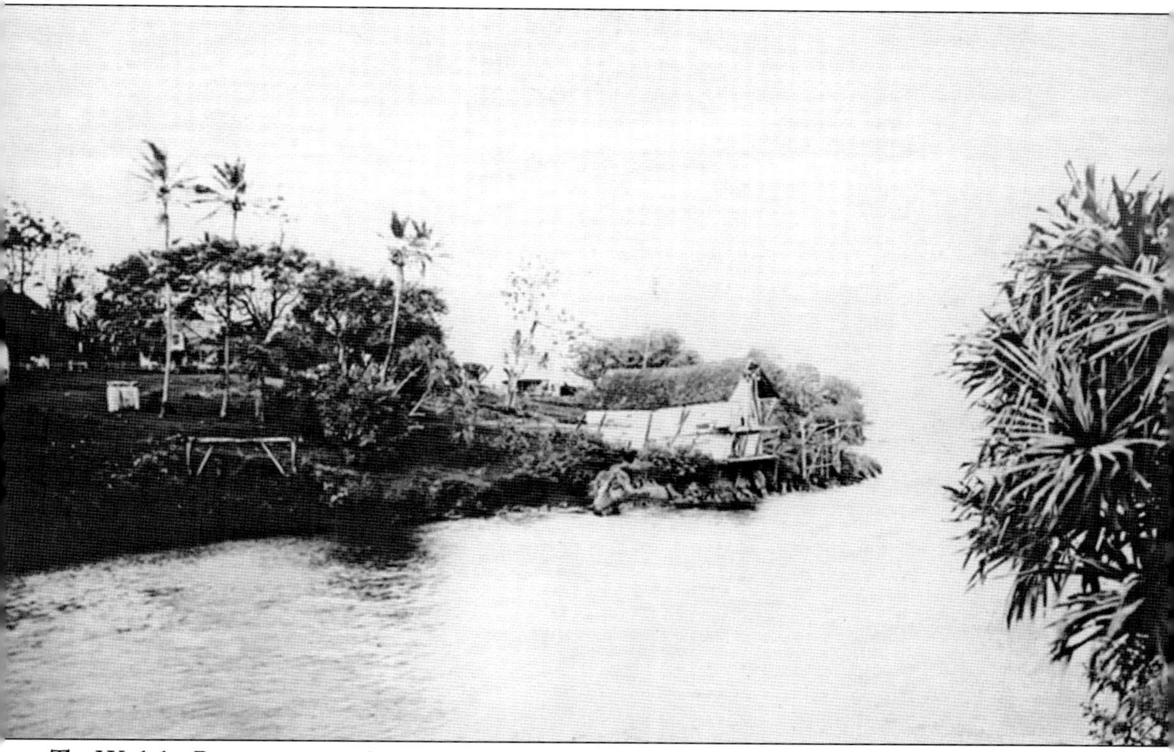

The Wailuku River was once the site of the common market for the Hawaiian people. Hawaiians of South Hilo, and even from as far away as Puna and Ka'ū, brought their produce and products to this area on the Hilo side of the river while those of North Hilo, including Hamākua and Kohala, brought theirs to the Hamākua side; the two groups would then bargain back and forth across the river. This is an early photograph of the area. Today, people from all over the island still visit Hilo for fresh produce at the famous Hilo Farmers' Market. (Courtesy of Hawai'i State Archives.)

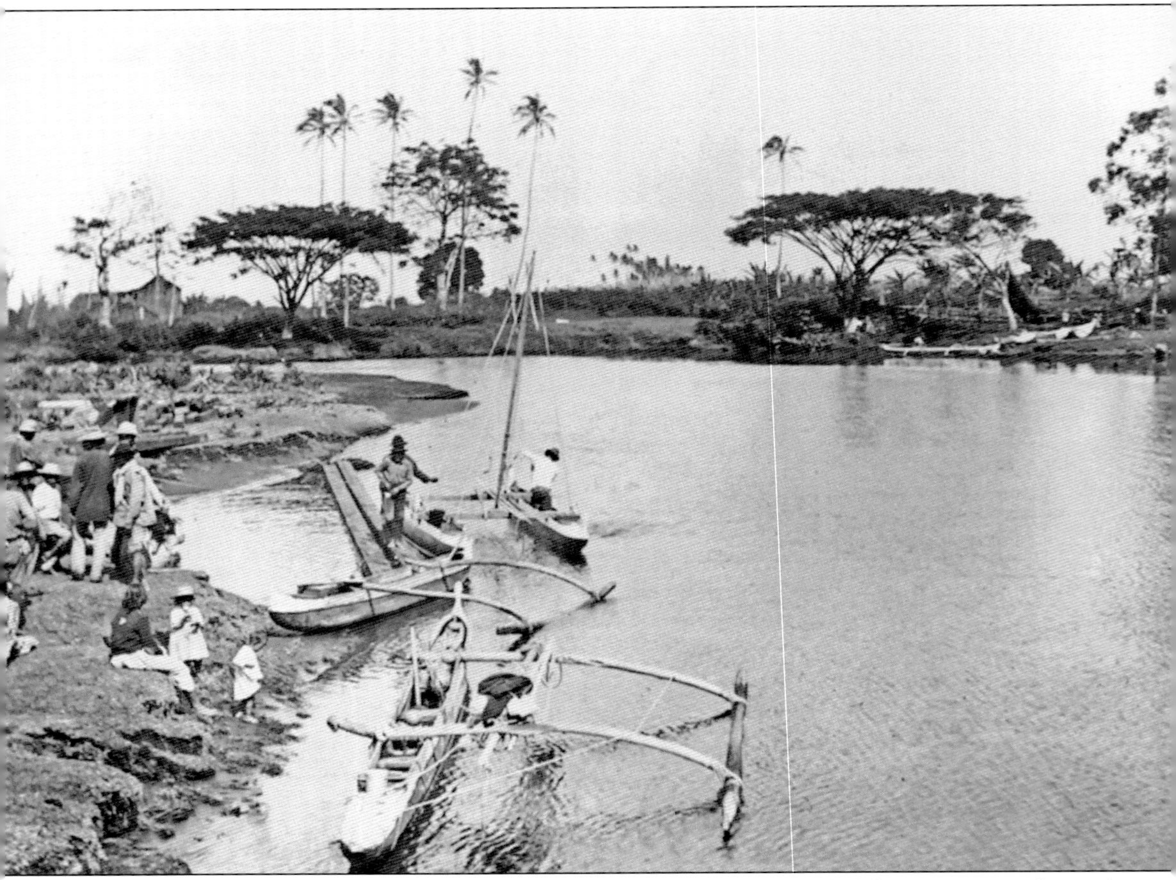

In this photograph of unknown date, Waiākea Stream is shown with fishing canoes and people gathered on the shore. Many streams and inlets in the area are fed by freshwater springs. (Courtesy of Hawai'i State Archives.)

Two

Volcanoes, Earthquakes, and Tsunami

Kīlauea Volcano has been a major attraction since the missionaries came in the early 1800s. Hilo, as the nearest city, serves as the point of embarkation for most. Also of special interest is Mauna Loa, a larger volcano that, though it has fewer eruptions, is more dangerous to residents. Perhaps coincidentally, at the time of the missionaries' coming, it erupted more than usual. Was the goddess Pele offended?, people wondered. One Hawaiian royal chiefess who had converted to Christianity wanted to test the new god's strength against the goddess went to the edge of the crater to challenge Pele and show the people. Hilo evangelist Titus Coan, who crossed the path of volcanic eruptions on his preaching tours to outlying areas, observed it perhaps 100 times, he stated, offering vivid descriptions of lava in all its forms. Drawn like a moth to a flame each time, he documented eruptions in 1843, 1852, 1855, 1868, 1877, and 1880–1881. At this last episode, lava came within half a mile of Hilo. Another flow threatened Hilo in 1935. The US Army Air Corps was called in by Dr. Jagger of Hawai'i Volcanoes Observatory to bomb the flow, which stood just 15 miles from Hilo.

A massive earthquake struck the island in 1868. Centered in Ka'ū, it was felt all over the Hawaiian Islands. Since it was before modern seismic measurements, its magnitude can only be estimated. However, it is said that it may have been the strongest earthquake ever to occur in the Pacific in recorded time. It was coincident with eruptions of Mauna Loa and Kīlauea, and it caused destructive tsunamis as well. Not a single building in Ka'ū was left standing, and houses in Hilo were badly damaged.

Settlements in all parts of the island have suffered damage from lava, tsunami, or tidal waves throughout recorded history. Some, like the coastal villages at Kapoho, Ho'opuloa, and Punalu'u, are gone forever. As a city with its major business district next to the open ocean, Hilo has been struck and yet has rebounded more than any other city in Hawai'i. Waters off its shoreline are unbroken by any other landmasses when waves are generated as far away as Alaska or South America. The most damaging events were in 1946 and 1960, with smaller ones in 1952 and 1957. The Reverend Titus Coan also recorded a spiritual conversion of one whaling captain who had just experienced a tsunami in Hilo Bay in 1837 and helped rescue a dozen people. He swore off drinking and whaling on the Sabbath after that.

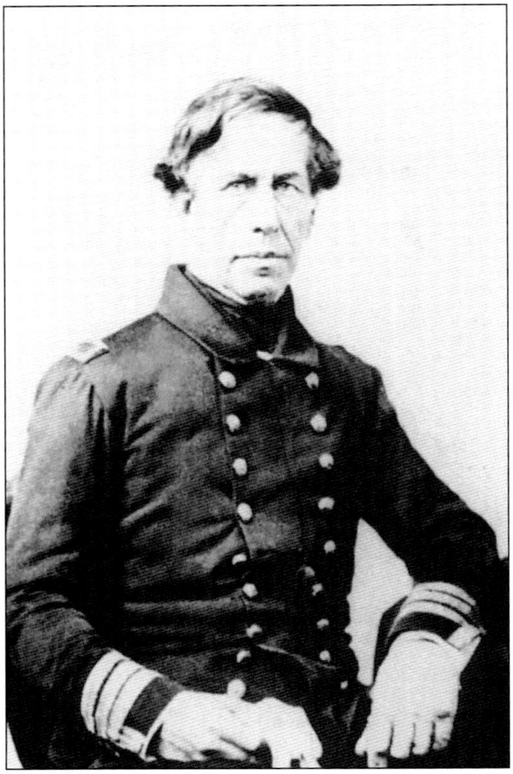

The first large-scale scientific investigation of volcanoes in Hawai'i began with the visit of the United States Exploring Expedition in 1840, which was under the command of Lt. Charles Wilkes, seen here. He sailed to Hilo on the USS *Vincennes* and led the expedition on foot from there. They drew the first maps of the volcanoes, including the summit of Mauna Loa and the crater of Kīlauea on the Big Island, and Haleakala on Maui.

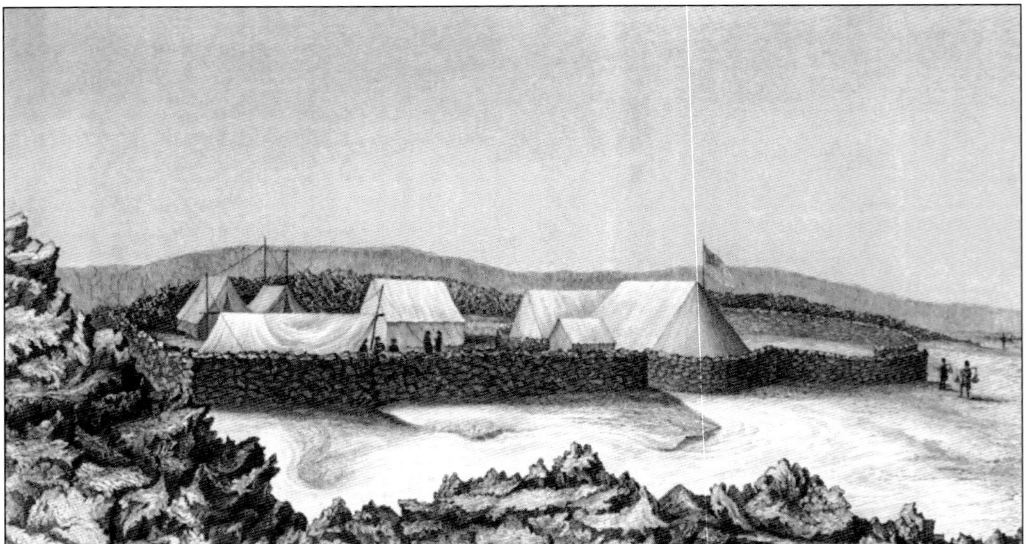

Wilkes hired more than 200 porters to carry his massive load of equipment. The botanical, zoological, and marine specimens brought back by the expedition formed the basic collection of the newly established Smithsonian Institution. The ruins of the Wilkes expedition's campsite are the only known physical evidence in the Pacific of the US Exploring Expedition. Its campsite at Mokuaweoweo, the summit of Mauna Loa, is listed in the National Register of Historic Places and is a state historic site. This illustration, dated January 1841, is from Wilkes's journal by ship artist Alfred Thomas Agate.

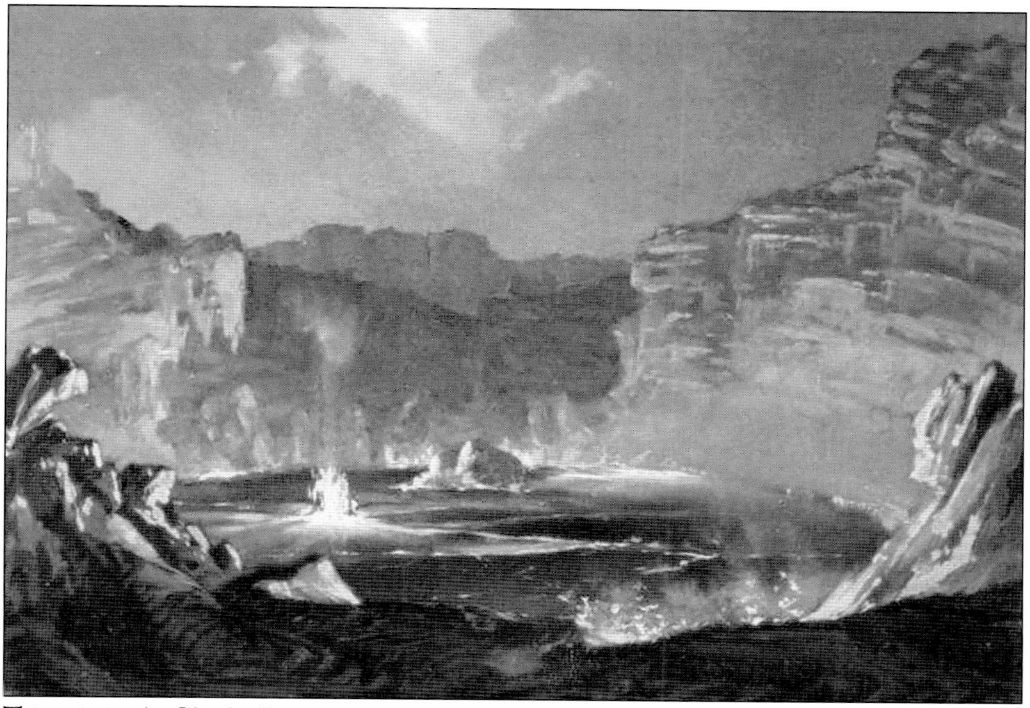

This painting by Charles Furneaux, *The Crater of Kilauea, Hawaii, USA*, shows the volcano at Kīlauea, site of a legendary event in 1824. High Chiefess Kapiʻolani of Kona was an important member of the Hawaiian nobility influenced by Christian missionaries. One of the first Hawaiians to read and write and sponsor a church, she decided in the fall of 1824 to show her people a dramatic demonstration of her faith. Although many other temples were destroyed by this time, the Native Hawaiians continued to honor the goddess Pele at Kīlauea, which was still active. The high chiefess traveled to the volcano on foot, gathering a large crowd as she walked about 60 miles. Reverend Goodrich from the Hilo mission met her at the volcano.

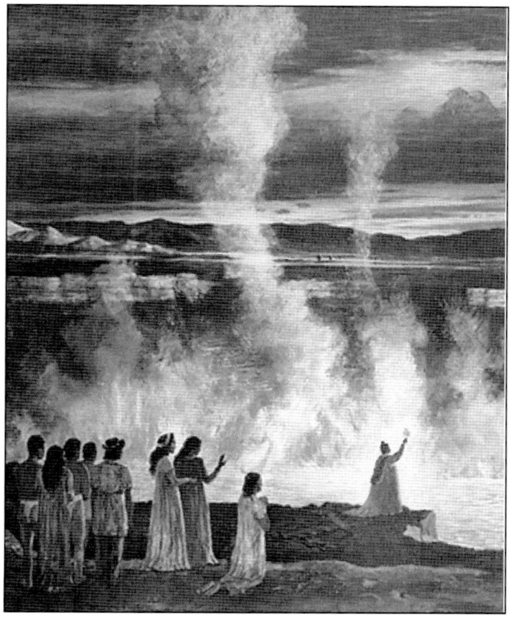

Despite the Hawaiians' admonition that she would surely be killed if she did not make the customary offerings, she said a Christian prayer instead of the traditional one to Pele, and then descended about 500 feet down into the main vent of Halemaʻumaʻu. There was a molten lava lake at the time, but no eruption, and she survived to tell the tale. This illustration of the event was commissioned by the sugar company American Factors, Ltd.

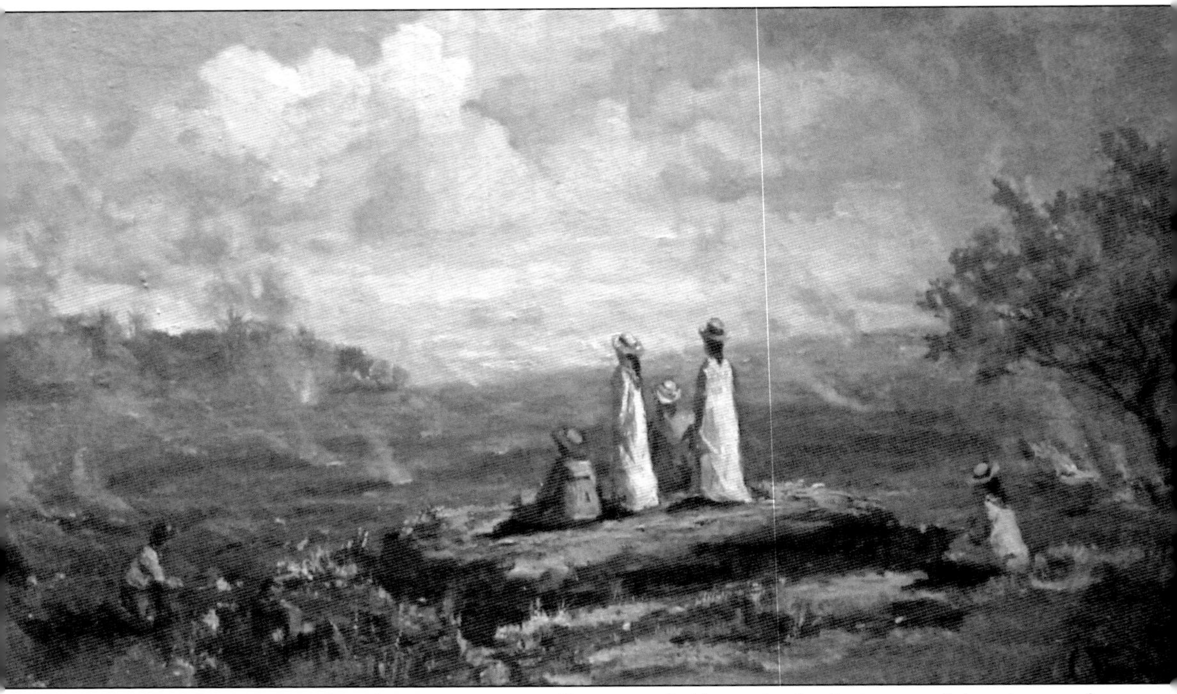

During the 1800s and earlier, events were often recorded by artists' paintings and drawings rather than photography. Charles Furneaux, who painted the oil on canvas *Natives Viewing the Hilo Flow, May 18, 1881*, above, was also an early photographer, though he is best known for his paintings of volcanic eruptions, as seen here and on page 31. The missionary evangelist Titus Coan described this event, an eruption of Mauna Loa that began on November 5, 1880: "Down came a third river of lava, in several channels, flowing in the direction of Hilo. . . . There was the sound as of a continuous cannonading as the lava moved on, rocks exploding under the heat, and gases shattering their way from confinement. We could hear the explosions in Hilo; it was like the noise of battle. Day and night the ancient forest was ablaze, and the scene was vivid beyond description. By the 25th of March the lava was within seven miles of Hilo, and steadily advancing. Until this time we had hoped that Hilo would not be threatened. But the stream pursued its way."

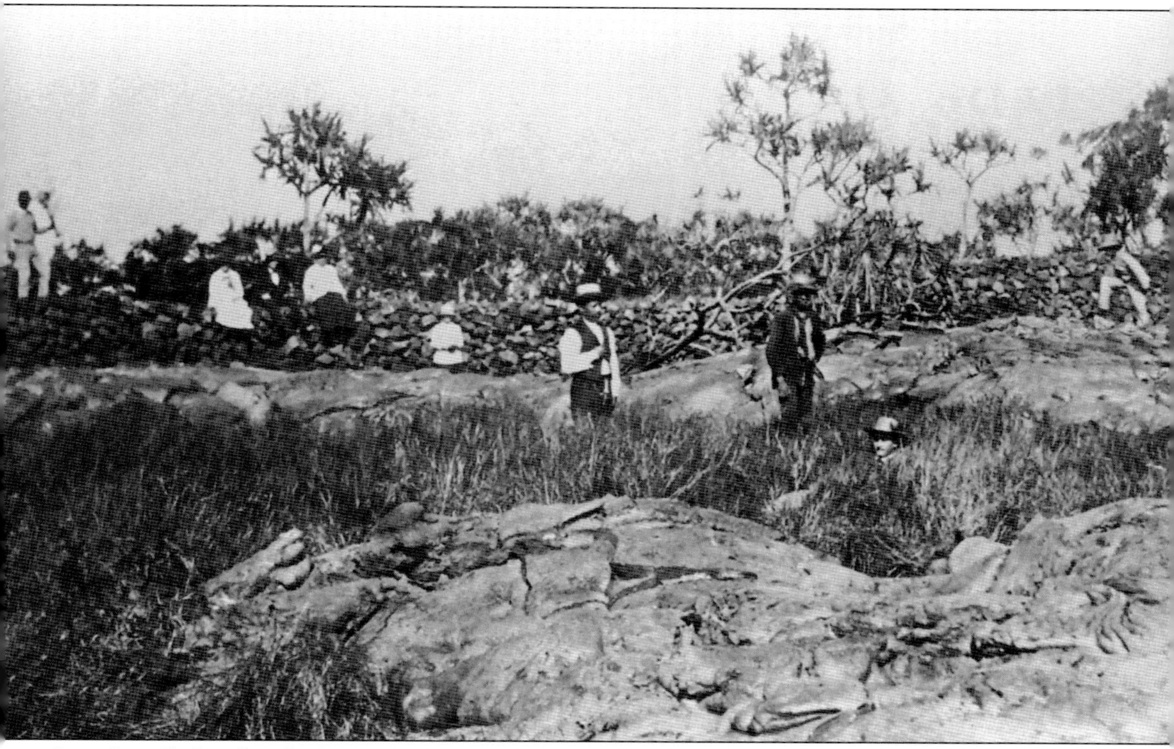

A rock wall five feet high was built to protect Waiākea Sugar Mill from the 1881 lava flow, illustrated in the painting *Natives Viewing the Hilo Flow* (pictured on the previous page). Lava breached the wall and hardened at that point. The lava stream from Mauna Loa was flowing directly toward the downtown area of Hilo. People could walk close to the flow, and its glow lit the city by night. Many visitors, including Princess Liliʻuokalani, came from the other islands to view the scene. Some residents packed up and left; others poked at the lava with sticks and made articles such as cups and other artifacts. Judge Luther Severance dug a moat around the prison. The stream halted around August 13, 1881. It was the closest the volcano has ever come to Hilo. More details may be found in Titus Coan's autobiographical work, *Titus Coan: Life in Hawaiʻi*. (Courtesy of Lyman Museum)

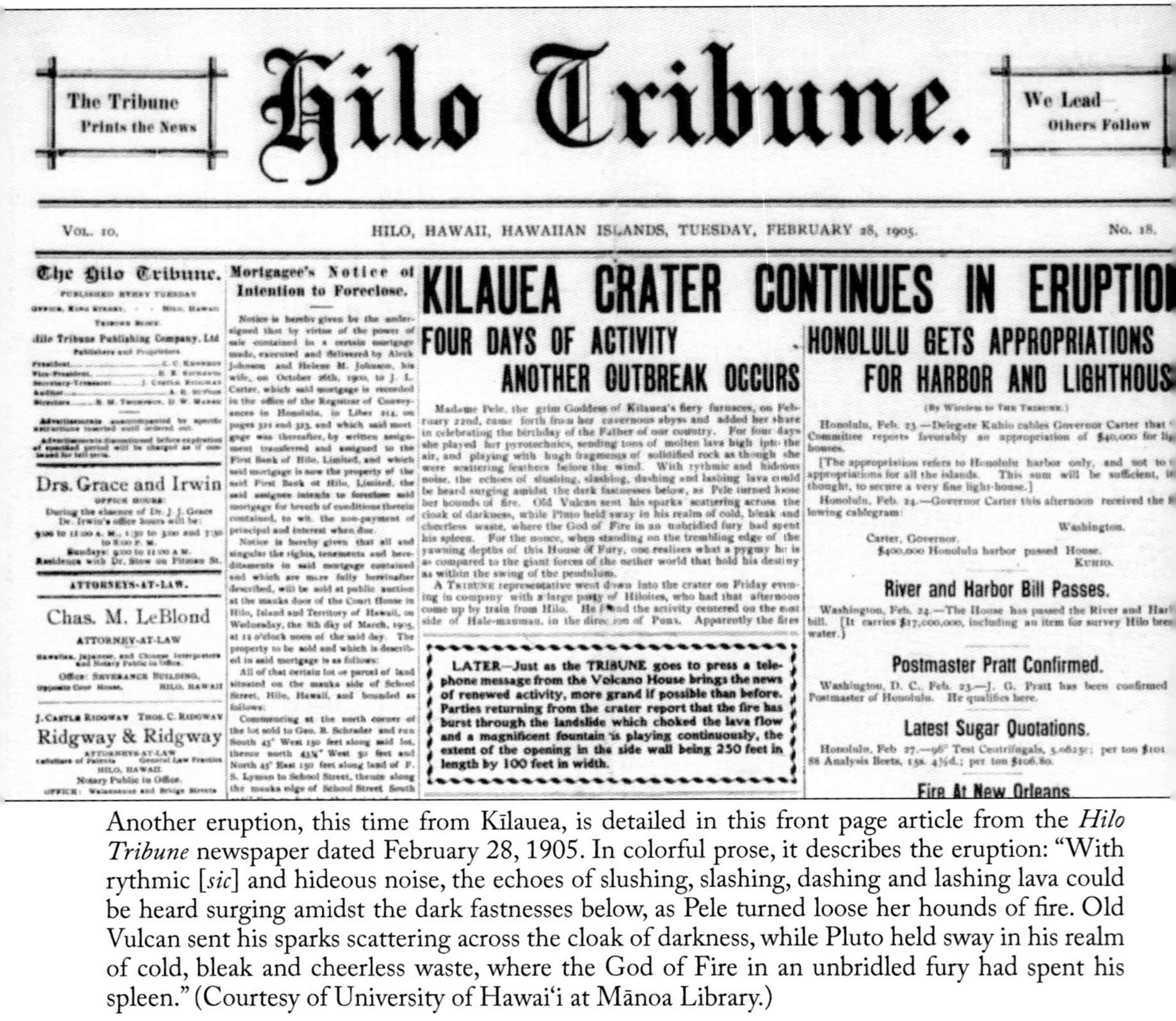

The Tribune Prints the News

Hilo Tribune.

We Lead Others Follow

VOL. 10. HILO, HAWAII, HAWAIIAN ISLANDS, TUESDAY, FEBRUARY 28, 1905. No. 18.

The Hilo Tribune.

PUBLISHED EVERY TUESDAY

Hilo Tribune Publishing Company, Ltd

Drs. Grace and Irwin

OFFICE HOURS:

During the absence of Dr. J. J. Grace Dr. Irwin's office hours will be:

9:00 to 11:00 A. M., 1:30 to 3:00 and 7:30 to 8:00 P. M.

Sundays: 9:00 to 11:00 A. M.

Residence with Dr. Stow on Pitman St.

ATTORNEYS-AT-LAW.

Chas. M. LeBlond

ATTORNEY-AT-LAW

Office: SEVERANCE BUILDING, Opposite Court House, HILO, HAWAII

J. CASTLE RIDGWAY THOS. C. RIDGWAY

Ridgway & Ridgway

ATTORNEYS-AT-LAW

HILO, HAWAII.

Notary Public in Office.

Mortgagee's Notice of Intention to Foreclose.

Notice is hereby given by the undersigned that by virtue of the power of sale contained in a certain mortgage made, executed and delivered by Aleck Johnson and Helene M. Johnson, his wife, on October 26th, 1900, to J. L. Carter, which said mortgage is recorded in the office of the Registrar of Conveyances in Honolulu, in Liber 214, on pages 322 and 323, and which said mortgage was thereafter, by written assignment transferred and assigned to the First Bank of Hilo, Limited, and which said mortgage is now the property of the said First Bank of Hilo, Limited, the said assignee intends to foreclose said mortgage for breach of conditions therein contained, to wit, the non-payment of principal and interest when due.

Notice is hereby given that all and singular the rights, tenements and hereditaments in said mortgage contained and which are more fully hereinafter described, will be sold at public auction at the mauka door of the Court House in Hilo, Island and Territory of Hawaii, on Wednesday, the 8th day of March, 1905, at 12 o'clock noon of the said day. The property to be sold and which is described in said mortgage is as follows:

All of that certain lot or parcel of land situated on the mauka side of School Street, Hilo, Hawaii, and bounded as follows:

Commencing at the north corner of the lot sold to Geo. R. Schrader and run South 45° West 150 feet along said lot, thence north 45½° West 50 feet and North 45° East 150 feet along land of F. S. Lyman to School Street, thence along the mauka edge of School Street South

KILAUEA CRATER CONTINUES IN ERUPTIO[N]

FOUR DAYS OF ACTIVITY ANOTHER OUTBREAK OCCURS

Madame Pele, the grim Goddess of Kilauea's fiery furnaces, on February 22nd, came forth from her cavernous abyss and added her share in celebrating the birthday of the Father of our country. For four days she played her pyrotechnics, sending tons of molten lava high into the air, and playing with hugh fragments of solidified rock as though she were scattering feathers before the wind. With rythmic and hideous noise, the echoes of slushing, slashing, dashing and lashing lava could be heard surging amidst the dark fastnesses below, as Pele turned loose her hounds of fire. Old Vulcan sent his sparks scattering across the cloak of darkness, while Pluto held sway in his realm of cold, bleak and cheerless waste, where the God of Fire in an unbridled fury had spent his spleen. For the nonce, when standing on the trembling edge of the yawning depths of this House of Fury, one realises what a pygmy he is as compared to the giant forces of the nether world that hold his destiny as within the swing of the pendulum.

A TRIBUNE representative went down into the crater on Friday evening in company with a large party of Hiloites, who had that afternoon come up by train from Hilo. He found the activity centered on the east side of Hale-maumau, in the direction of Puna. Apparently the fires

LATER—Just as the TRIBUNE goes to press a telephone message from the Volcano House brings the news of renewed activity, more grand if possible than before. Parties returning from the crater report that the fire has burst through the landslide which choked the lava flow and a magnificent fountain is playing continuously, the extent of the opening in the side wall being 250 feet in length by 100 feet in width.

HONOLULU GETS APPROPRIATIONS FOR HARBOR AND LIGHTHOUS[E]

(By Wireless to THE TRIBUNE.)

Honolulu, Feb. 23.—Delegate Kuhio cables Governor Carter that Committee reports favorably an appropriation of $40,000 for lig[ht]houses.

[The appropriation refers to Honolulu harbor only, and not to appropriations for all the islands. This sum will be sufficient, i[t is] thought, to secure a very fine light-house.]

Honolulu, Feb. 24.—Governor Carter this afternoon received the [fol]lowing cablegram:

Washington.

Carter, Governor.

$400,000 Honolulu harbor passed House.

KUHIO.

River and Harbor Bill Passes.

Washington, Feb. 24.—The House has passed the River and Har[bor] bill. [It carries $17,000,000, including an item for survey Hilo bre[ak]water.]

Postmaster Pratt Confirmed.

Washington, D. C., Feb. 23.—J. G. Pratt has been confirmed Postmaster of Honolulu. He qualifies here.

Latest Sugar Quotations.

Honolulu, Feb 27.—96° Test Centrifugals, 5.0625c; per ton $101 88 Analysis Beets, 15s. 4½d.; per ton $106.80.

Fire At New Orleans

Another eruption, this time from Kīlauea, is detailed in this front page article from the *Hilo Tribune* newspaper dated February 28, 1905. In colorful prose, it describes the eruption: "With rythmic [*sic*] and hideous noise, the echoes of slushing, slashing, dashing and lashing lava could be heard surging amidst the dark fastnesses below, as Pele turned loose her hounds of fire. Old Vulcan sent his sparks scattering across the cloak of darkness, while Pluto held sway in his realm of cold, bleak and cheerless waste, where the God of Fire in an unbridled fury had spent his spleen." (Courtesy of University of Hawai'i at Mānoa Library.)

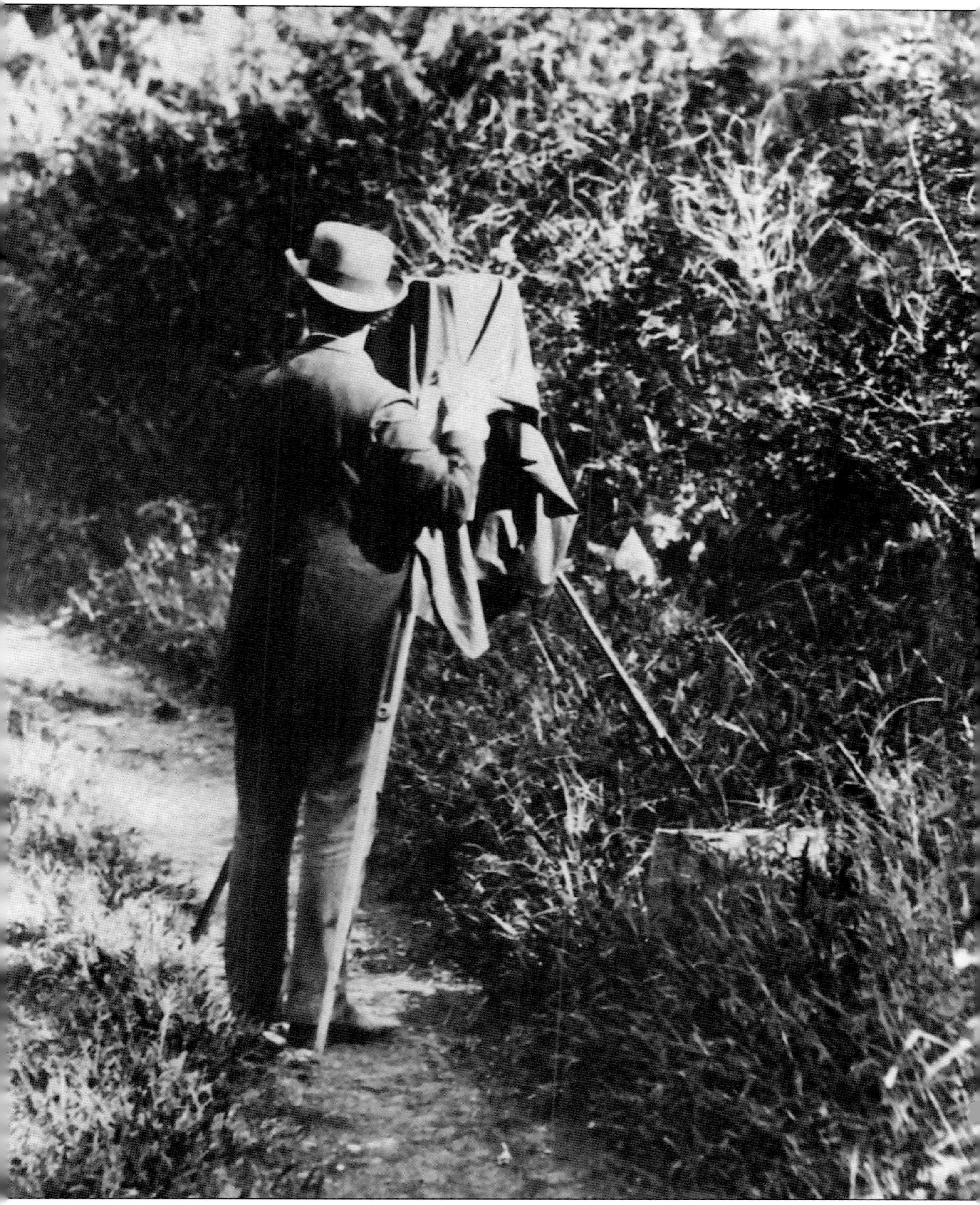

Artist Charles Furneaux is shown here taking a picture with his camera. The artist came to Hawai'i from Boston in 1880, just in time to illustrate the infamous 1880–1881 volcanic eruption that threatened Hilo. Furneaux also taught art at Punahou School in Honolulu and had commissions from King Kalākaua and other members of the royal family. (Courtesy of Lyman Museum.)

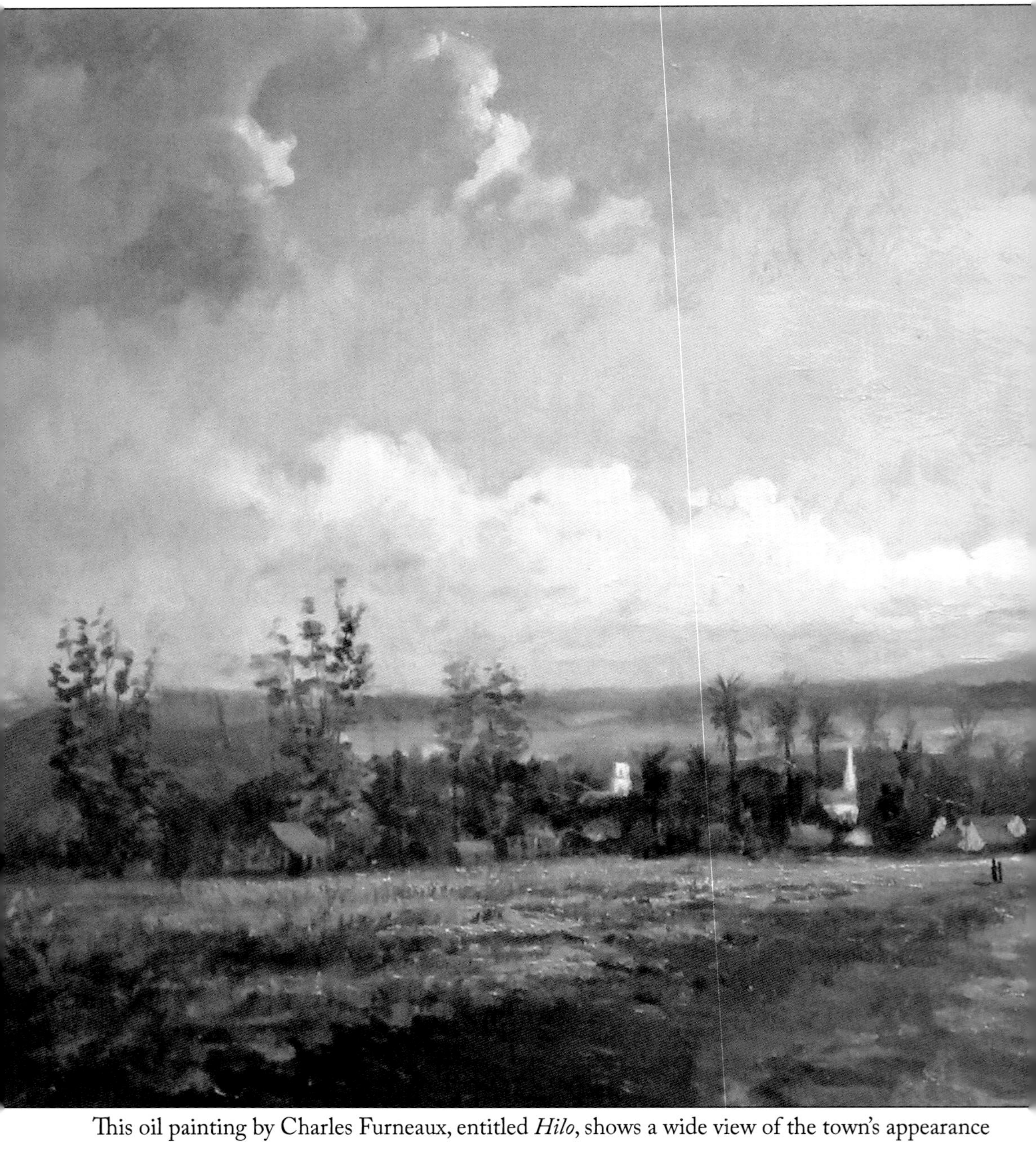

This oil painting by Charles Furneaux, entitled *Hilo*, shows a wide view of the town's appearance

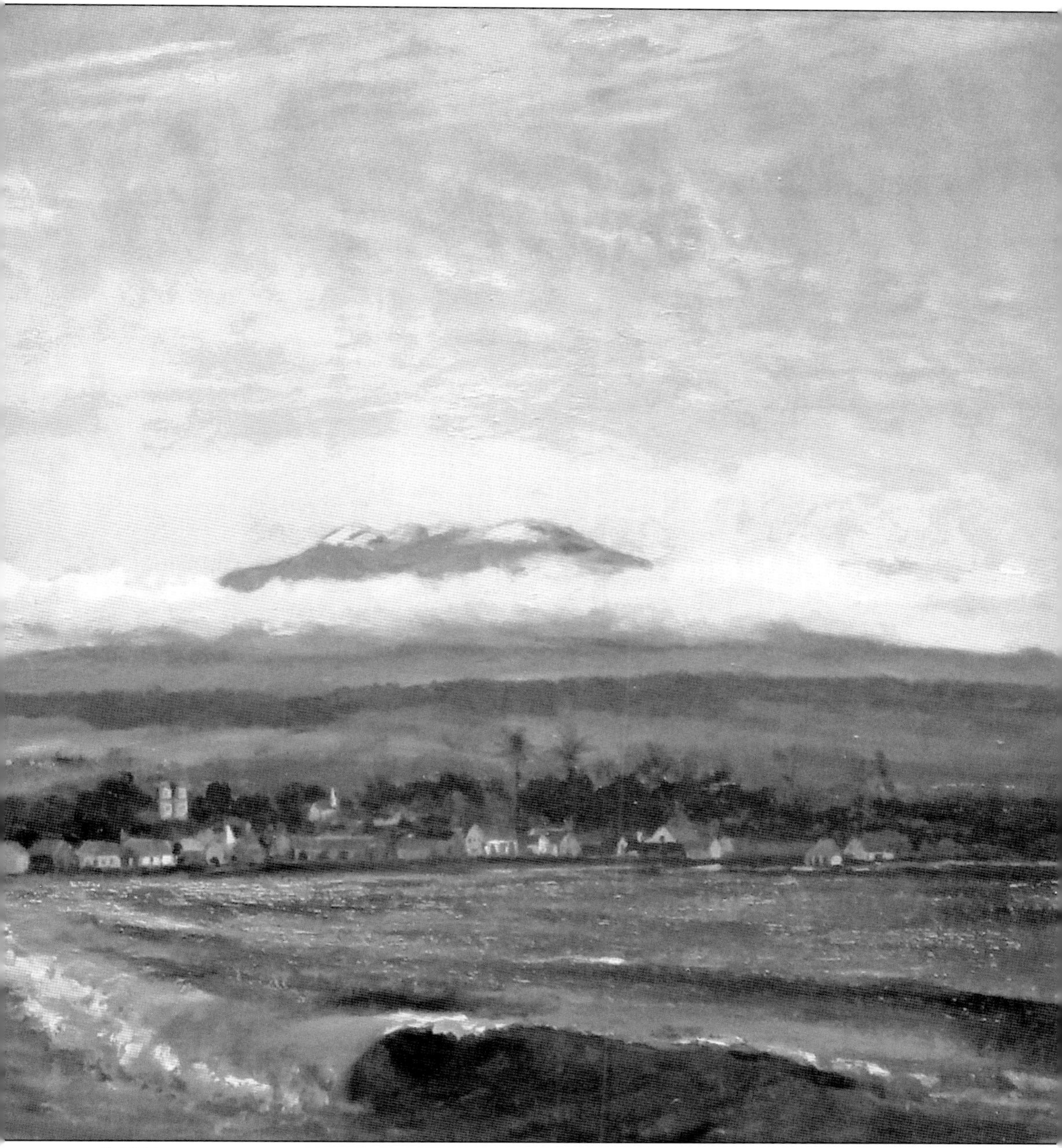

around 1880.

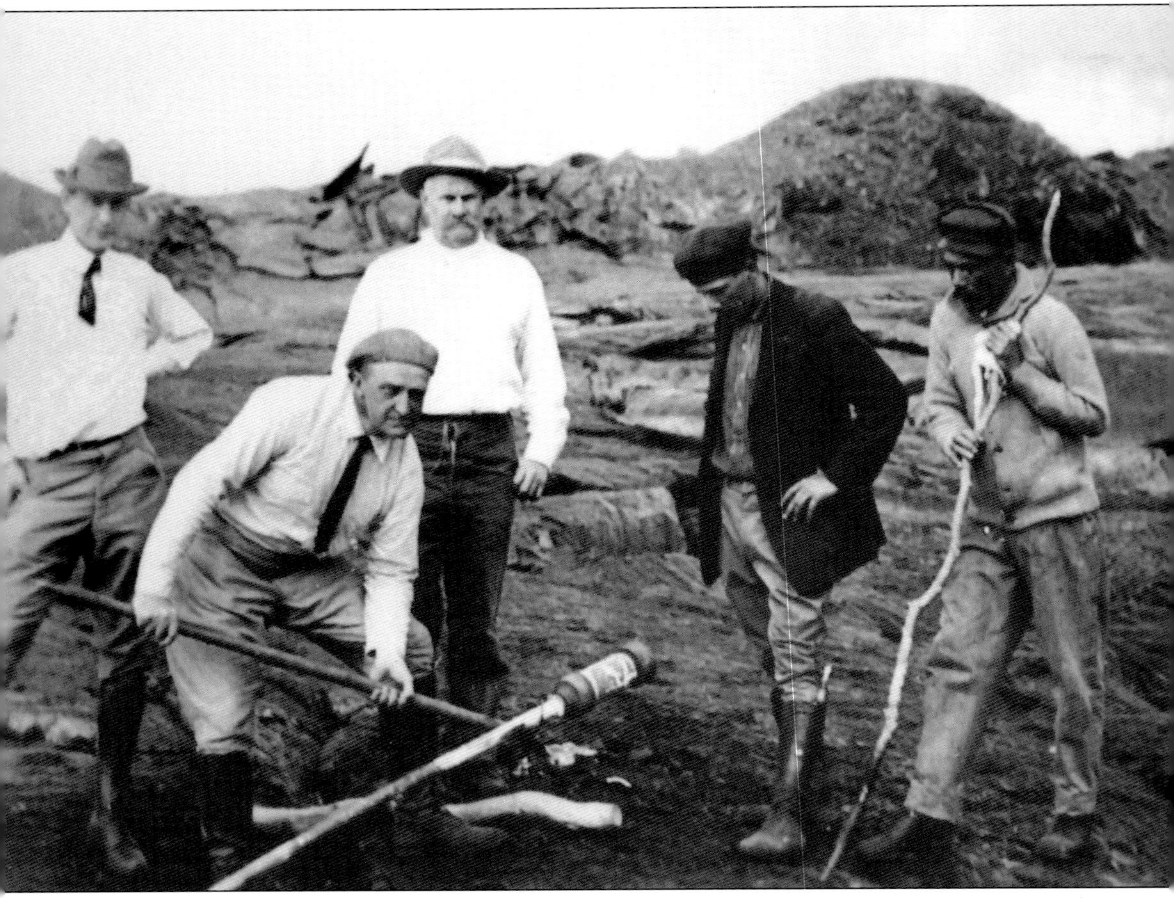

Thomas A. Jaggar, founder of the Hawaiian Volcano Observatory (HVO) in 1912, is shown here as he prepares to measure the temperature of the Halema'uma'u lava lake in 1917. Pictured from left to right are Norton Twigg-Smith, Jaggar, Lorrin Thurston, Joe Monez, and Alex Lancaster. In November 1935, an eruption of Mauna Loa was again threatening Hilo, and Dr. Jaggar, who had been experimenting with using TNT to dynamite lava tubes and divert the flows, decided to take drastic action. As the flow was threatening Hilo's water works, he called in the US Army Air Corps to drop bombs on the lava. (Courtesy of USGS, HVO.)

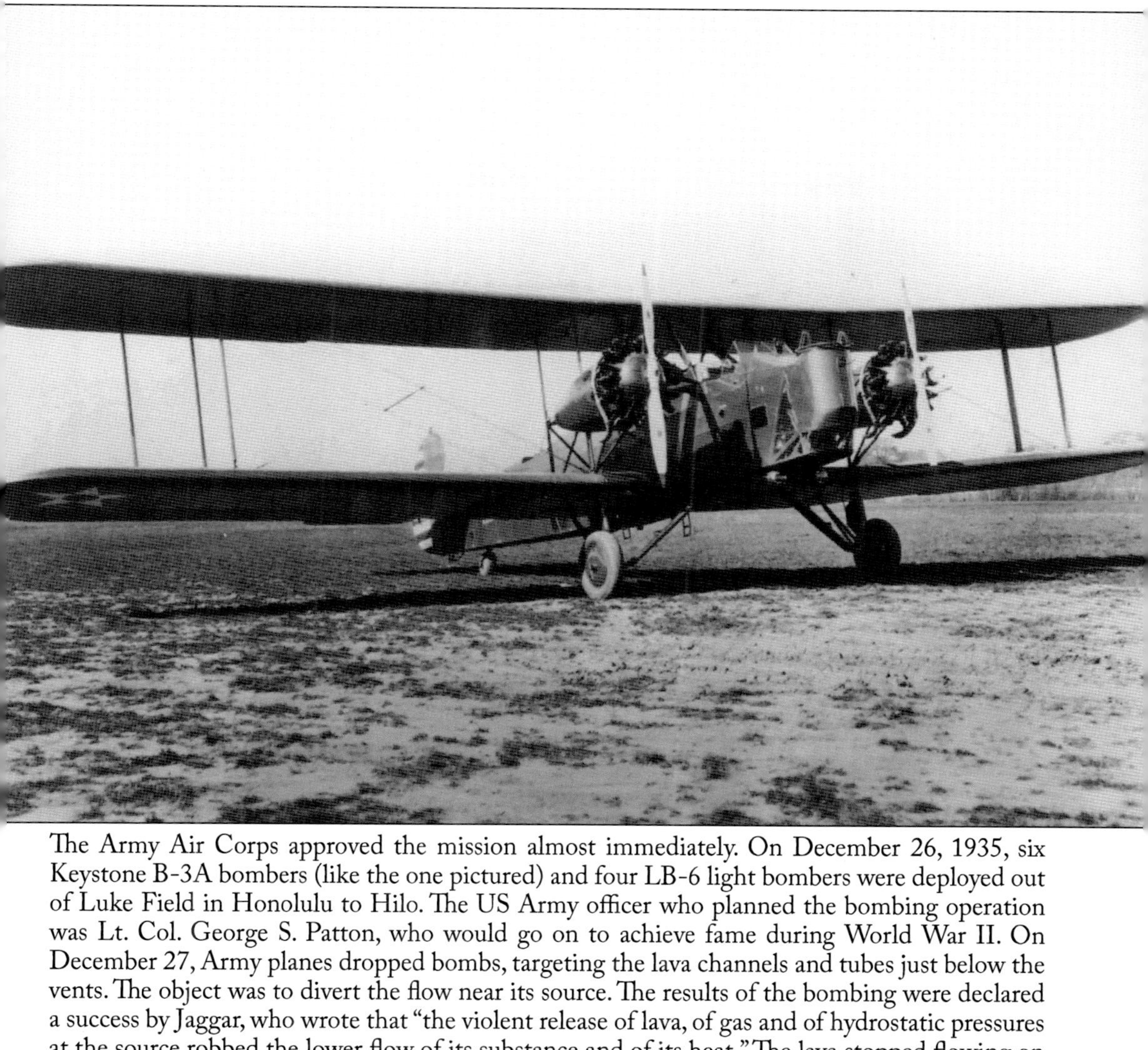

The Army Air Corps approved the mission almost immediately. On December 26, 1935, six Keystone B-3A bombers (like the one pictured) and four LB-6 light bombers were deployed out of Luke Field in Honolulu to Hilo. The US Army officer who planned the bombing operation was Lt. Col. George S. Patton, who would go on to achieve fame during World War II. On December 27, Army planes dropped bombs, targeting the lava channels and tubes just below the vents. The object was to divert the flow near its source. The results of the bombing were declared a success by Jaggar, who wrote that "the violent release of lava, of gas and of hydrostatic pressures at the source robbed the lower flow of its substance and of its heat." The lava stopped flowing on January 2, 1936. The efficacy of this lava bombing is disputed by some volcanologists. (Courtesy the US Air Force Museum.)

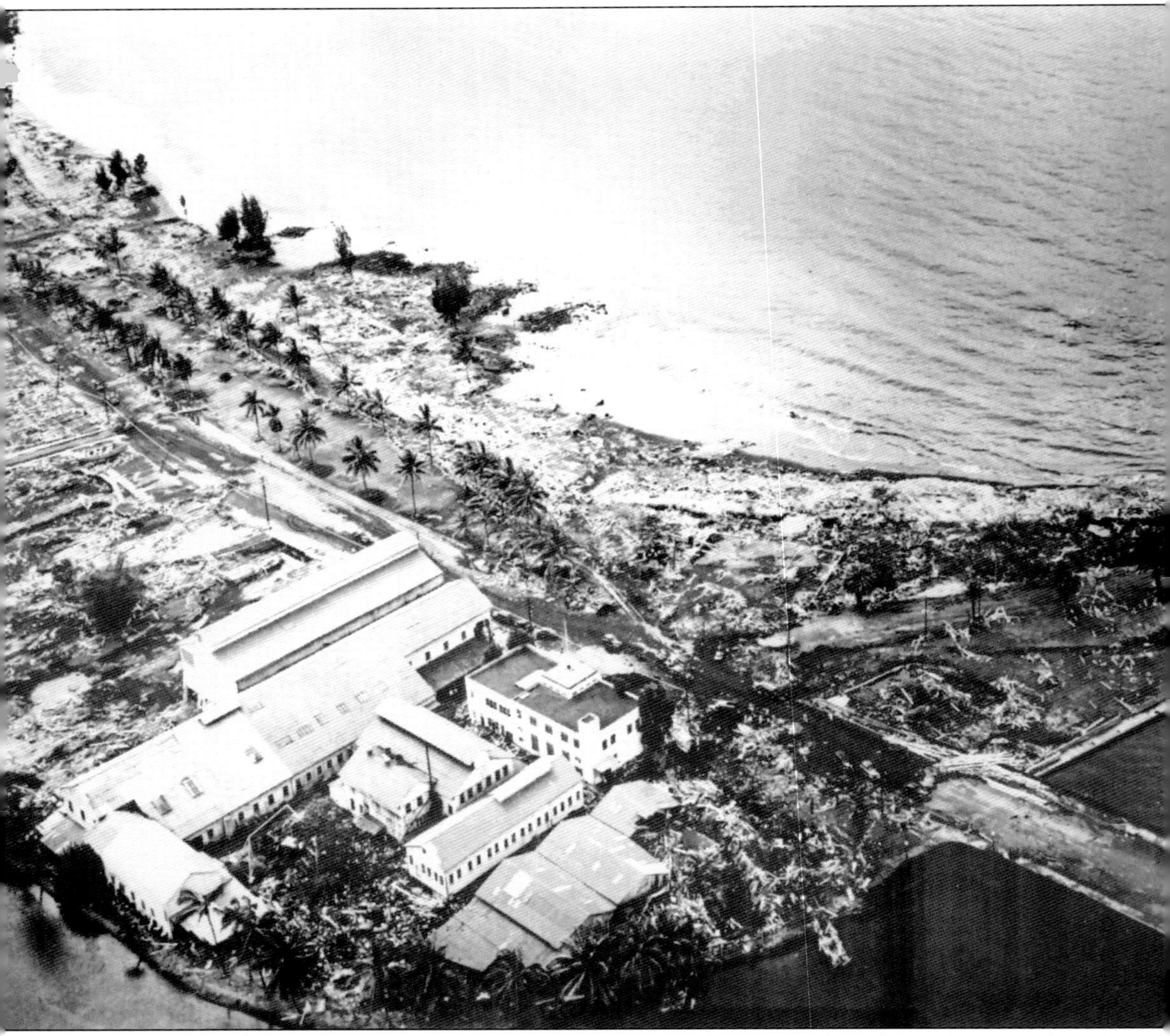

As it was happening, the major tsunami of 1946 was documented in these photographs and the ones on following pages. It struck Hilo on April Fool's Day, 1946, at 6:54 a.m. HST. It originated with a 7.1-magnitude earthquake at the Aleutian Unimak Island, Alaska. Maximum wave height measured or estimated was 50 feet. It resulted in damages of $26 million ($300 million today) and the loss of 159 lives. This aerial photograph shows the extent of the wave and resulting destruction around the Hilo Ironworks and the Wailoa River Bridge. (Courtesy of NOAA/NGDC Natural Hazards Photo Archive.)

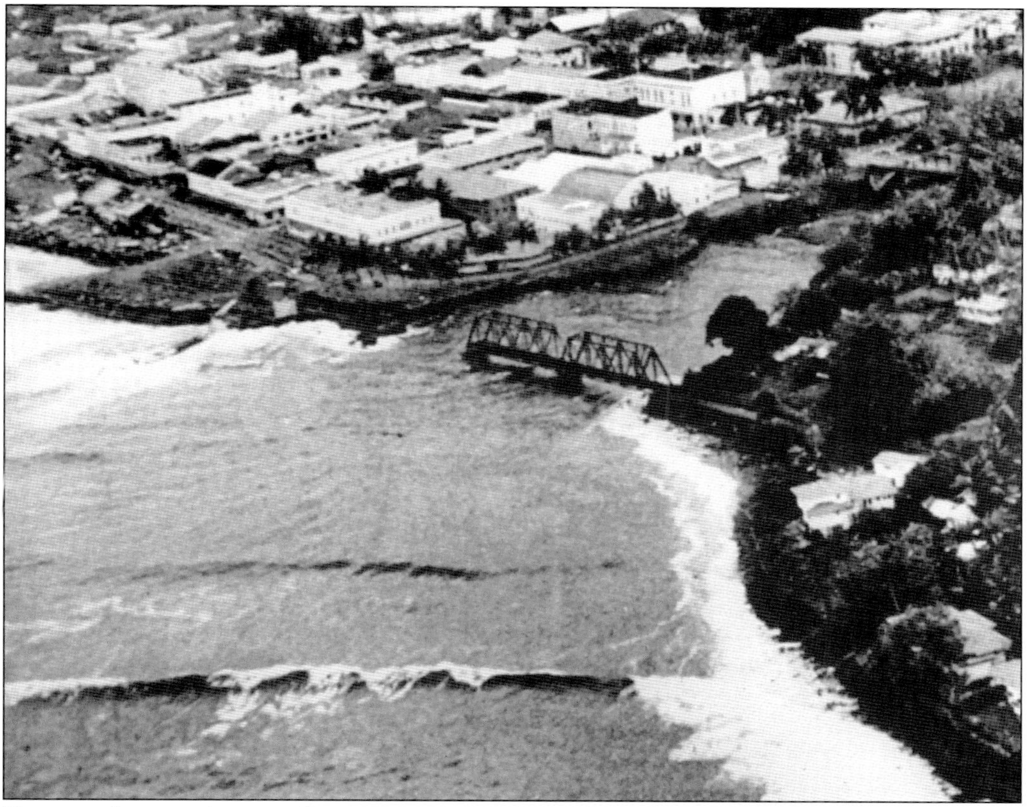

This aerial view shows a later wave approaching the Wailuku River; the railroad bridge had already been washed out by the first wave. (Courtesy of NOAA/NGDC Natural Hazards Photo Archive.)

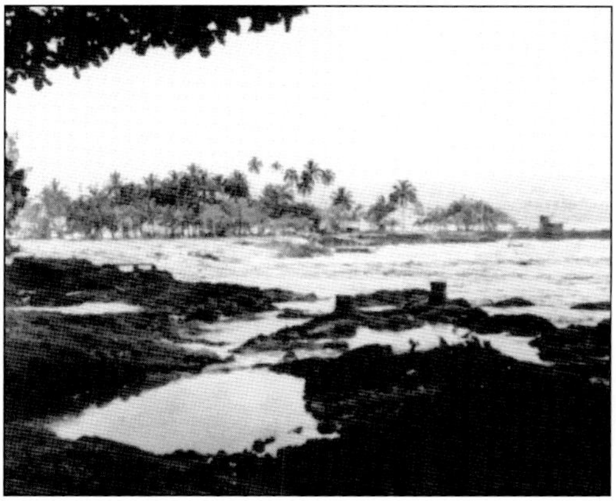

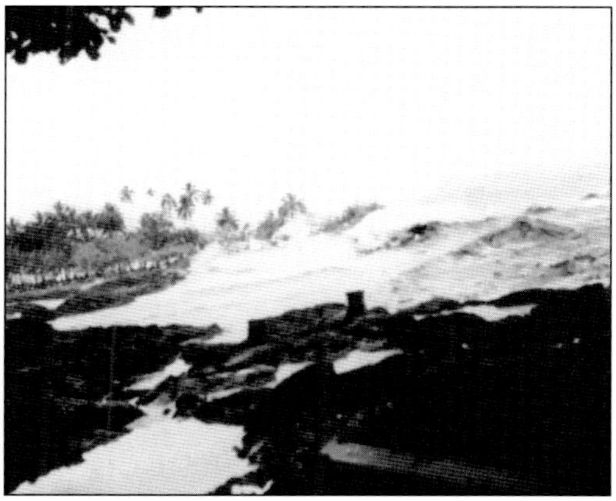

The photographer captured these images as the wave approached Coconut Island and then washed completely over it. (Both, courtesy of NOAA/NGDC Natural Hazards Photo Archive.)

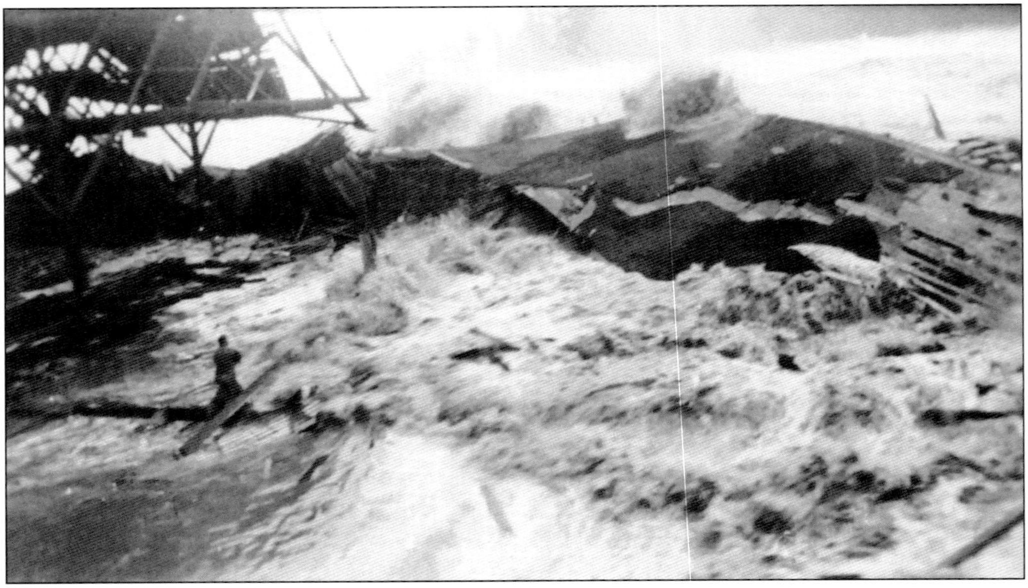

A tsunami wave breaks over Pier 1 in Hilo Harbor in this photograph taken aboard the US Navy ship *Brigham Victory*, which was in the harbor at the time of the event. The man in the foreground about to be overcome by the wave is Antone "Tony" Aguiar. He cut the hawser of the ship, allowing it to escape to safety in the open sea; in doing so, he became one of the fatalities. The ship was caught by the waves and tossed about, but was able to use its own power to avoid the reefs and get past the breakwater to the open sea. (Courtesy of NOAA/NGDC Natural Hazards Photo Archive.)

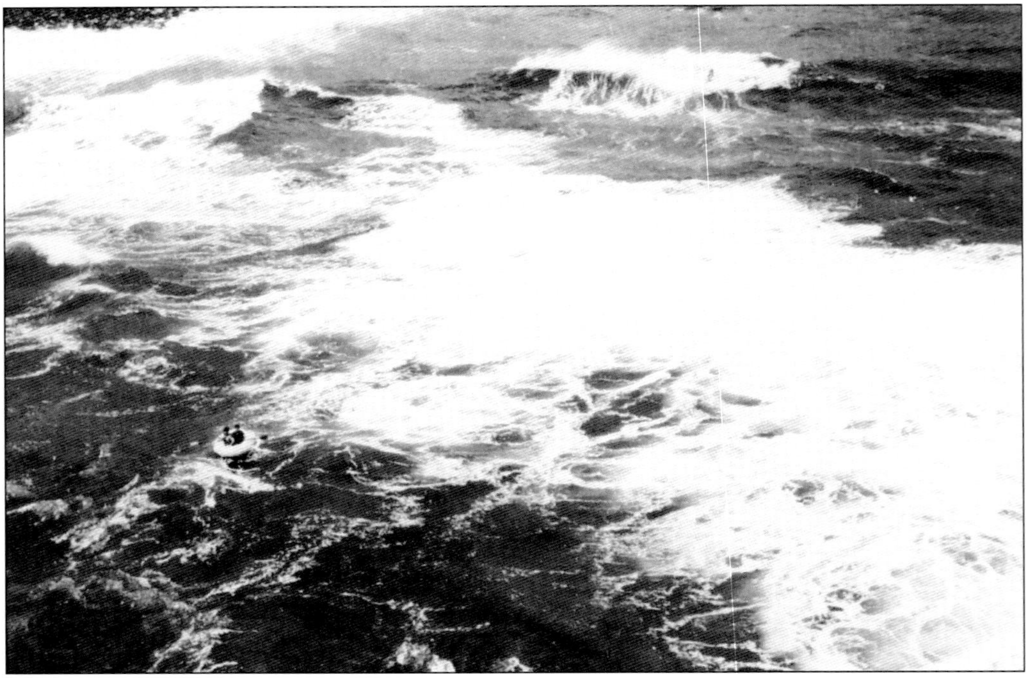

Two days after the tsunami, the plane shooting photographs spotted these two children approaching perilously close to the breakers in their air-sea rescue rubber boat. The pilot watched as they reached safety in a small cove to the left (not visible). (Courtesy of NOAA/NGDC Natural Hazards Photo Archive.)

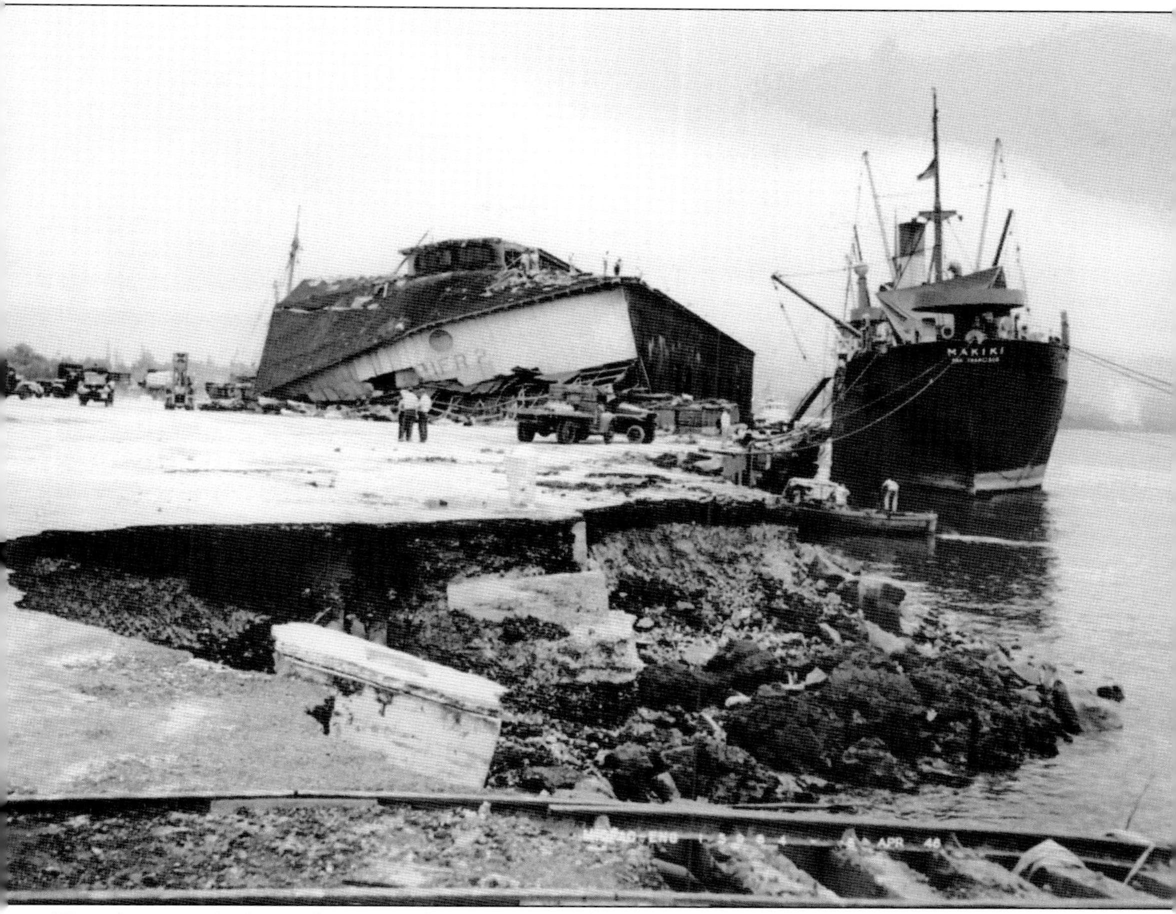

This photograph shows the severe damage done to Territorial Pier No. 2 and its storage building. (Courtesy of NOAA/NGDC Natural Hazards Photo Archive.)

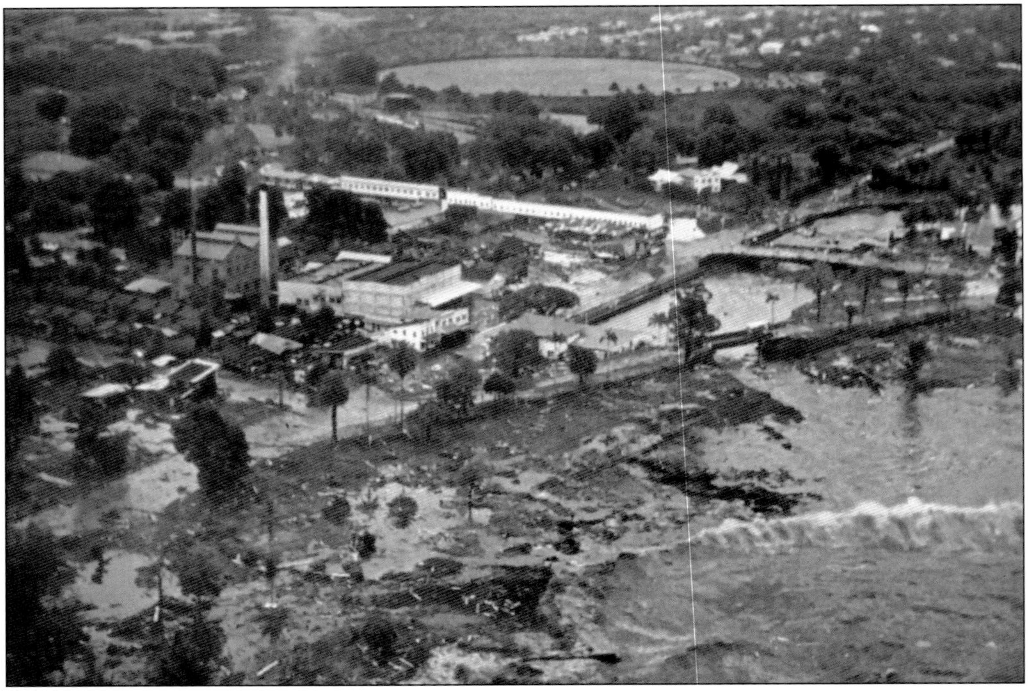

This aerial view shows the extent of inundation resulting from the first wave as a secondary wave approaches the shoreline and entrance to the Wailoa River and a small boat harbor. The large building is Hilo Electric Company. (Courtesy of NOAA/NGDC Natural Hazards Photo Archive.)

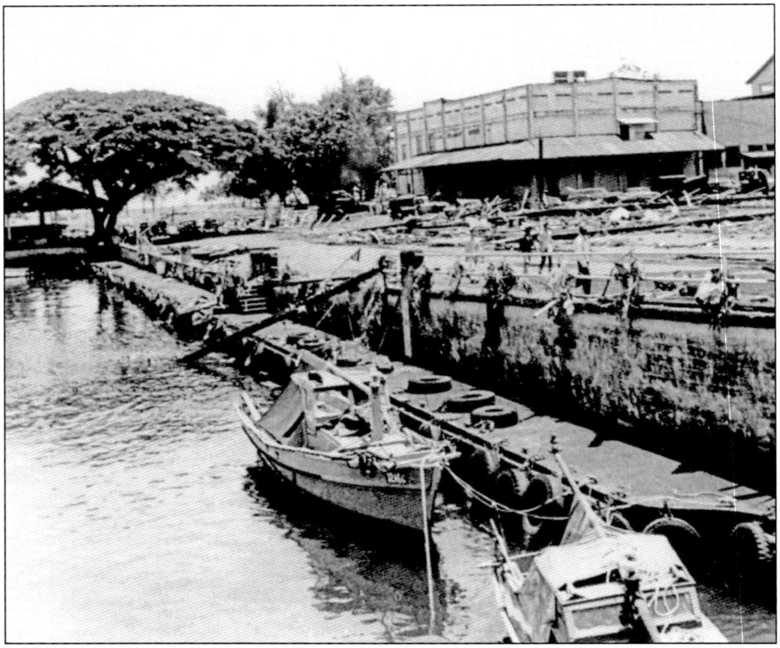

Sampans (fishing boats) are tied up near Suisan Company on Banyan Drive after the tsunami. In the background is Hilo Electric Light Company's power plant, which was damaged. (Courtesy of NOAA/NGDC Natural Hazards Photo Archive.)

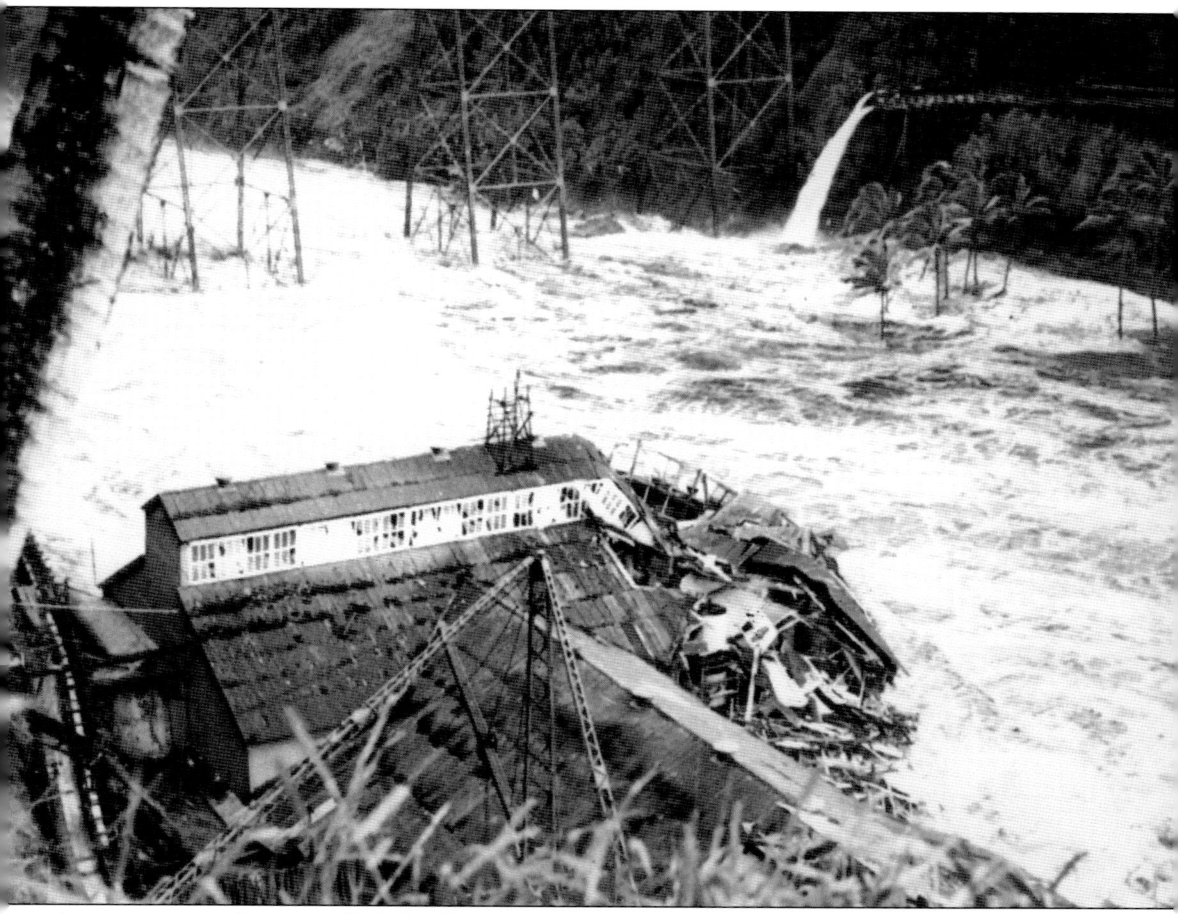

A tsunami wave destroys a Hakalau Sugar Mill building. This gulch is normally dry except for a small stream. (Courtesy of NOAA/NGDC Natural Hazards Photo Archive.)

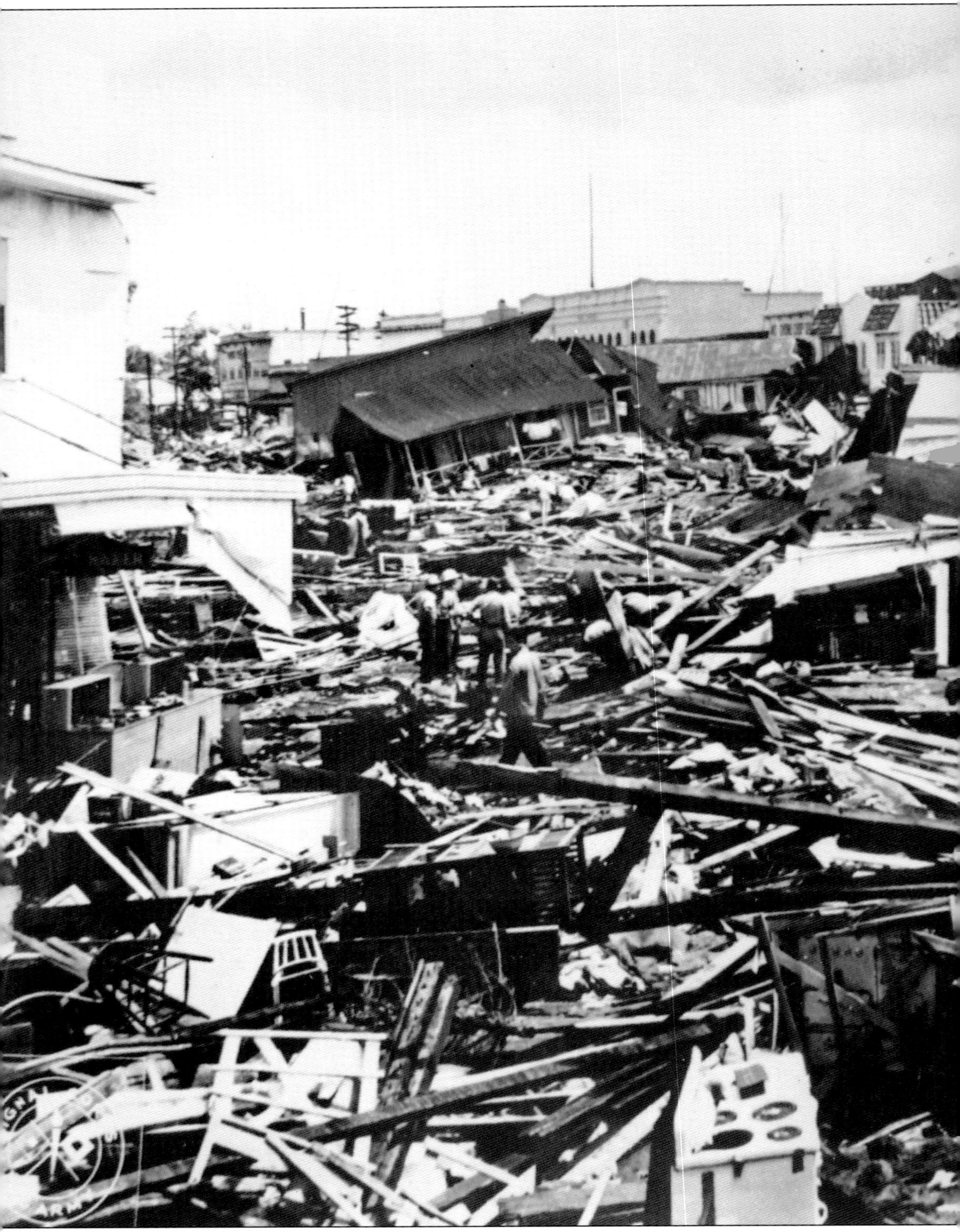

This is a graphic view of the devastation along Kamehameha Avenue, showing the wreckage of business buildings left by the huge wave. One business, P.C. Beamer's Hardware Store, was

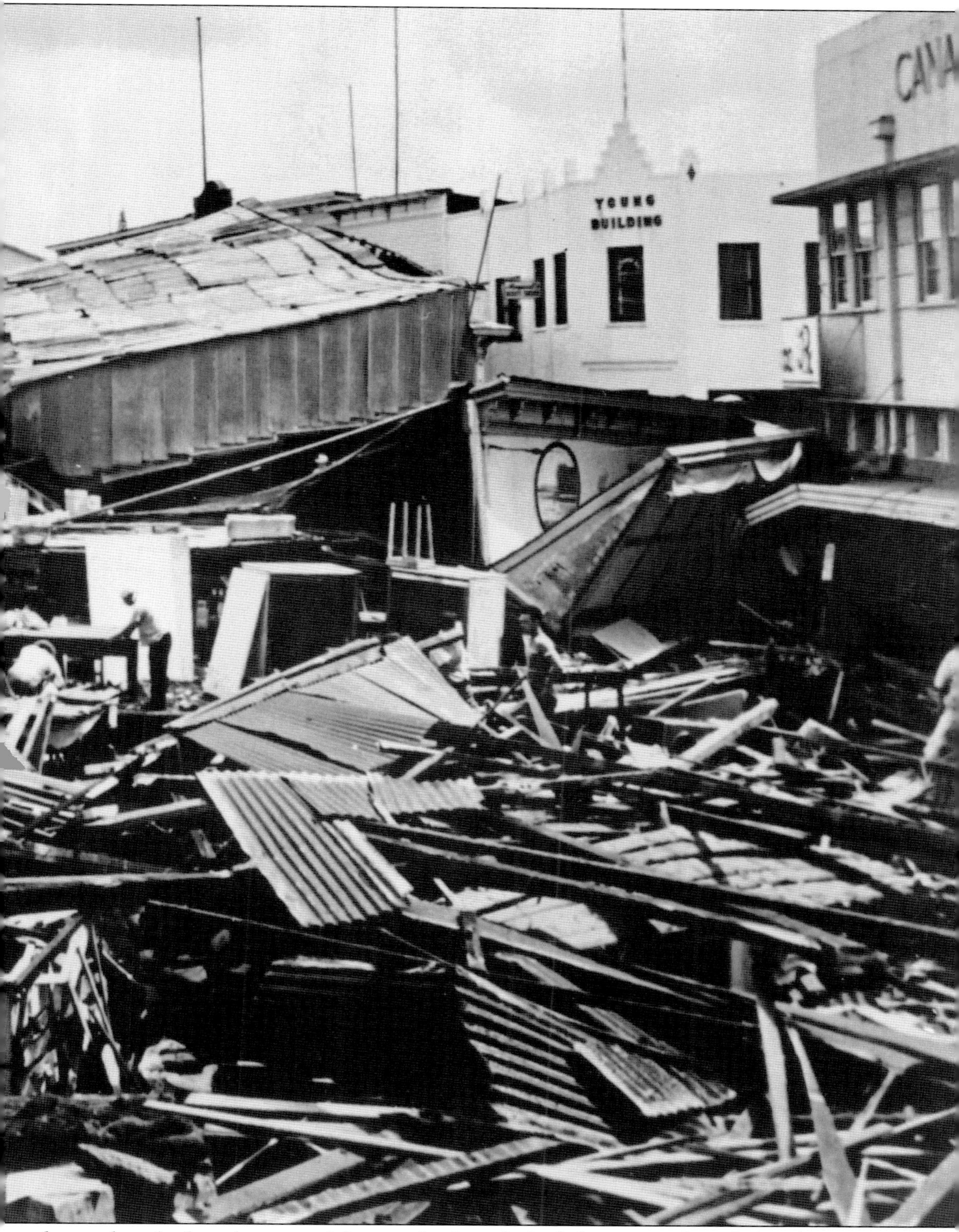

damaged on the front, but opened the next day from the back door to supply tools for rebuilding and cleanup. (Courtesy of NOAA/NGDC Natural Hazards Photo Archive.)

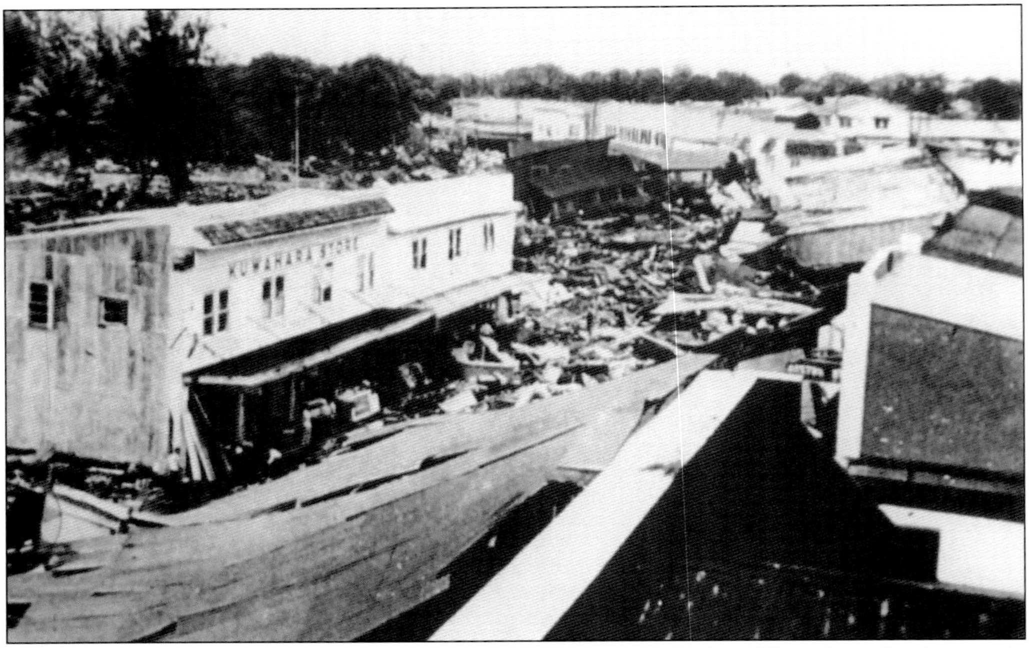

Kuwahara Store is the only building left standing on the ocean side of Kamehameha Avenue in this image. It reopened and remained in this location until the early 1950s, when a parking lot was built here. (Courtesy of NOAA/NGDC Natural Hazards Photo Archive.)

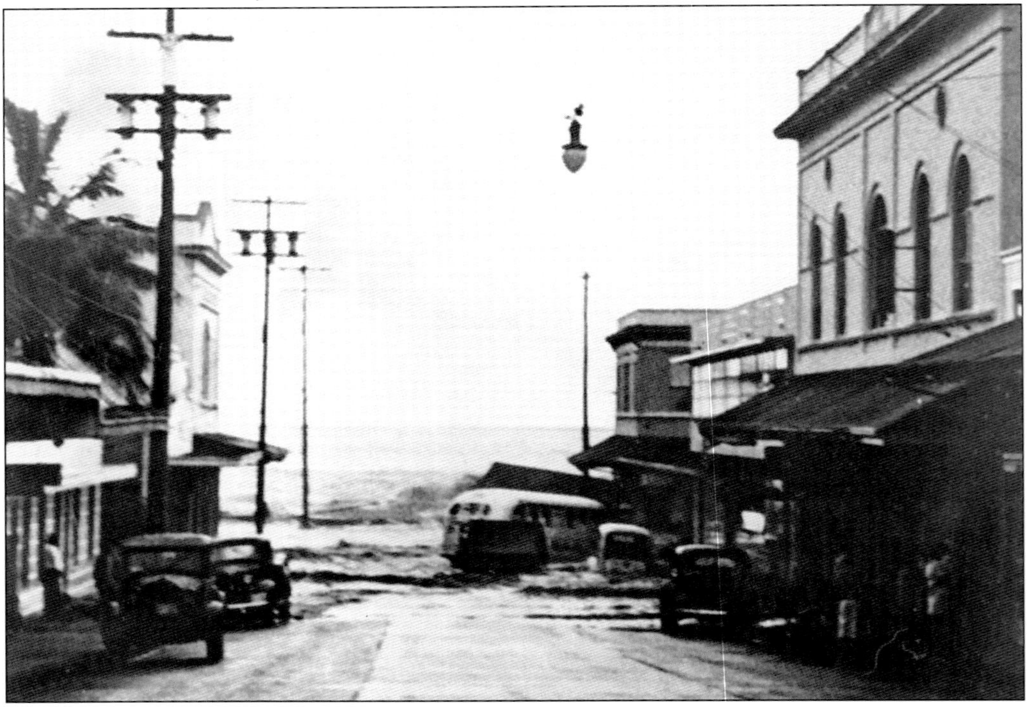
This view looks down Wai'ānuenue Street as the breakwater in the distance is being breached by the third or fourth wave. The wave reaching the shoreline in this photograph is the second wave, according to an employee of a business on the far right corner of the street. (Courtesy of NOAA/NGDC Natural Hazards Photo Archive.)

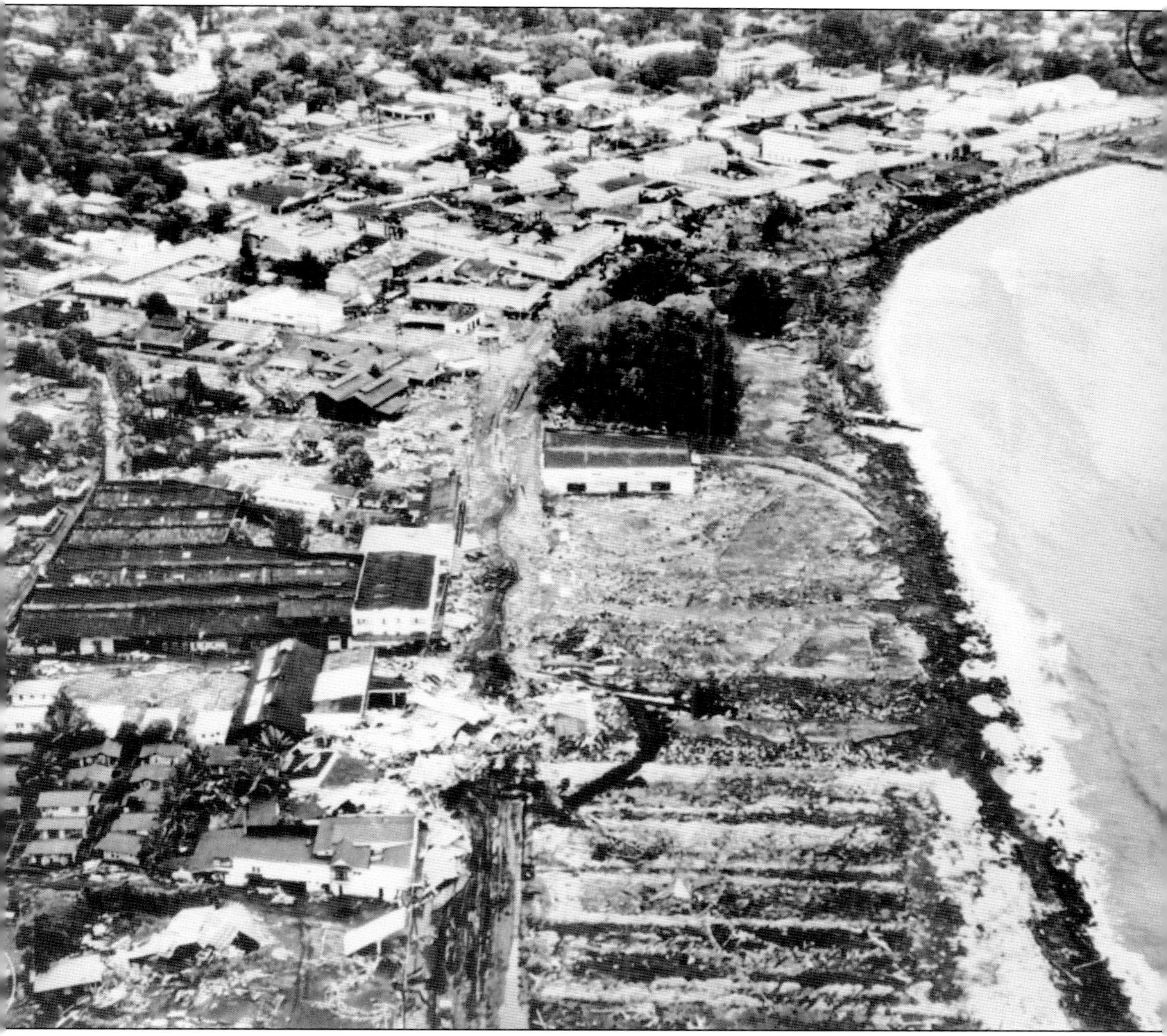

This wide aerial view of tsunami damage looks up Kamehameha Avenue. A string of scenic parks has replaced most of the shoreline. (Courtesy of NOAA/NGDC Natural Hazards Photo Archive.)

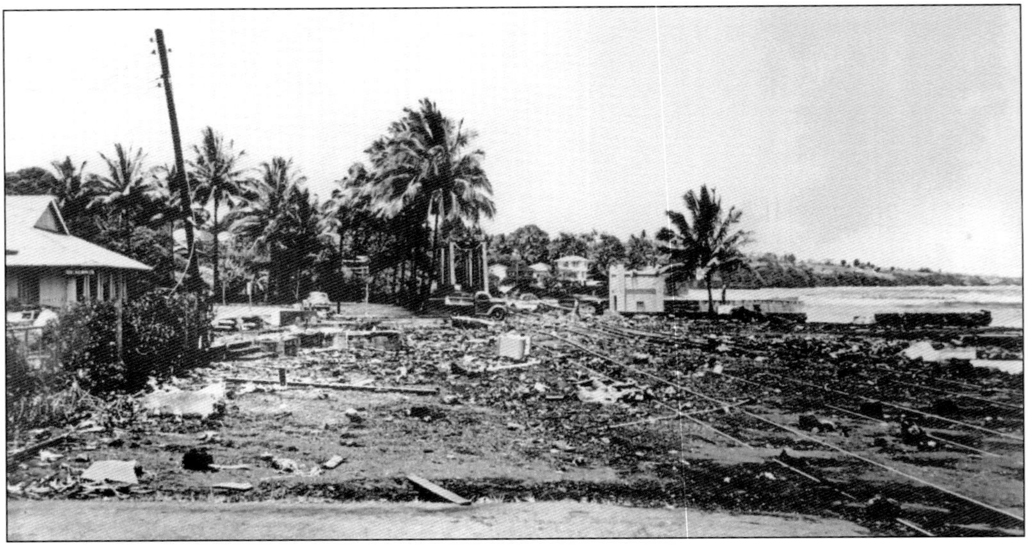

This rubble is all that remained of the railroad station. The railroad tracks once ran along the shoreline. The tsunami of 1946, in fact, ended the railroad for Hilo and the eastern side of the island. The cost of reconstructing tracks, bridges, trestles, locomotives, and buildings was just too much to justify. (Both, courtesy of NOAA/NGDC Natural Hazards Photo Archive.)

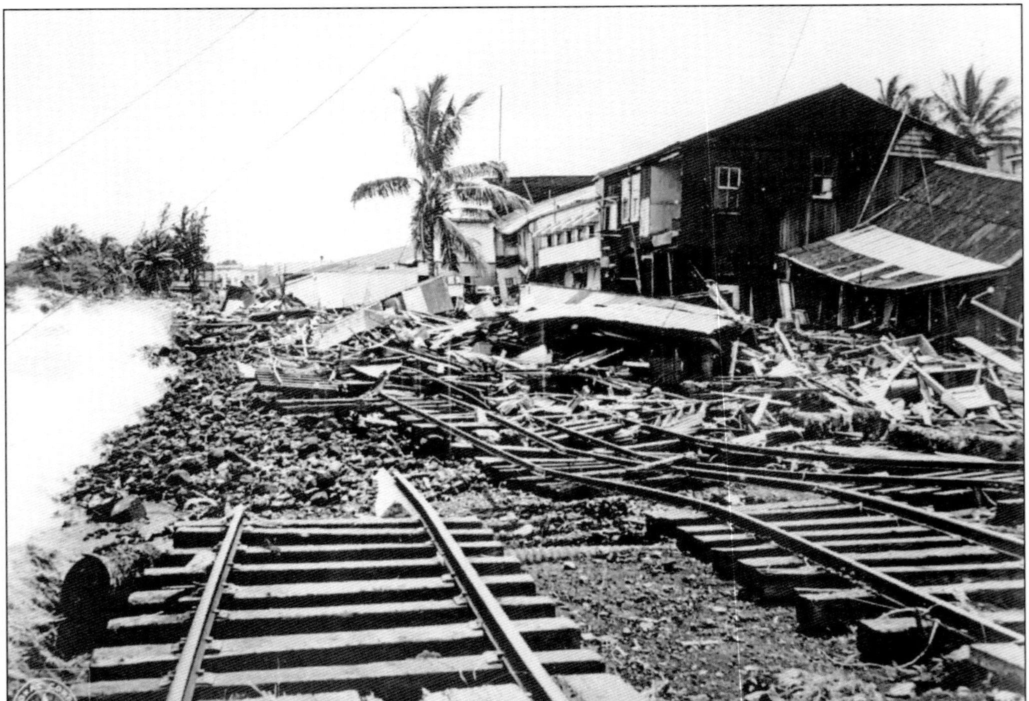

Three

Hawai'i, a Kingdom

When the first western foreigners arrived and moved onto the Hawaiian islands in the late 1700s, King Kamehameha the Great, who had a strategic and provisioning base at Hilo, was in the process of uniting all the islands under one kingdom, creating a monarchy. After his success, he and his successors to the throne adapted rapidly to the changes occurring around them. Being savvy and intelligent, they realized it was important to learn the ways of the world; they established formal diplomatic relationships, particularly with the United Kingdom, a country with a monarchy they wished to emulate. The Hawaiian kings and queens began dressing as the English did and adopted a flag that includes the flag of the United Kingdom in its corner. The eight stripes designate the eight main islands.

The people of Hilo, as did all Hawaiians, loved their kings and queens and accepted their rule as benevolent. They looked to their monarchs to guide them through the turbulent times to come. Happy that the wars between the chiefdoms were over, the Hawaiians turned to adapting themselves to the new foreign influences. As the city took form around a bay that was becoming more and more populated with foreign trading vessels, businesses sprouted up. Kamehameha realized that the islands could profit from trading resources, including sandalwood, which was prized by the Chinese. This resulted in a changing landscape as the sandalwood forests were scraped to the ground.

Following western ways and at the urging of the arriving New England missionaries, one by one the monarchs converted to Christianity. The concept of land ownership was adopted, as were new laws. In the following generations, descendants of missionaries and sailors who stayed accumulated land and began to raise crops, the greatest of which was to be sugar. Hilo thrived. In the end, the monarchy did not, and it was overthrown in 1893 as a direct result of sugar business interests.

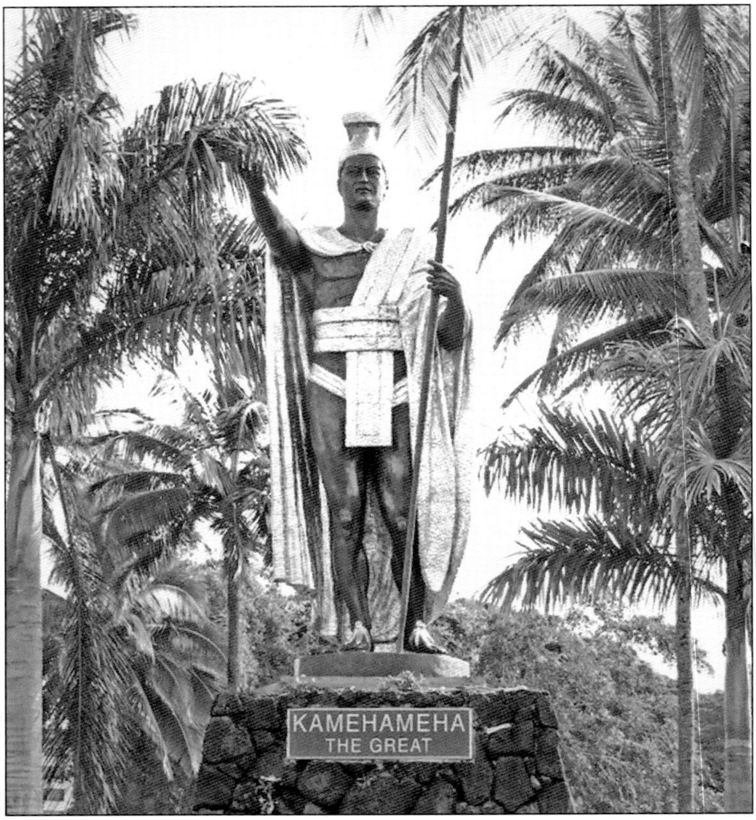

Kamehameha the Great was born at North Kohala on the Island of Hawai'i around 1758. He became a great warrior with the assistance of those who recognized his potential, training first in Waipi'o Valley and later in the district of Ka'ū. This statue in Hilo's Wailoa Park is one of four of similar design. The others are in North Kohala, near his birthplace; in Honolulu; and in National Statuary Hall, in Washington, DC. (Courtesy of Library of Congress.)

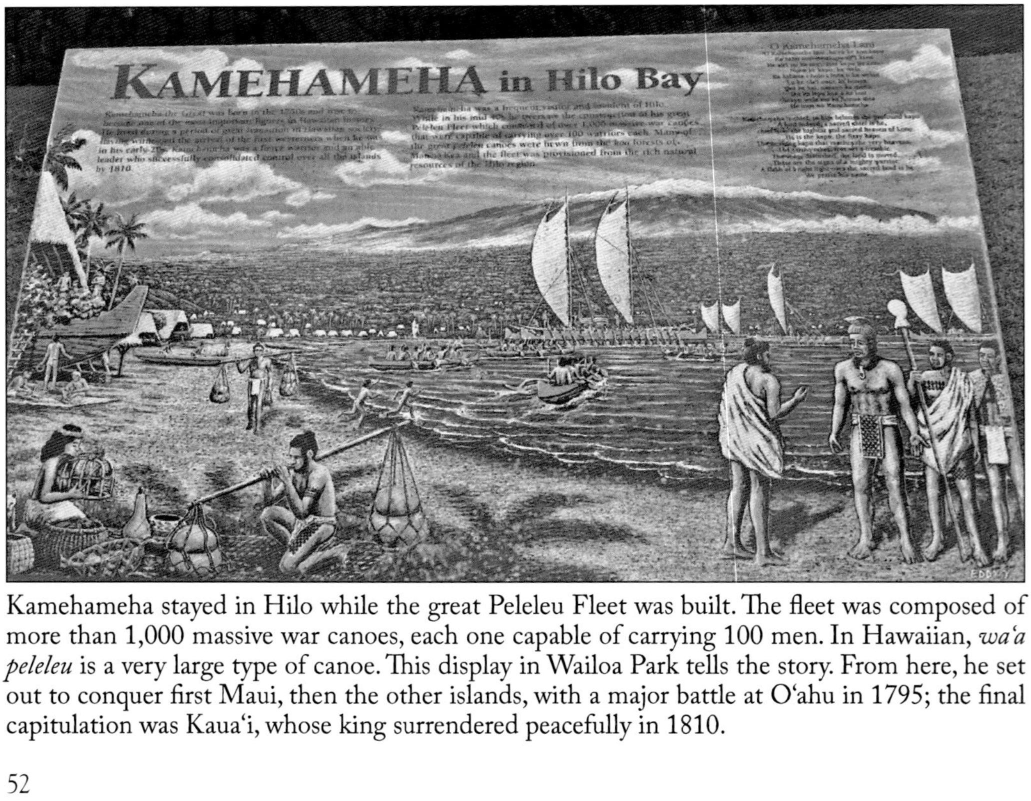

Kamehameha stayed in Hilo while the great Peleleu Fleet was built. The fleet was composed of more than 1,000 massive war canoes, each one capable of carrying 100 men. In Hawaiian, *wa'a peleleu* is a very large type of canoe. This display in Wailoa Park tells the story. From here, he set out to conquer first Maui, then the other islands, with a major battle at O'ahu in 1795; the final capitulation was Kaua'i, whose king surrendered peacefully in 1810.

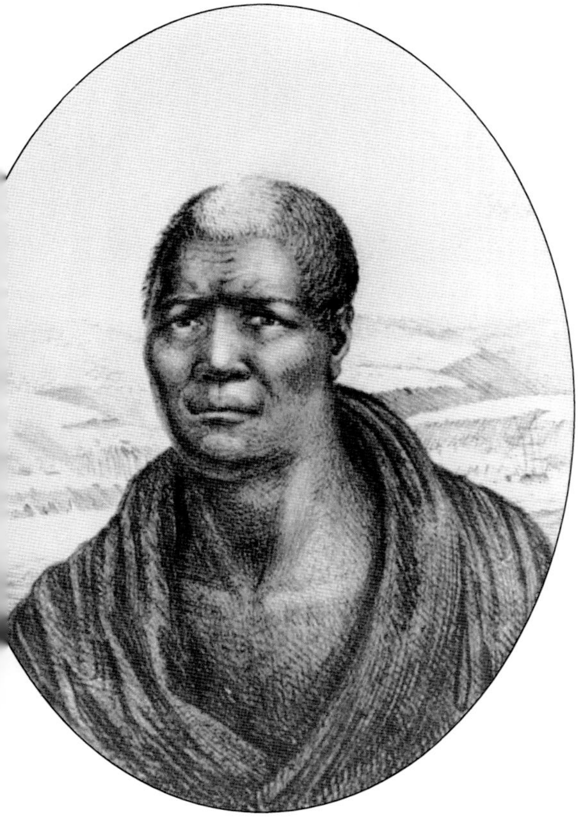

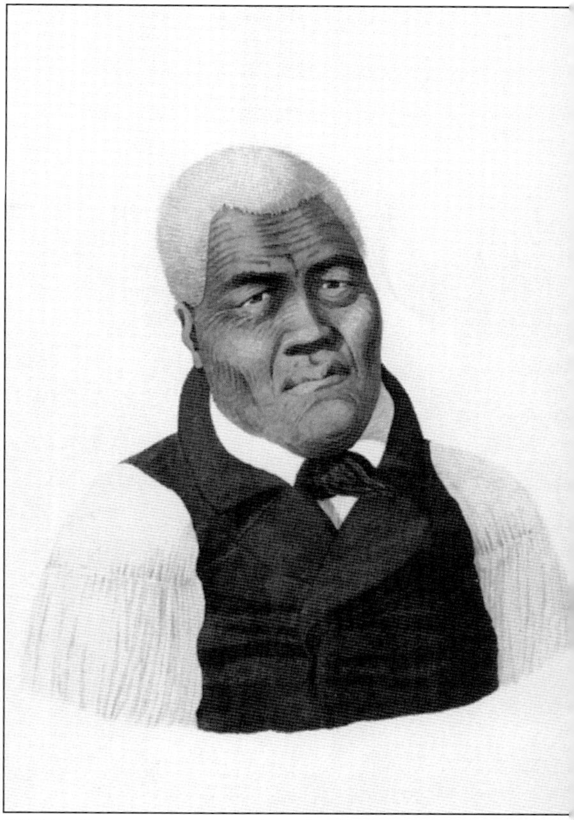

The journal of Capt. George Vancouver, who visited Hilo Bay in January 1794, tells of several shipboard discussions he had with the 36-year-old King Kamehameha, who he said was "a willing and astute listener." On May 8, 1819, the king died at Kailua-Kona at the age of 61. The two portraits above were done by German Russian artist and explorer Louis Choris. It appears evident that Kamehameha was more comfortable in native dress than in the English style he adopted to be considered an equal regent. (Both, courtesy of Hawai'i State Archives.)

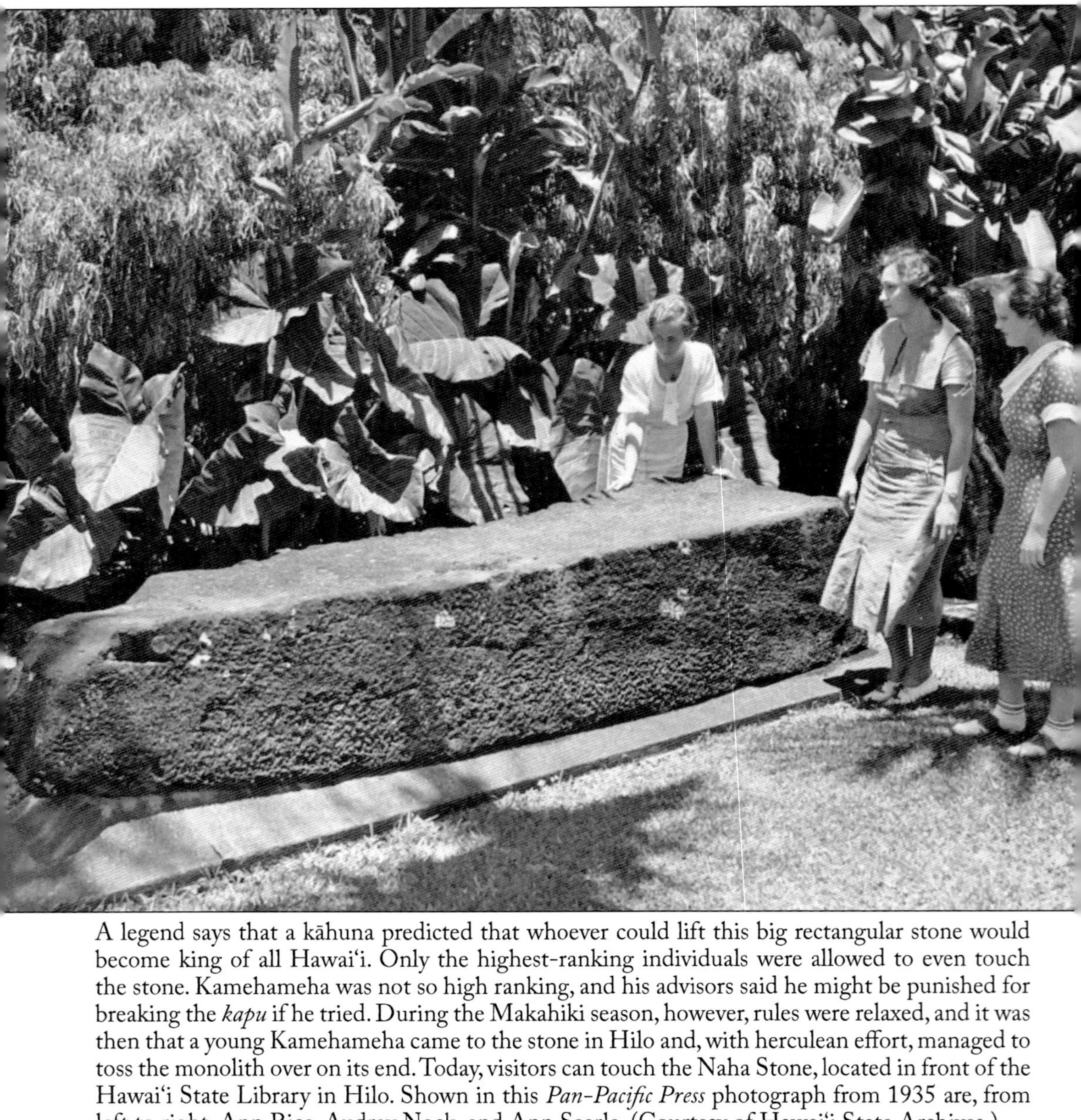

A legend says that a kāhuna predicted that whoever could lift this big rectangular stone would become king of all Hawai'i. Only the highest-ranking individuals were allowed to even touch the stone. Kamehameha was not so high ranking, and his advisors said he might be punished for breaking the *kapu* if he tried. During the Makahiki season, however, rules were relaxed, and it was then that a young Kamehameha came to the stone in Hilo and, with herculean effort, managed to toss the monolith over on its end. Today, visitors can touch the Naha Stone, located in front of the Hawai'i State Library in Hilo. Shown in this *Pan-Pacific Press* photograph from 1935 are, from left to right, Ann Rice, Audrey Nock, and Ann Searle. (Courtesy of Hawai'i State Archives.)

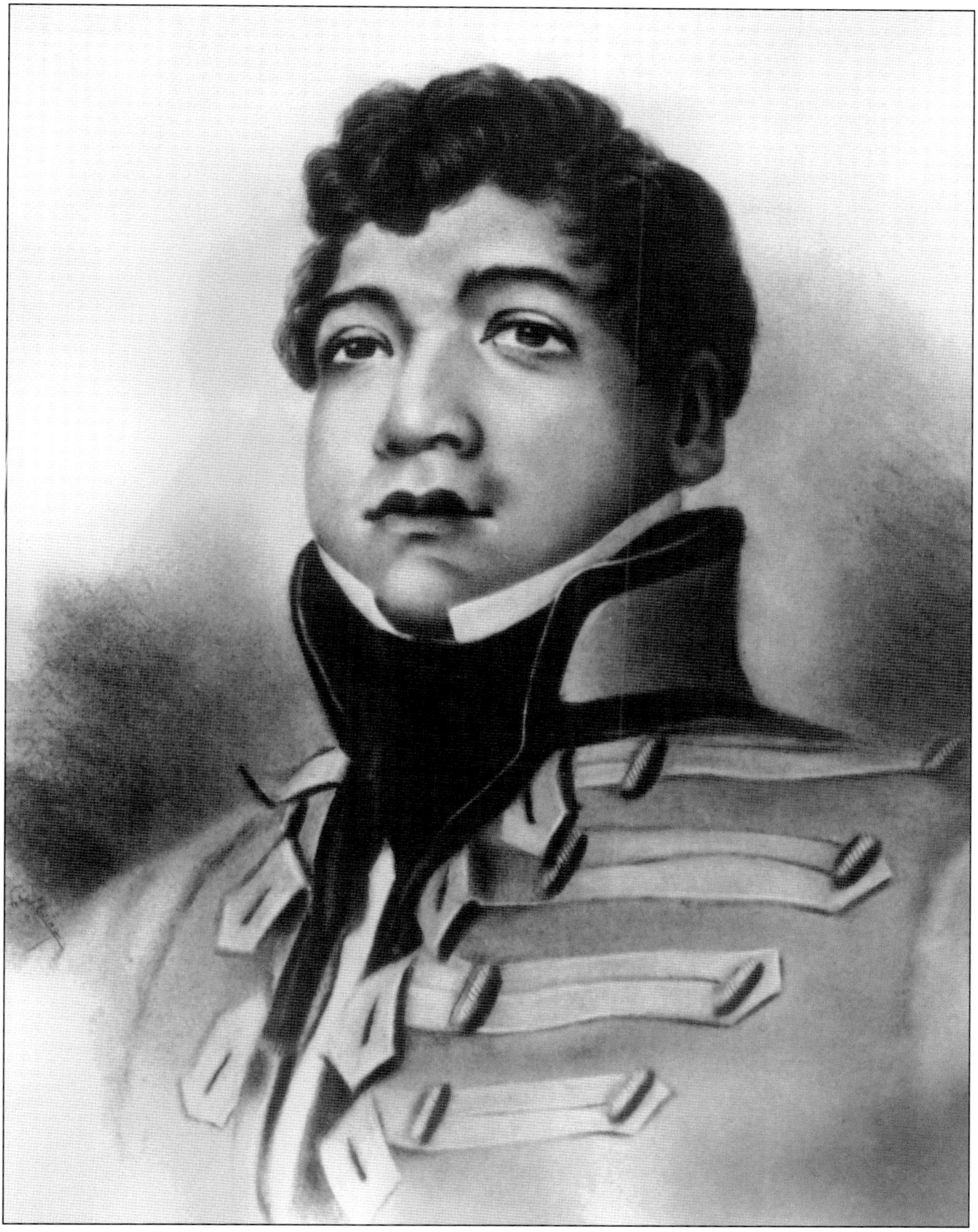

The great King Kamehameha I ruled from the Big Island and had more than 20 wives, but only three were the highest-ranking ali'i whose children were heirs to the throne. Kamehameha II (depicted here), born Liholiho in 1796 or 1797 in Hilo, became king upon the death of his father in 1819. Keōpuōlani, his father's most kapu (sacred) wife, was his mother, but he was raised by Ka'ahumanu, his father's favorite wife, who then became queen regent, or coruler. During his reign, many of the old ways were put aside and many Hawaiians, including Ka'ahumanu, became Christian converts. Change was relentless; Liholiho continued the sandalwood trade for foreign goods, and Hilo became a center of business for the east side of the island. (Courtesy of Hawai'i State Archives.)

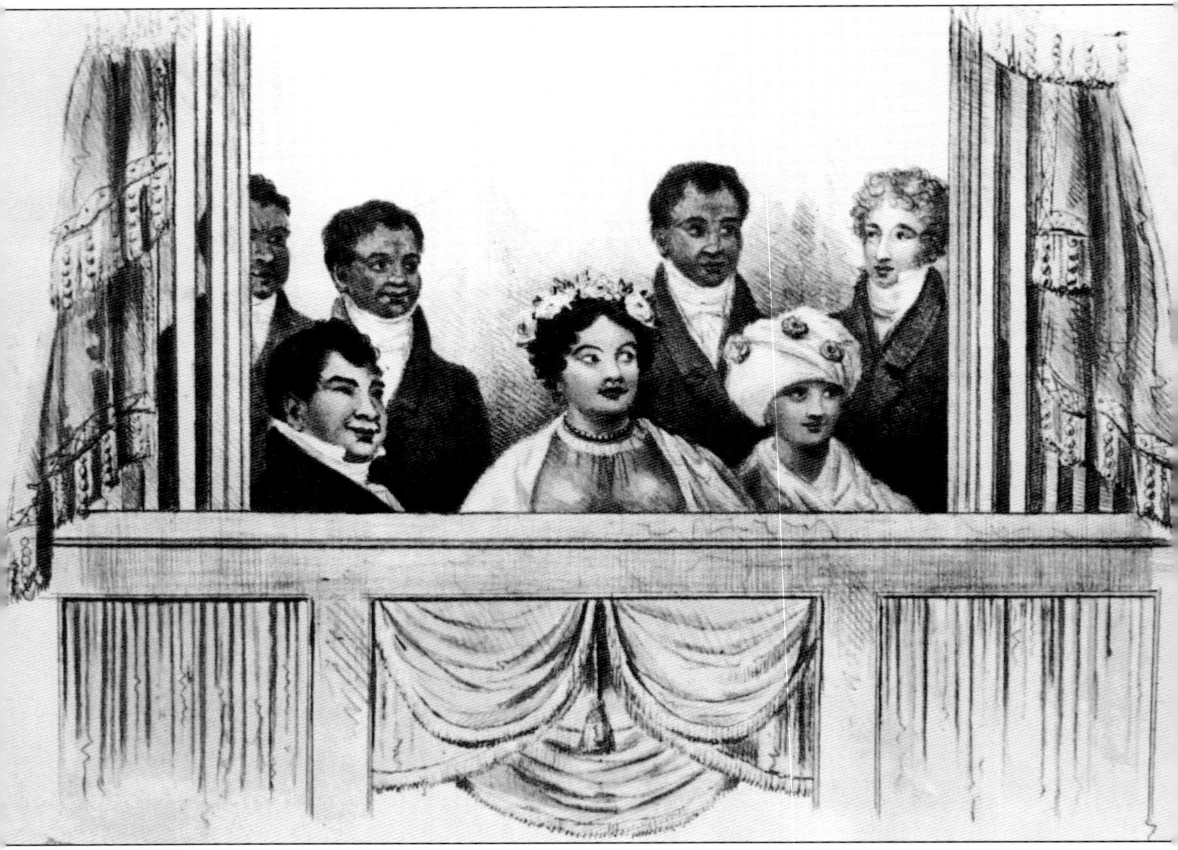

Foreign contact proved disastrous for Hawaiians, who had no immunity to common diseases like measles, which killed large numbers. In 1824, Kamehameha II and his queen, Kamāmalu, visited Great Britain on a diplomatic mission, the first Hawaiian monarchs to do so. This drawing, dated June 4, 1824, is from an English newspaper with an article titled "British Press Greets the King of the Sandwich Islands: Kamehameha II in London, 1824." Shown seated in King George IV's Royal Box at the Theatre Royal on Drury Lane are, from left to right, (first row) King Kamehameha II; Queen Kamāmalu; and Chiefess Liliha; (second row) two unidentified Hawaiians; Boki, the governor of O'ahu; and Frederick C. Byng. The royal couple fell ill and died of measles before leaving Britain. It was then Boki who led the Hawaiian delegation to meet with King George IV and receive the king's assurances of British protection for Hawai'i from foreign intrusion. (Courtesy of Hawai'i State Archives.)

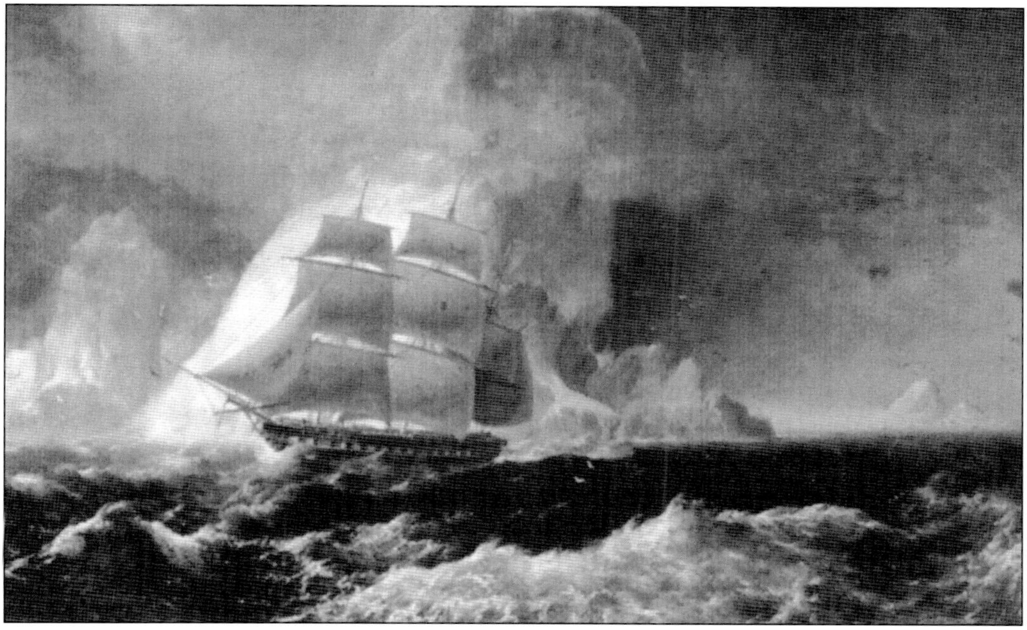

Carrying the king and queen's bodies back to Hawai'i on a famous voyage was the HMS *Blonde*, under the command of Lord George Anson Byron, cousin of the famous poet. Also aboard were naturalist Andrew Bloxam and ship's artist, Robert Dampier, who made several important paintings on the voyage. This painting, *HMS Blonde*, hangs at Washington Place, the historic home of Queen Lili'uokalani in Honolulu. (Courtesy of Hawai'i State Archives.)

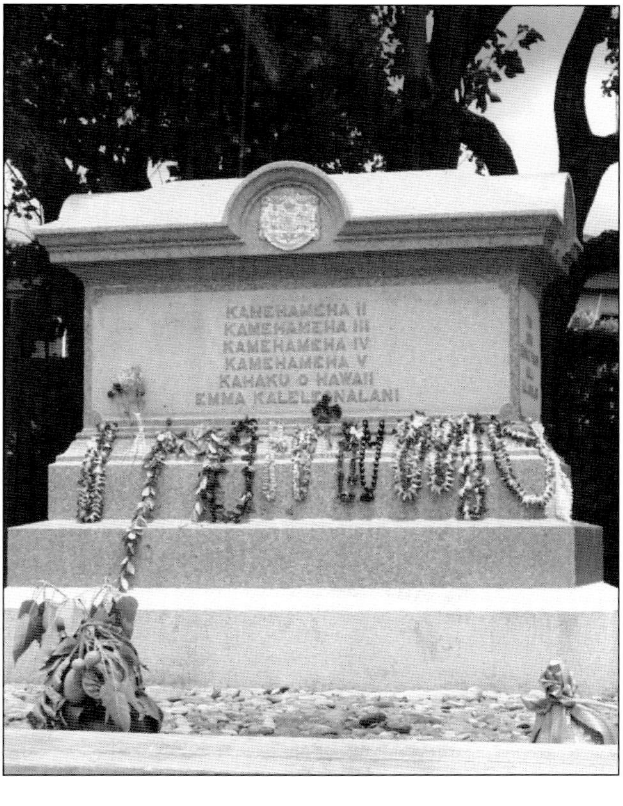

They reported first sighting land off the coast of Hilo, but they continued on to Honolulu, where a state funeral was held for the late king and queen. The *Blonde* then sailed back to Hilo, where church services were held on Sunday, June 12, 1825. For a time after that, Hilo Bay was called Byron's Bay by Europeans. A party from the ship visited Kīlauea volcano before departing Hilo and returning to Honolulu and, later, back to Kealakekua Bay. There, they built a monument at the site where Capt. James Cook died and visited the *heiau*, Hale o Keawe, at Pu'uhonua o Hōnaunau, removing most of the wooden carvings and other artifacts, which Byron considered pagan symbols. Seen here is the Kamehameha Dynasty Tomb at the Royal Mausoleum in Honolulu, Hawai'i. (Courtesy of Wikicommons.)

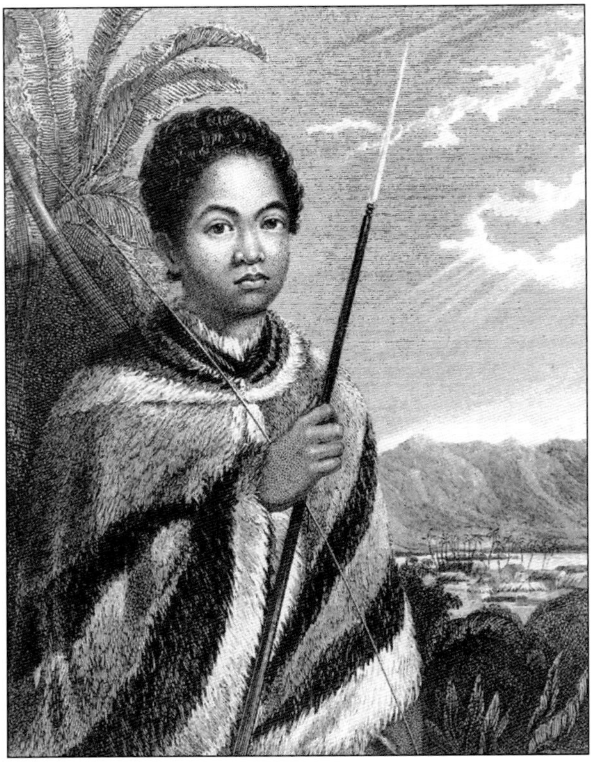

Kamehameha III was born Kauikeaouli at Keauhou, Kona, in 1817. He was chosen successor at the age of seven, when his older brother, Kamehameha II, sailed to Great Britain and died in 1824. They were both natural sons of Kamehameha I and Keōpuōlani. His hanai mother, Queen Ka'ahumanu, continued as queen regent. Kamehameha III was greatly influenced by American Christian missionaries during his lifetime. This engraving was made from a painting by Robert Dampier, ship's artist aboard the HMS *Blonde*. (Courtesy of Hawai'i State Archives.)

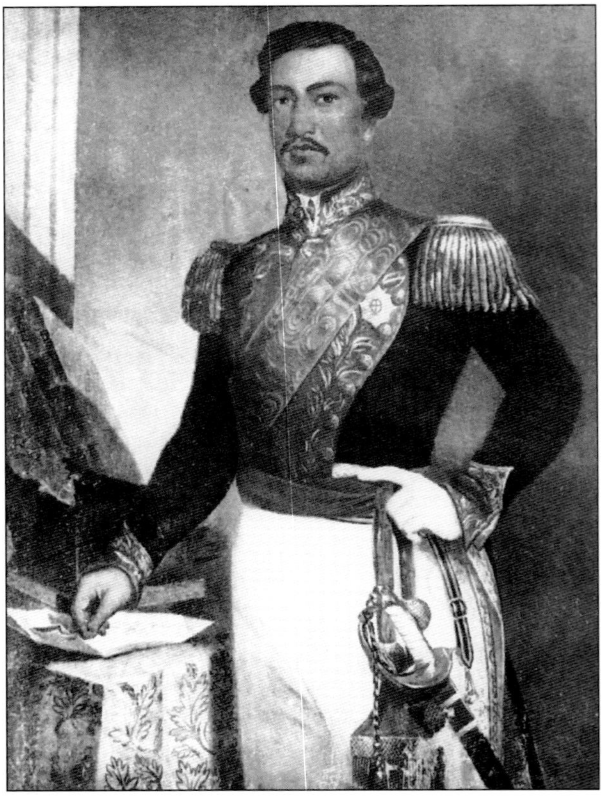

Great changes in government were made during the 30-year reign of Kamehameha III, including the first time Hawaiians held the right to vote and the first constitution, which was adopted in 1840. In 1848, Kamehameha III permitted an unprecedented system of land division and ownership under the Great Mahele, dividing lands among the ali'i, the government, and the people. This was followed by the Resident Alien Act, which gave foreigners the right to own land. Total population had plummeted from a high of about 300,000 in 1778 to a low of about 60,000 by 1850, reflecting the decimation of Native Hawaiians. Kamehameha III died in 1854 at age 37. (Courtesy of Hawai'i State Archives.)

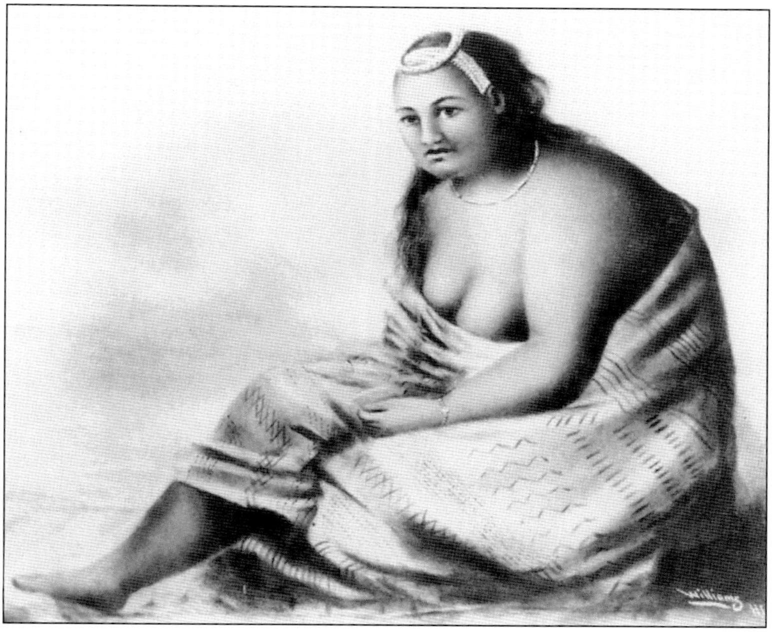

Ka'ahumanu, the favorite wife and queen consort of King Kamehameha I, continued to wield considerable power in the kingdom as the *Kuhina Nui* (regent) of the Kingdom of Hawai'i during the reigns of his first two successors. She managed to end ancient kapu against women, thereby changing the rules of Hawaiian society. (Courtesy of Hawai'i State Archives.)

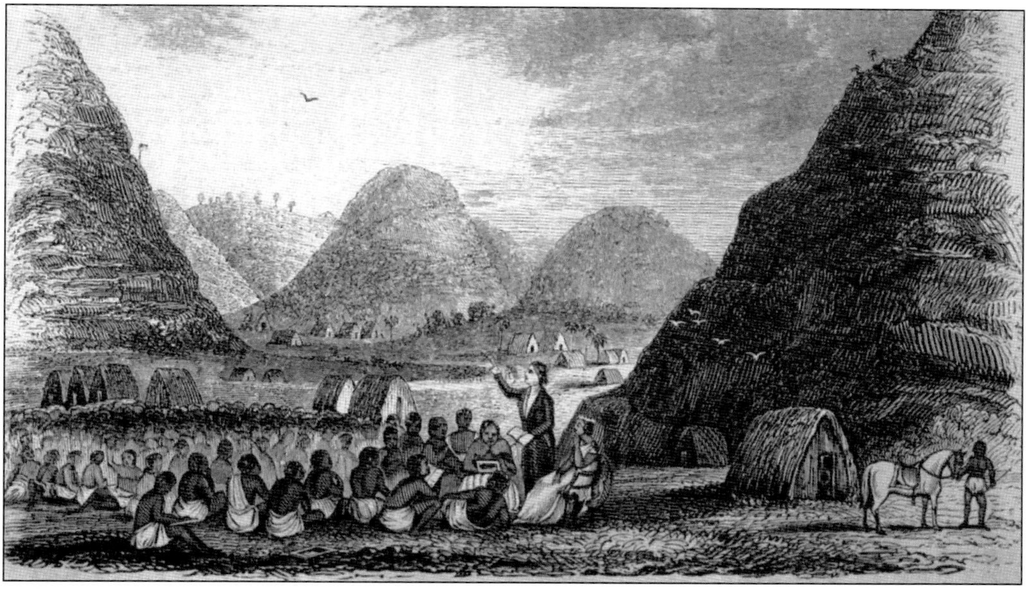

Ka'ahumanu publicly acknowledged her embrace of Protestant Christianity and encouraged her subjects to be baptized into the faith. In order to preserve the loyalty of the island of Kaua'i, which had never been forcibly conquered by Kamehameha, she and her sons conspired to convince its king, Kaumuali'i, to marry Ka'ahumanu in political alliance. After he died, she went on to marry one of his sons. Ka'ahumanu and King Kamehameha III negotiated the first free trade treaty between the Kingdom of Hawai'i and the United States in 1826. The queen, who was known to be an accomplished surfer, died of an intestinal illness in 1832 in Honolulu. This 1826 illustration shows missionary Hiram Bingham preaching to the queen and her subjects. (Courtesy of Hawai'i State Archives.)

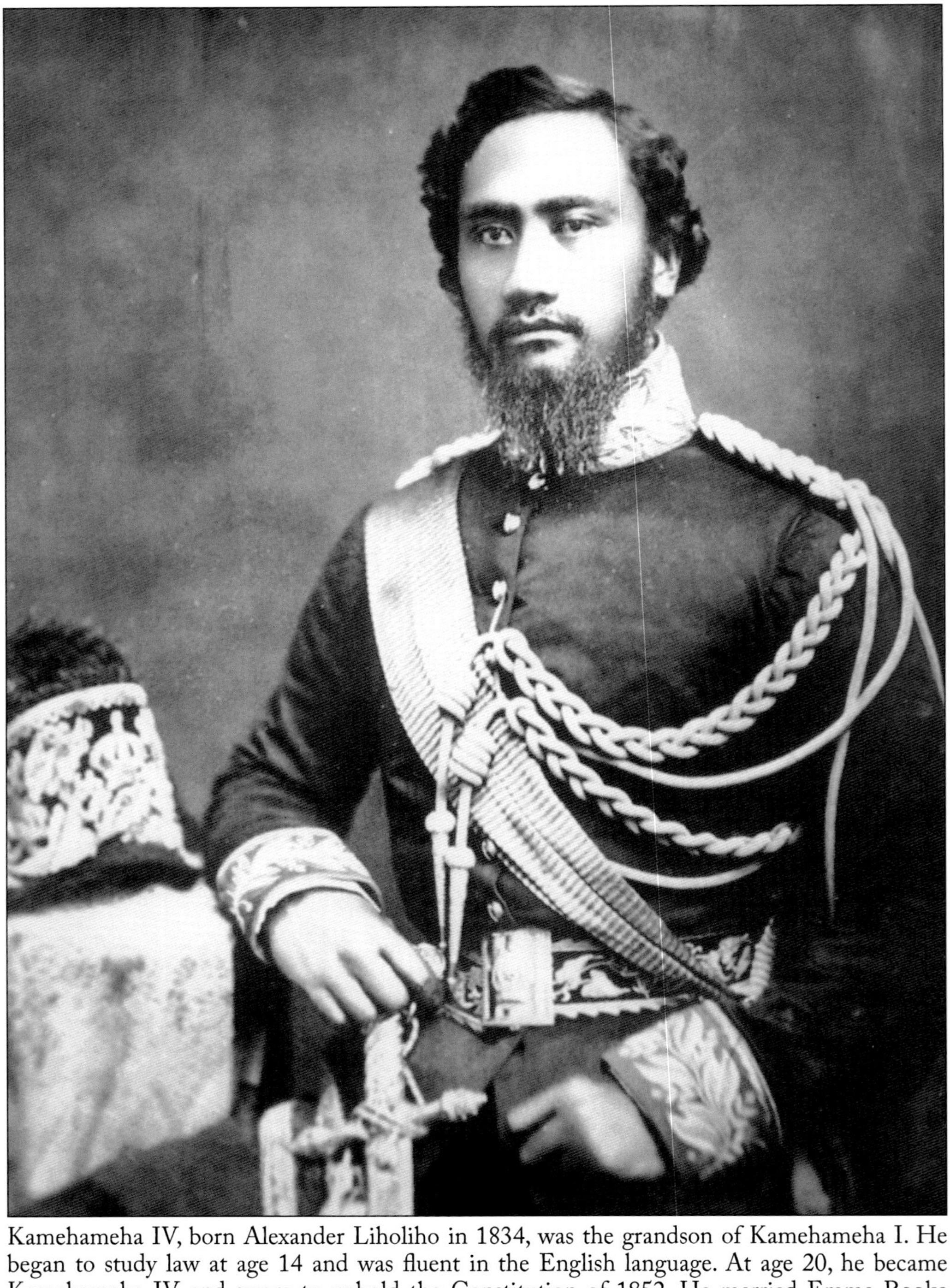

Kamehameha IV, born Alexander Liholiho in 1834, was the grandson of Kamehameha I. He began to study law at age 14 and was fluent in the English language. At age 20, he became Kamehameha IV and swore to uphold the Constitution of 1852. He married Emma Rooke in 1856. They had one son, Albert Edward, who died at age four. Kamehameha IV did not agree that annexation to the United States was in the best interest of his people, but American sugar planters were becoming economically and politically powerful. In 1860, the king and queen founded the Queen's Hospital in Honolulu for their sick and dying people. Kamehameha IV, too, died young, at the age of 29 in 1863. (Courtesy of Hawai'i State Archives.)

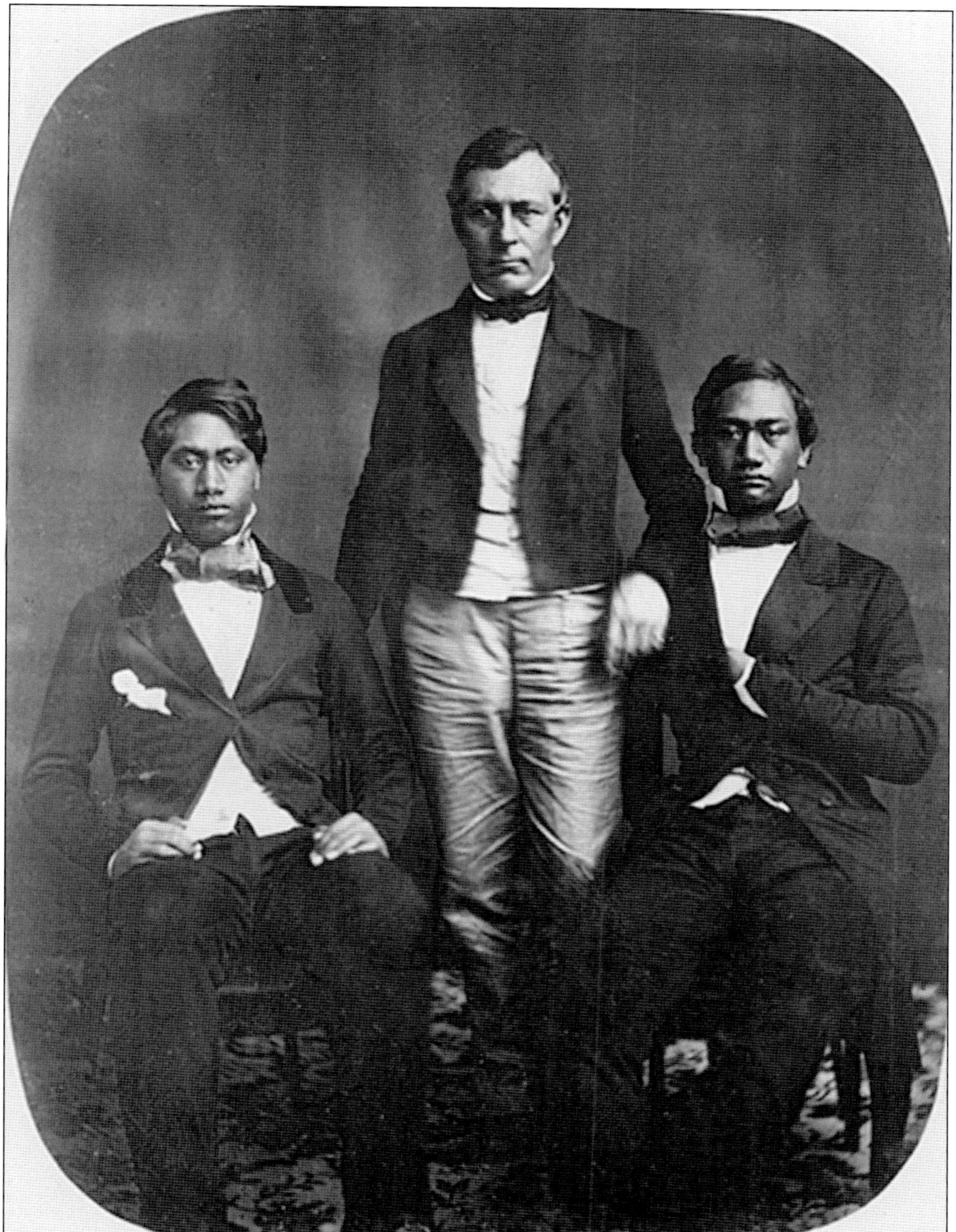

In 1849, Alexander Liholiho, and his older brother, Lot, began their yearlong trip to the United States and Europe, traveling with Dr. Gerrit P. Judd, who was a missionary, physician, and cabinet minister of finance. When they returned, Alexander Liholiho was made king and Lot was appointed a member of the house of nobles and began government service. In this 1850 photograph, the 19-year-old Lot is on the left, Judd in the center, and 15-year-old Alexander Liholiho at right. (Courtesy of Hawai'i State Archives.)

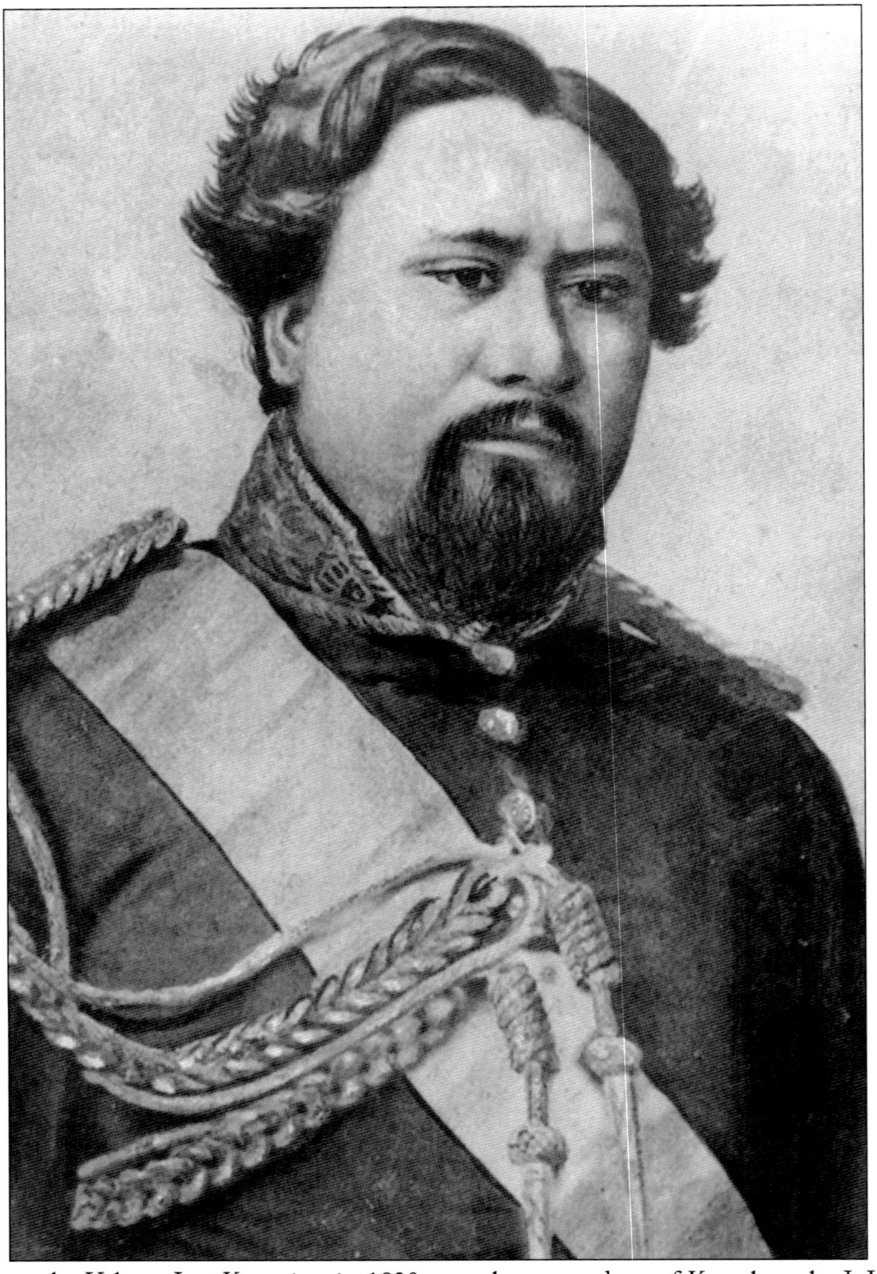

Kamehameha V, born Lot Kapuaiwa in 1830, was also a grandson of Kamehameha I. He was trained in western as well as Hawaiian traditions. A visit to Hilo was reported in 1862. He became king upon the death of Alexander Liholiho in 1863. Like his brother, Kamehameha V preferred the British and their traditions and opposed American annexation of Hawaiʻi. Because the Hawaiian population was at its lowest in the 1850s, Kamehameha V agreed with the sugar planters to hire workers from other countries. Chinese immigrated to the area in 1852, then Japanese, and many others followed. More ships came to Hilo and other ports, and new buildings were constructed. His reign of a decade saw the continuing growth of what would soon become Hawaiʻi's major industry: sugar. The king died in 1872 without a successor. (Courtesy of Hawaiʻi State Archives.)

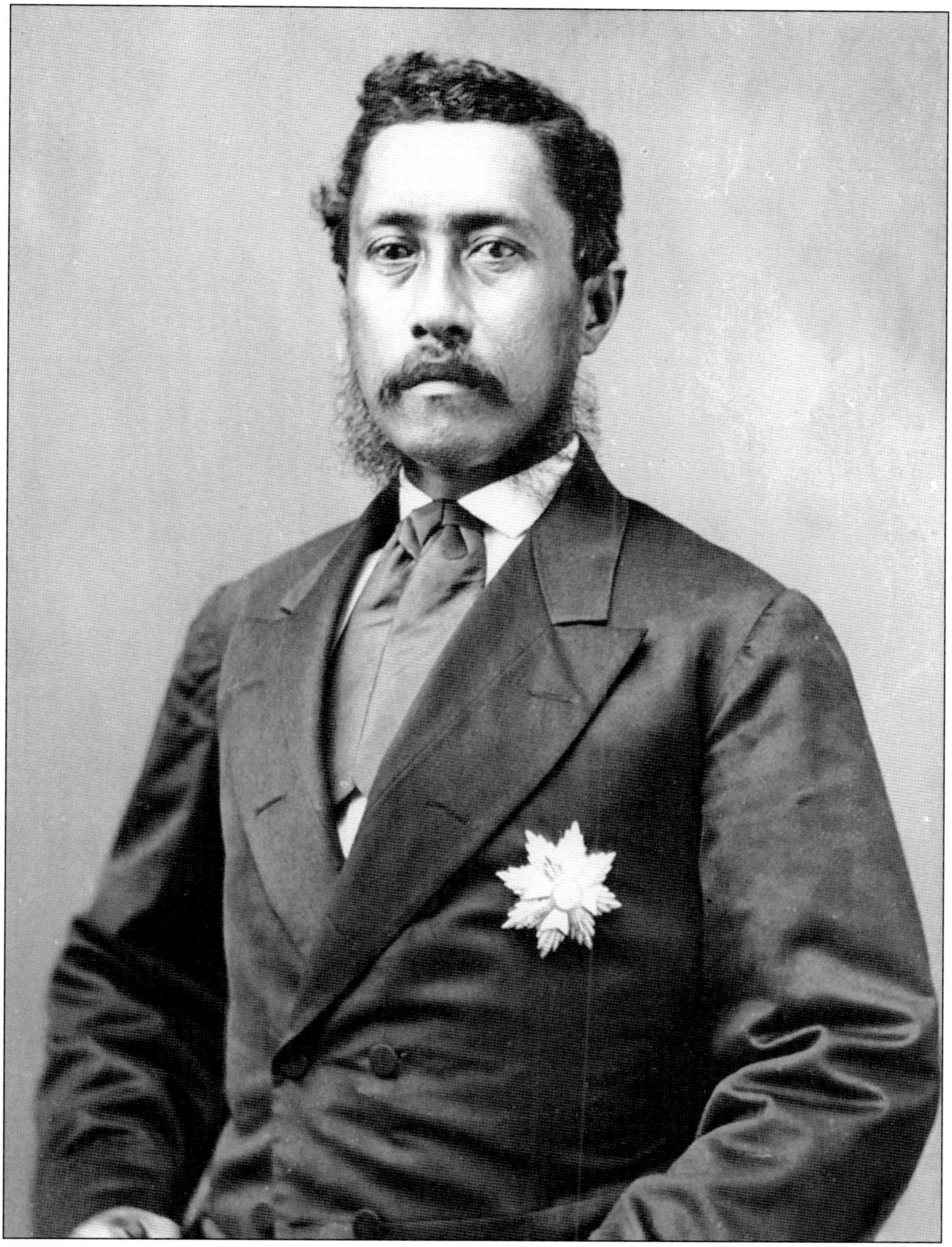

The constitution directed the legislature to elect a king from the ali'i when an heir was not provided. William "Billy" Charles Lunalilo, a grandnephew of Kamehameha I, was chosen on January 1, 1873. Prince Billy was named William in honor of the English monarch William IV. He died of tuberculosis on February 3, 1874. During his short reign, he made a memorable visit to Hilo on the USS *Benicia*, which is recorded in the journal of Isabella Bird: "Lieutenant-Governor Lyman and Mr. Severance, the sheriff, went out to the Benicia, and the king landed at 10 o'clock, being graciously pleased to accept the Governor's house as his residence during his visit." The people of Hilo made a big celebration of the king's visit. (Photograph by Menzies Dickson, courtesy of Hawai'i State Archives.)

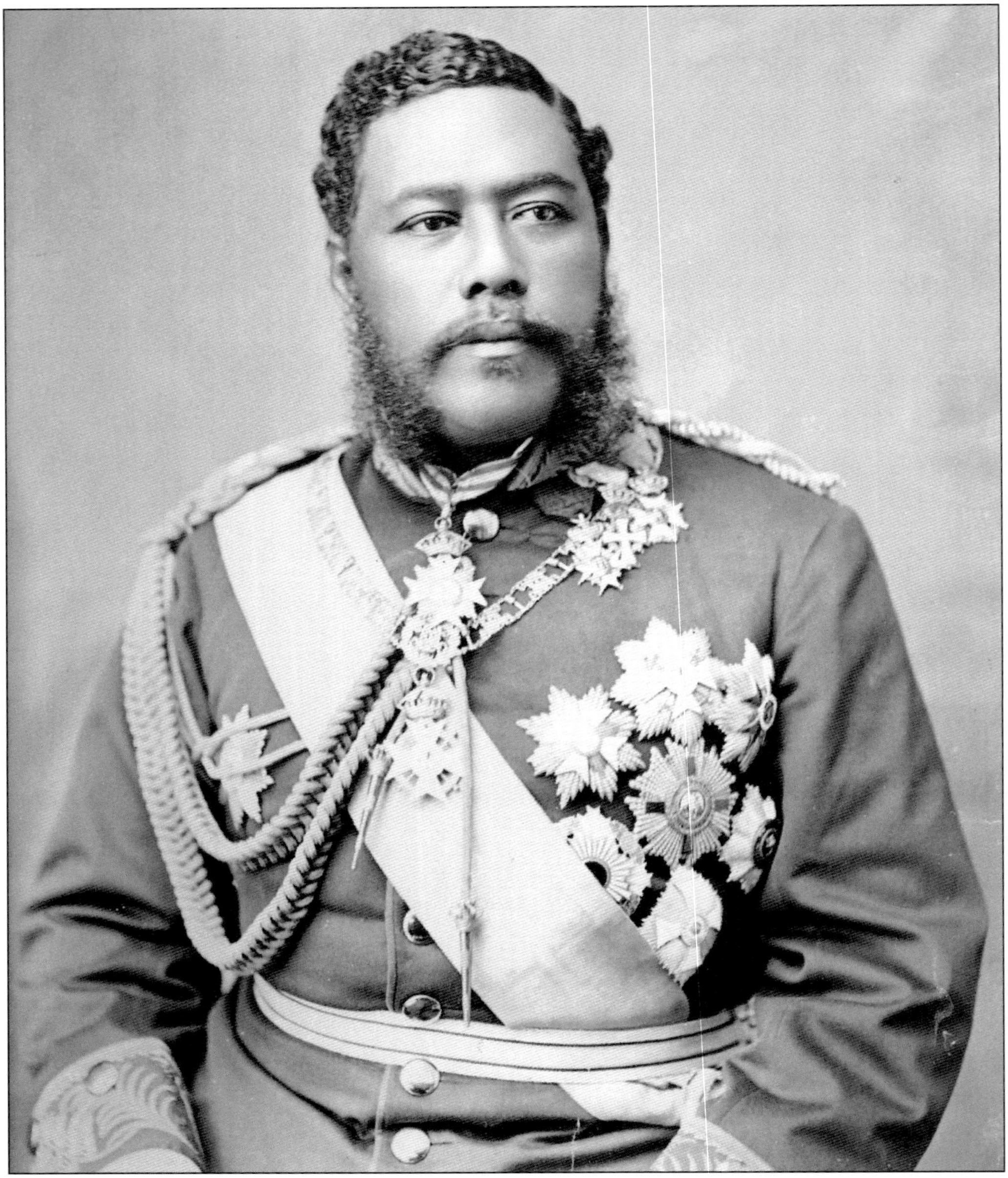

David Kalākaua, born on November 16, 1836, on O'ahu, was the son of a chief and chiefess. His wife was Kapi'olani. He studied law and became a major on King Kamehameha IV's staff, a member of the Privy Council and the House of Nobles, postmaster general, and the king's chamberlain under Kamehameha V. In 1873, David Kalākaua became the kingdom's first popularly elected monarch. A renaissance man, he was interested in music, science, technology, and languages. A world traveler, he built 'Iolani Palace, met with Thomas Edison, and installed electric lights in the palace before the White House had them. His regency was challenged with increasing pressure from business interests to become a territory of the United States. Business interests wanting more control forced Kalākaua to sign the Bayonet Constitution in 1887, reducing his power to that of a figurehead. After a bruising legislative session in 1890, Kalākaua sailed to San Francisco, hoping to rest and restore his health. He died there on January 20, 1891, of Bright's disease, a kidney ailment. (Courtesy of Hawai'i State Archives.)

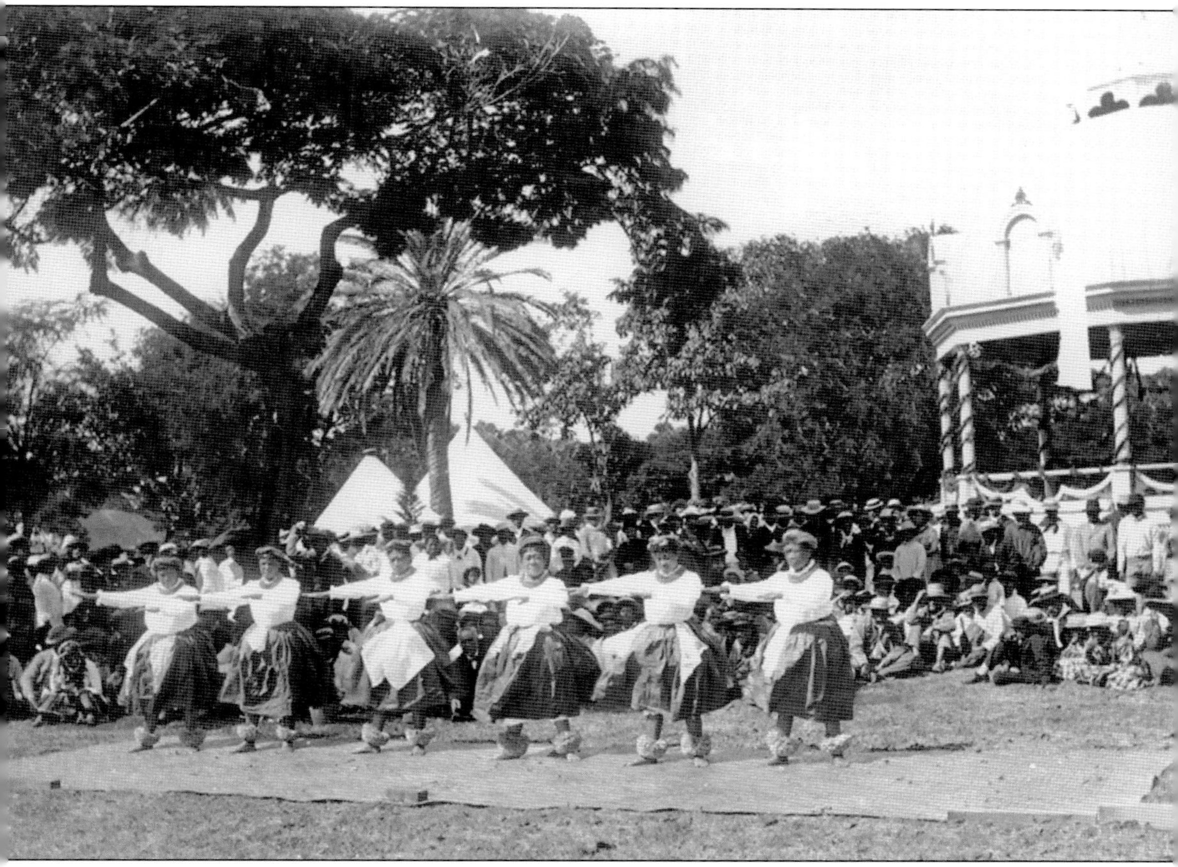

Kalākaua was known as the "Merrie Monarch" because of his love of pomp, ceremony, and celebrations. One of his most significant acts was to revive the performance of hula in public, after it had been suppressed by missionary influences. He was a supporter of traditional Hawaiian music and was an accomplished writer and composer. At the king's 49th birthday celebration at 'Iolani Palace in 1885, a number of hula performances were seen, including this one by Honolulu dancers. More than 100 years later, the Merrie Monarch Festival would be created in Hilo and become the most famous celebration and competition in the hula world. A landmark in the center of downtown Hilo is Kalākaua Park, named after the king. Located there is a bronze statue of Kalākaua, who dedicated the park around 1877. (Photograph by Dr. Edward Arning, courtesy of Hawai'i State Archives.)

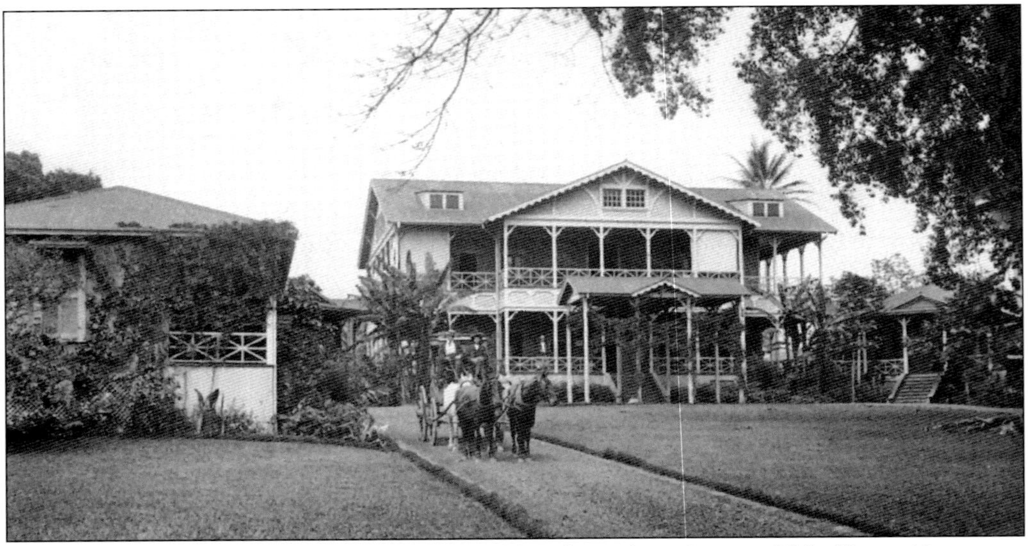

The old Hilo Hotel was on the site of King Kalākaua's royal residence in Hilo. The residence was a modest and humble house that stood in the rear of the property sold to John D. Spreckels, who built the hotel in 1888. The photograph shows the hotel with a horse-drawn carriage coming down the driveway. (Courtesy of Lyman Museum.)

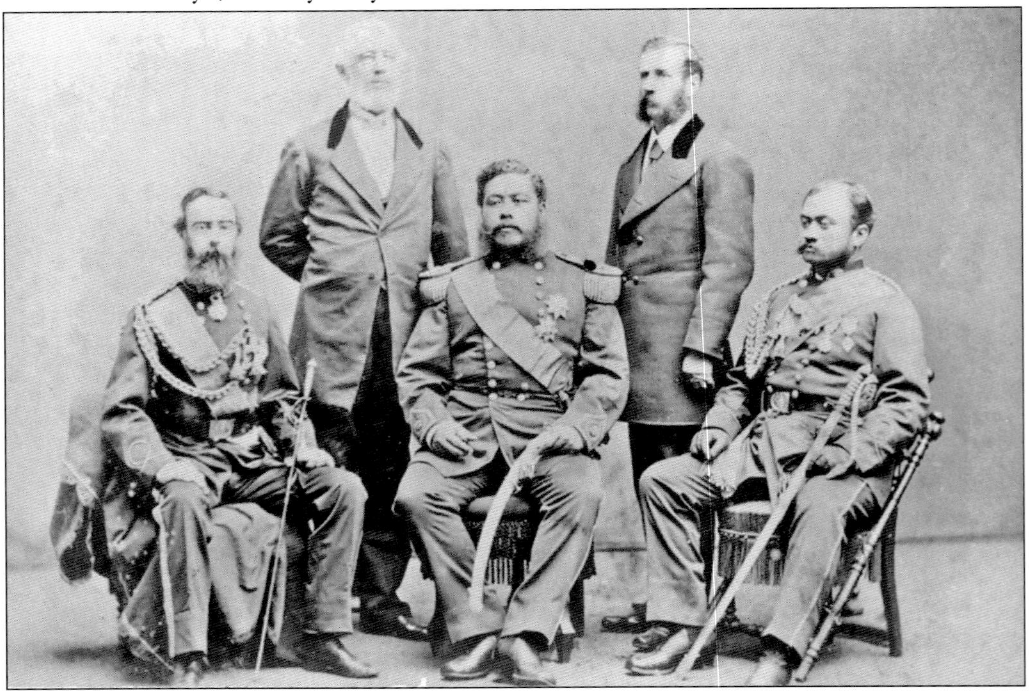

The Reciprocity Commission traveled to San Francisco to sign the Reciprocity Treaty of 1875. Seated, from left to right, are John O. Dominis, husband of Kalākaua's sister Lydia (Lili'uokalani); King Kalākaua, and John M. Kapena. Standing are Henry A. Peirce, right, and Luther W. Severance from Hilo. This treaty gave free access to the United States market for sugar and other Hawaiian products in return for lands granted to the United States to be used for the Pearl Harbor naval base. The treaty led to large investment by resident Americans in sugar plantations in Hawai'i. (Courtesy of Hawai'i State Archives.)

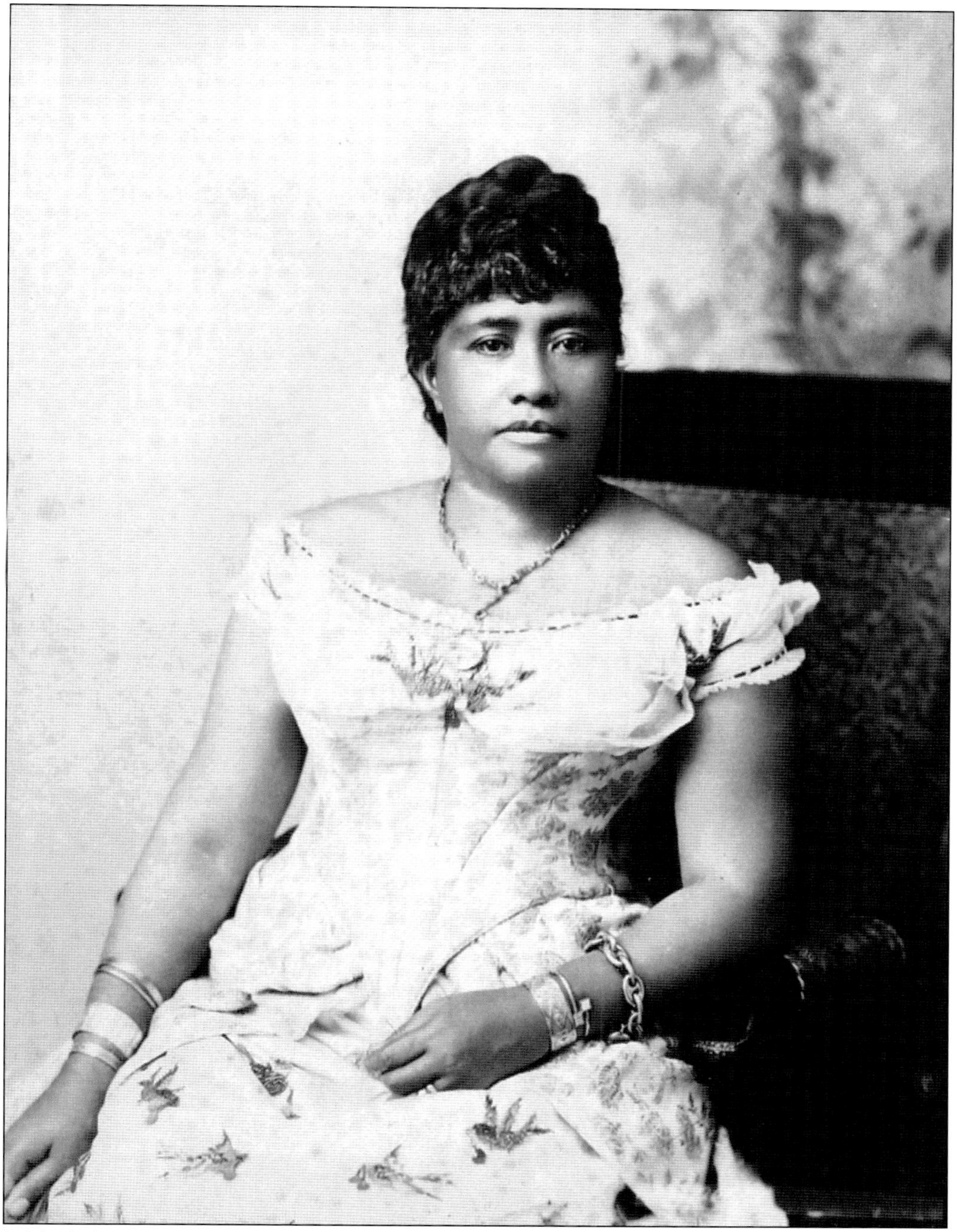

Lili'uokalani was born on September 2, 1838. She was well educated and married John Owen Dominis when she was 24. When her brother became king, she became a princess and performed ceremonial duties. She was a gifted musician and composer, writing the popular "Aloha 'Oe." She is pictured here as crown princess. Upon the death of Kalākaua in 1891, Lili'uokalani became queen. The cards were stacked against her as the forces for annexation were already underway. In the end, she was forced to resign and was taken prisoner in her own palace in a coup d'état on January 17, 1893. After the queen's release, she lobbied in Washington, DC, but it was to no avail. On July 7, 1898, Hawai'i became a territory of the United States. (Courtesy of Wikicommons.)

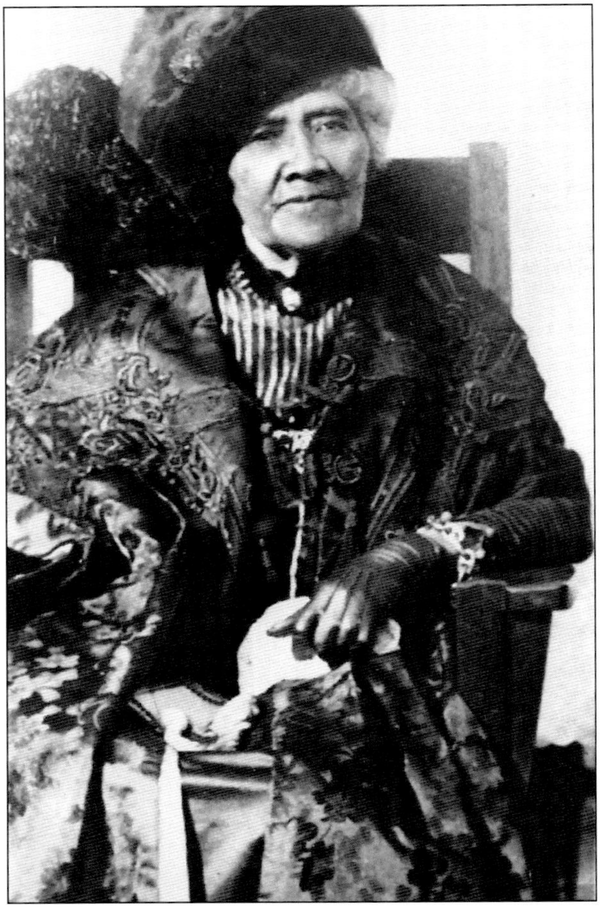

In her book, *Hawai'i's Story by Hawai'i's Queen*, Lili'uokalani describes several visits to Hilo. She accompanied Prince Lot on a visit here in 1824 as a newlywed and reports staying at his own residence. On another trip in 1880, she brought a friend to visit the volcano. Lili'uokalani is shown here during her last visit to Hilo in 1913. (Courtesy of Lyman Museum.)

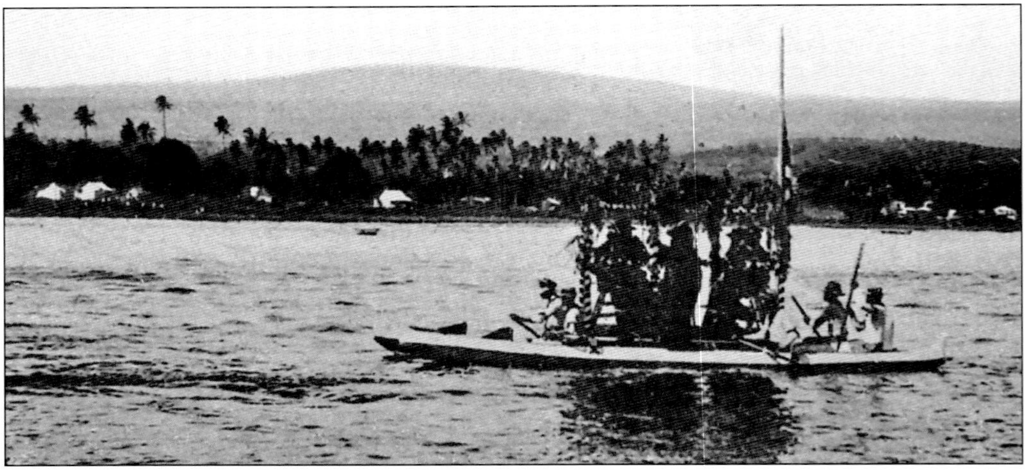

This postcard image shows the queen arriving in a canoe at Hilo Bay on an unknown date. She donated the 30-acre site now known as Lili'uokalani Park and Gardens on Banyan Drive adjacent to the Hilo Hawaiian Hotel, Coconut Island, and Hilo Bay. Built in the early 1900s, the park now consists of Edo-style Japanese gardens, and is said to be the largest such gardens outside Japan. Each year, the city holds a celebration in honor of the queen's birthday. (Courtesy of Lyman Museum.)

Four

Missionaries Change Life Forever

American missionaries arrived in Hawai'i in 1820 after hearing stories about the islands and the Hawaiian people. The first group to tour the island of Hawai'i, sent by the American Board of Commissioners for Foreign Missions, included William Ellis, whose *Journal of William Ellis, a Narrative of an 1823 Tour Through Hawai'i* is a detailed description of the terrain and population of the time, and includes his many adventures. The task force, which also included Asa Thurston, Artemis Bishop, and Joseph Goodrich, scouted for sites to place missions. The Waiākea Mission Station, also known as the Hilo Station, was set up as the first Christian mission on the eastern side of the island.

On May 19, 1824, a simple grass hut was dedicated as the first church, with Joseph Goodrich as preacher and Samuel Ruggles as teacher. The Hawaiian village at the time was called Waiākea in the district of Hilo.

In 1825, a larger grass structure was built at the present-day site of Kalākaua Park. David Belden Lyman and his wife, Sarah Joiner Lyman, arrived in 1832 and Goodrich returned to New England. The Lymans' real passion was education; in order to supplement their preaching, they established the Hilo Boarding School. In 1835, Rev. Titus Coan and his wife, Fidelia, arrived. He learned the Hawaiian language, enabling him to travel through the districts of Puna and Ka'ū to the south while gathering converts. Titus developed a reputation a great evangelist and made a big impact on Hilo.

As church attendance became widespread over the next two decades, the missionaries suppressed many traditional Hawaiian cultural practices, operated over 1,000 common schools, instructed the natives in wearing apparel, banned alcohol and other activities deemed immoral, and instructed the ali'i in western political economy.

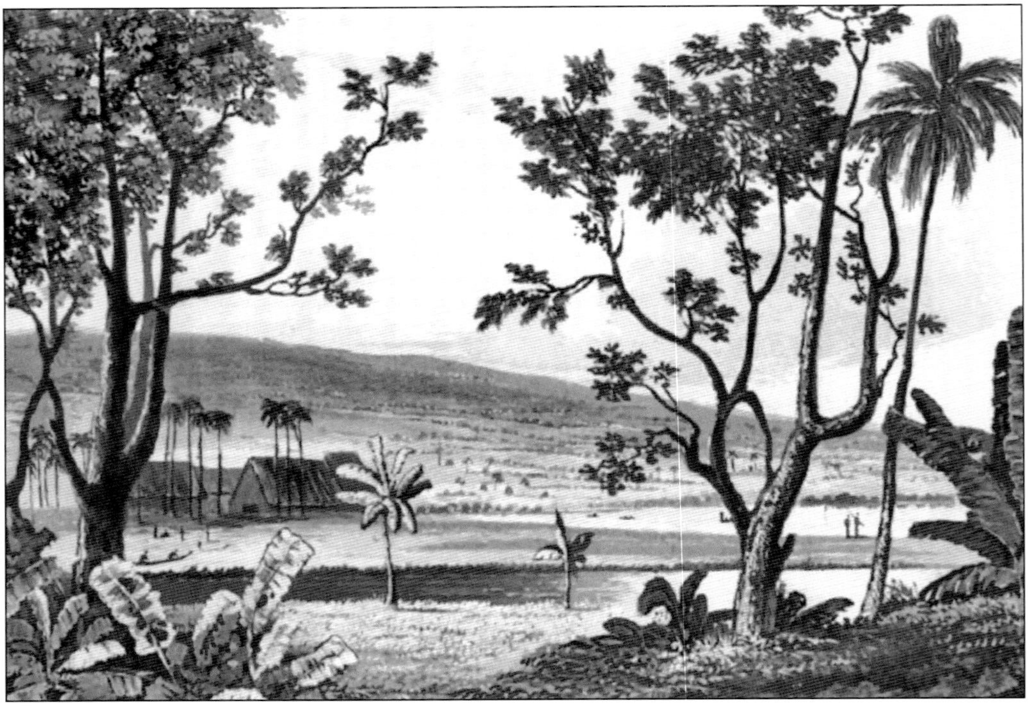

The Waiākea Mission as it appeared in 1825 was illustrated by HMS *Blonde*'s artist, Robert Dampier, during its visit to Hilo after returning the bodies of King Kamehameha II and his queen, who had died in London. Only a few thatched huts were there at the time.

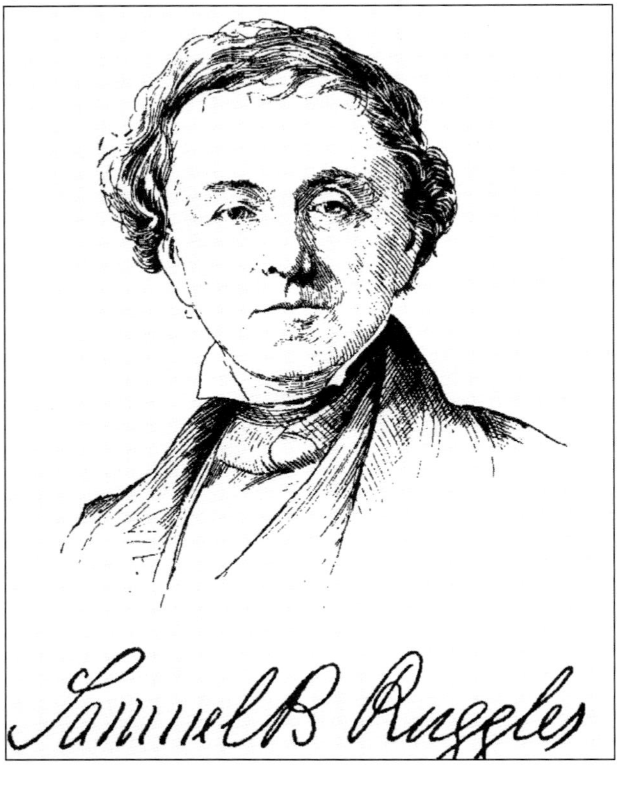

Samuel Ruggles was in the first Protestant missionary company to Hawai'i in 1820. He served in Hilo from 1822 to 1828. He is credited with bringing the first slips of coffee to the Kona district when he transferred to Kealakekua in 1828. The artist of this drawing is unidentified. (Courtesy of Wikicommons.)

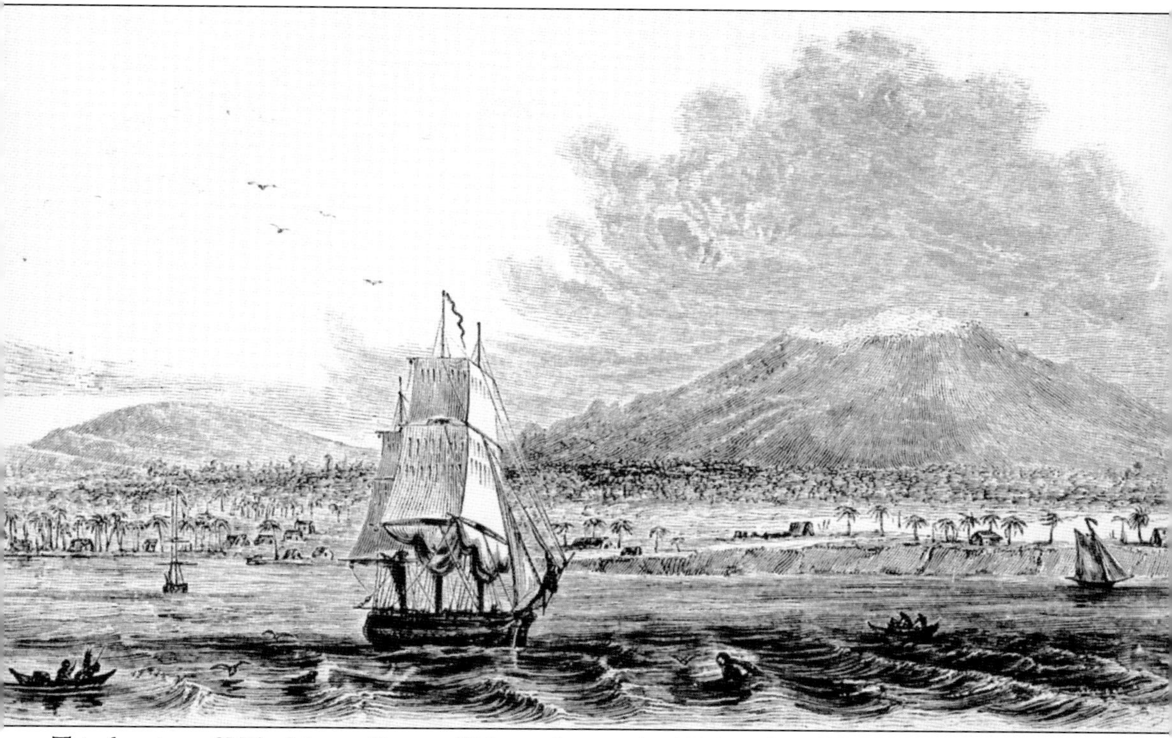

This drawing of Hilo, Mauna Kea, and Mauna Loa in the 1820s is from Hiram Bingham's book *A Residence of Twenty-one Years in the Sandwich Islands.* Bingham was an influential missionary who served in Honolulu.

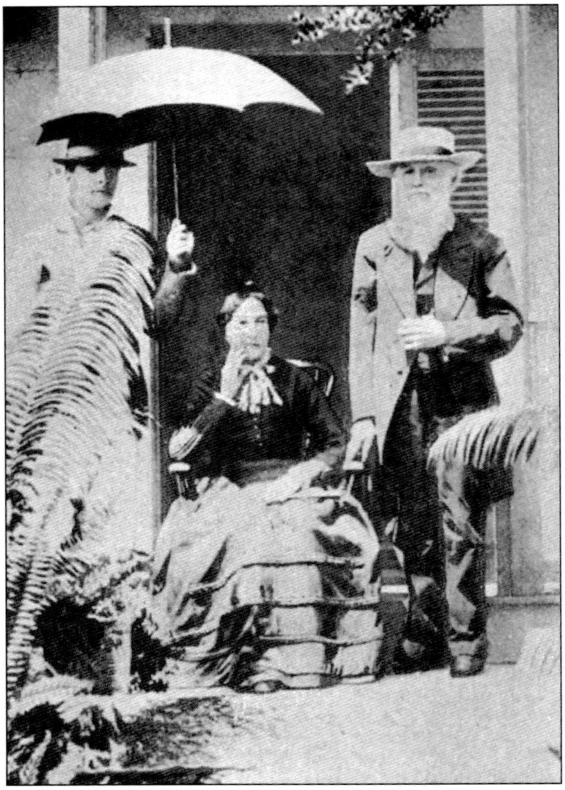

The Reverend David Belden Lyman and Sarah Joiner Lyman were the first permanent missionary family to be located in Hilo. In 1836, Lyman established the Hilo Boys' Boarding School, a vocational school that also offered preparatory courses for the high school at Lahainaluna. The couple is shown here around 1881 with an unidentified young man holding an umbrella on the front porch of their home. This building is now restored and part of the Lyman Museum. (Courtesy of Hawaiian Mission Children's Society Library.)

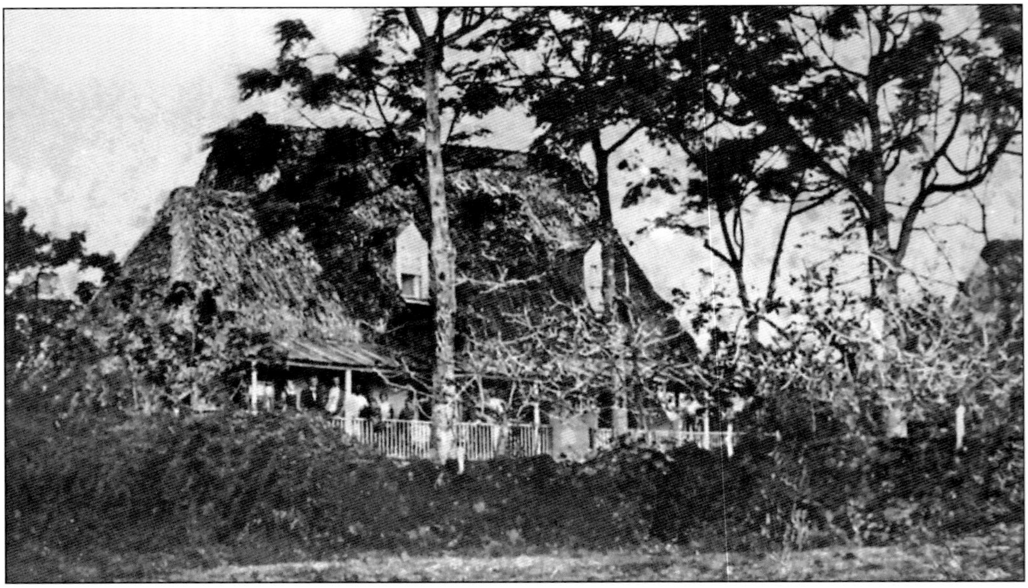

This image is taken from a daguerreotype from about 1850 to 1855 of the Lyman Mission House, with the Lyman family and others on the front porch. It appears here as originally built in 1839, with a native Hawaiian thatched roof and New England dormer windows. Later, a second story was added. Before any hotels were built in Hilo, the Lymans often welcomed guests into their home. King Kalākaua was an early visitor, as were all the kings and queens of Hawai'i who reigned after 1825. (Courtesy of Lyman Museum.)

An engraving from a drawing by Rev. Edward Bailey shows the missionary houses and original campus of the Hilo Boarding School, built in 1836 under the direction of Sarah Joiner and Rev. David Belden Lyman. (Courtesy of *Hawai'i Journal of History*, 1977)

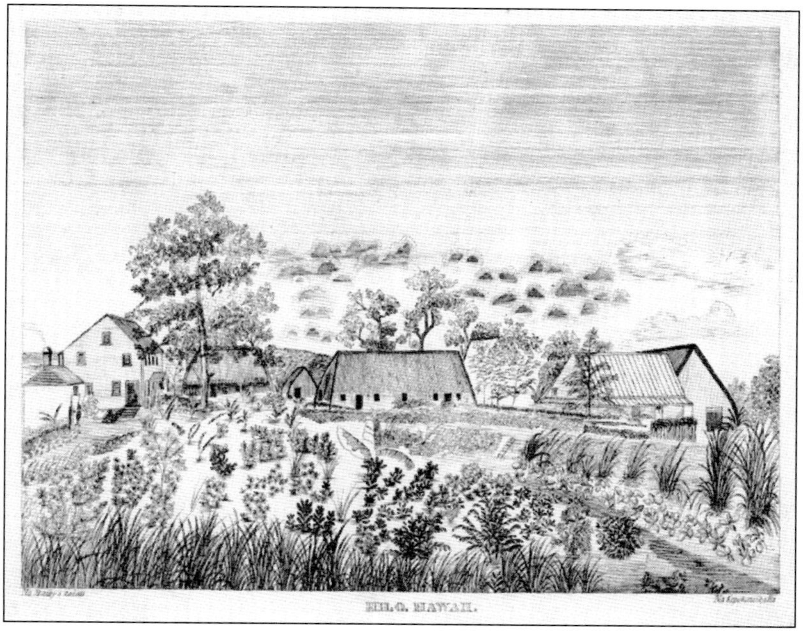

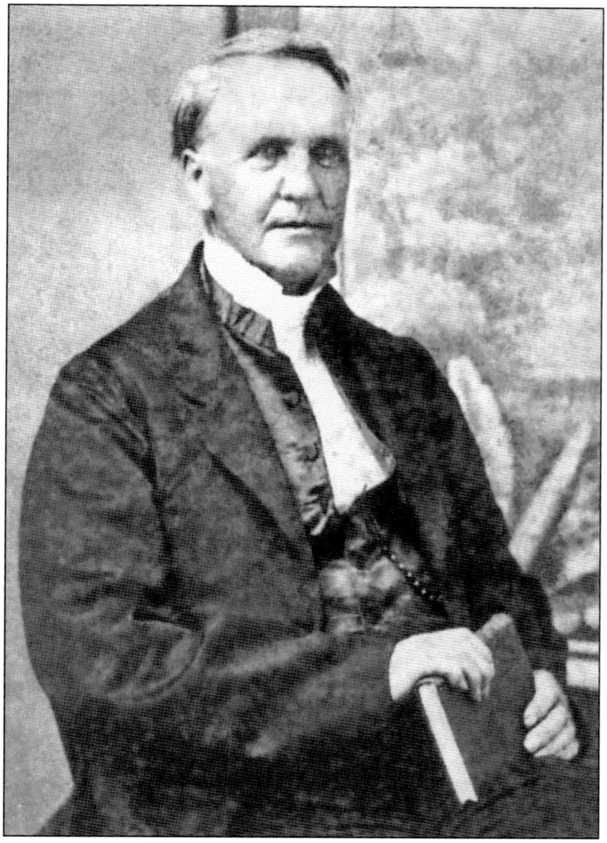

The Reverend Titus Coan and his wife, Fidelia, arrived in Hilo in July 1835. He was a charismatic preacher and adventurer who traveled throughout the districts of Hilo, Puna, and Ka'ū. He officially took over preaching duties at the Haili Church in Hilo. When the United States Exploring Expedition visited Hilo in 1840–1841, Coan met geologist James Dwight Dana. Over the next four decades, Coan regularly sent him observations of eruptions of volcanoes. Coan was known as "the bishop of Kīlauea," and his observations were invaluable to subsequent scientists. Fidelia Coan was among the first American women to publish in a scientific journal with an 1852 article in the *American Journal of Science*. Titus directed the construction of Haili Church from 1855 to 1859. He visited the Marquesas Islands in 1860 and 1867. From 1870 to 1871, he and Fidelia returned to the United States, where they made an extensive speaking tour.

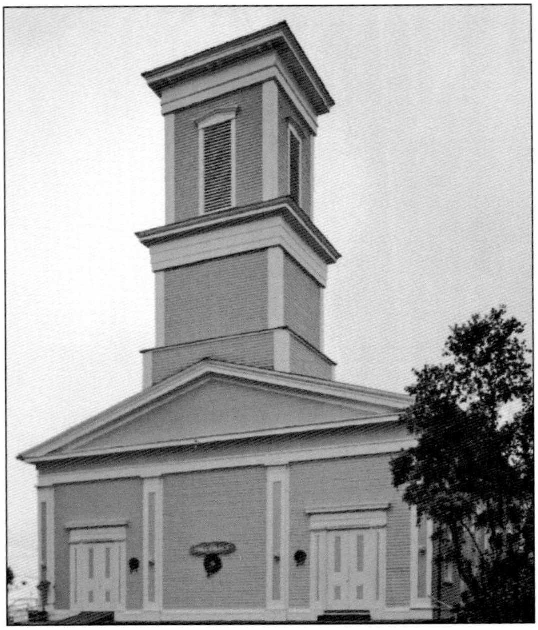

The first church building in Hilo was a large grass canoe shed near the site of the present Hilo Iron Works. By 1825, another grass building was constructed at the site of Kalākaua Park facing Kinoʻole Street. Several other structures were built before the present Haili Church building was finished in 1859. The name of this church comes from the forest where the ʻōhiʻa wood was gathered for its construction.

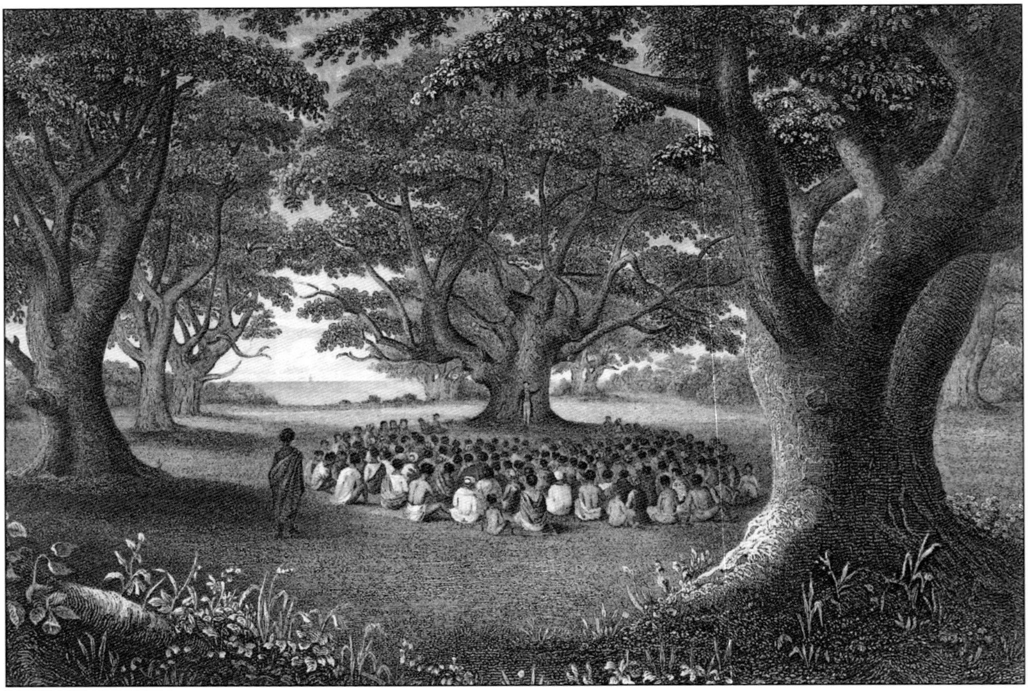

This drawing is entitled *A New England Missionary Preaches in a Kukui Grove in Hawaiʻi*, as depicted in an engraving appearing in Wilkes's *Narrative of the United States Exploring Expedition*. The man preaching could very well be Titus Coan. A good description of the evangelist is found in Emmett Cahill's *The Shipmans of East Hawaiʻi*: "This Hilo minister was renowned not only as a spell-binding preacher but also as an evangelist without peer. His fame was not confined to the Hawaiian Islands but extended to the United States and other corners of the world. He is credited with having converted over 7,000 Hawaiians to his Hilo district churches." Coan himself, in his book, relates that on one memorable Sunday in July 1838 he baptized 1,700 Hawaiians.

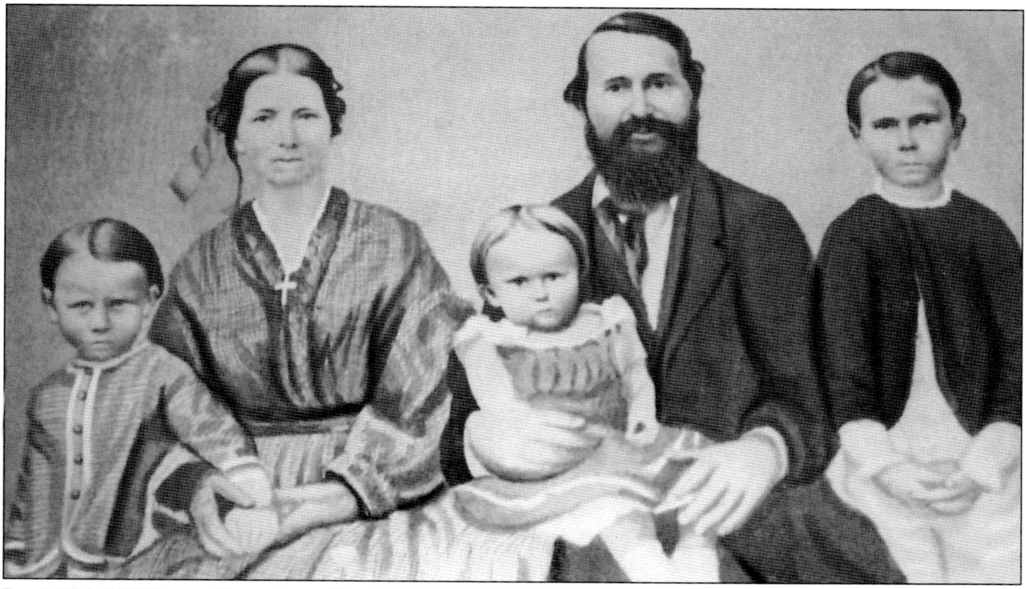

In 1855, William Cornelius Shipman and Jane Stobie Shipman were assigned the outpost of Wai'ōhinu, from which they were responsible for ministry in the entire Ka'ū District. On December 21, 1861, William died from typhoid fever. Jane considered moving the family back to America. However, Titus Coan encouraged her to start a school, and Jane moved the family to Hilo and began teaching both Hawaiian and white children to support her family. On July 8, 1868, she married businessman William H. Reed (for whom Reed's Bay and Reed's Island in Hilo are named). The Shipmans are shown in this photograph with their children, from left to right, Oliver Taylor, Margaret Clarissa, and William Herbert.

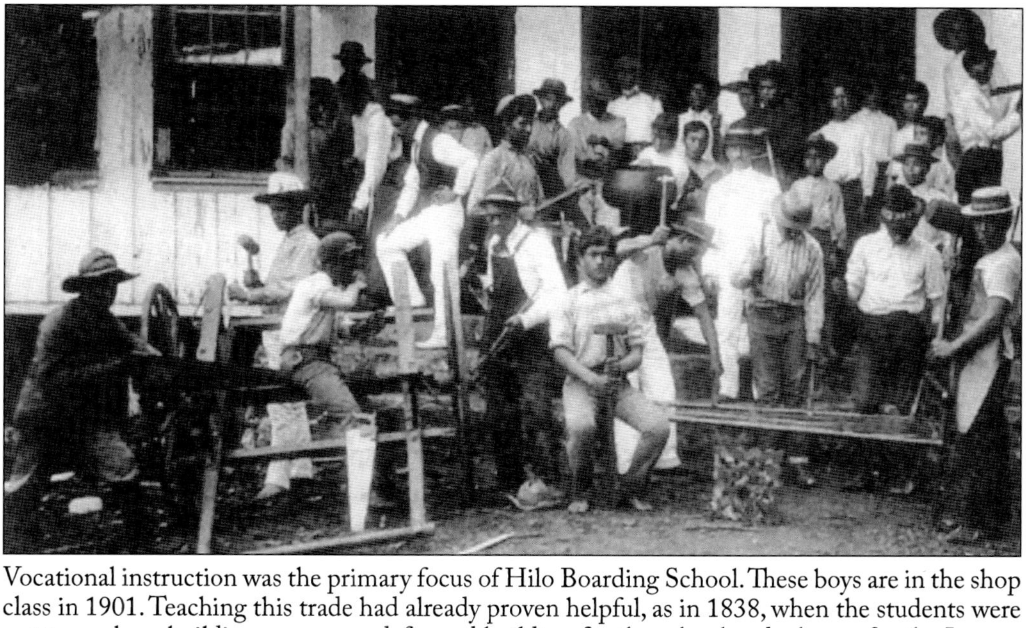

Vocational instruction was the primary focus of Hilo Boarding School. These boys are in the shop class in 1901. Teaching this trade had already proven helpful, as in 1838, when the students were put to work on building a new wood-framed building for the school and a house for the Lyman family. Sarah Lyman opened a school for girls in 1839. Students tended a garden to grow their own food and to raise some cash crops to support expenses. By 1840, thousands of pounds of sugar and molasses were being produced each year.

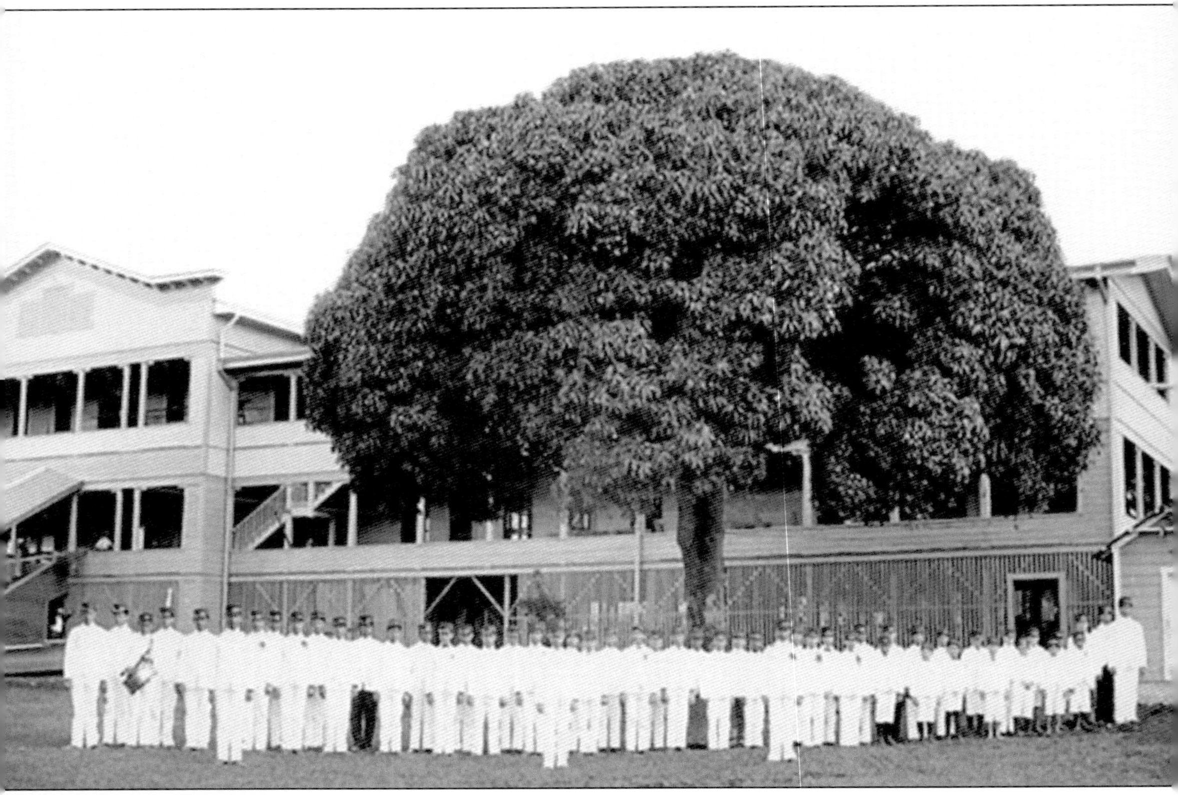

This is the third and final school campus of Hilo Boarding School, opened in 1856 about half a mile inland from the church and the Lyman's house. The photograph shows students around 1909. The Lymans founded the Hilo Boarding School in 1836 with a grant of $500 to build two grass huts for 12 boarders. In 1846, King Kamehameha III granted the school water rights to the Wailuku River. In 1848, the school was officially incorporated, and the Great Mahele formally acknowledged property of 40 acres. By 1849, the Hilo school shifted its emphasis to educating teachers and other vocations. The Lymans enforced strict discipline, dismissing students at a high rate because of the large demand to be admitted. Classes were taught in the Hawaiian language. In 1853, despite Lyman's protest, instruction in the English language was added to that in the Hawaiian language. On November 2, 1853, the school was destroyed by fire and was rebuilt and expanded with the help of fundraising by local businesses and an appropriation from the Hawaiian Kingdom. The school became the first building with electricity in Hilo when a dynamo was installed on the river in 1892. The school would later sell the power to the new company formed by the Lymans' son. Similar manual training schools would become popular on the mainland many years after the Hilo school, which closed in 1925 after public schools were established.

Five

Hilo as a Port City and Hilo Bay

Hilo Bay is a natural harbor; the first sailing ships found it to be the only safe anchorage on the windward side of the island. Safe was relative, however, to ocean conditions, and they were not always ideal for a calm berth. The coastline is marked by shipwrecks that occurred when the sea clashed with the unyielding rocks and ships got caught in the middle. In early days, the bay was somewhat protected by a natural reef that was formed by a stream of lava. This reef, named Blonde Reef after the HMS *Blonde*, served as the only protection before the Hilo Breakwater was built in the early 1900s. Ships started visiting in the early 1800s after King Kamehameha's fleet of war canoes left Hilo Harbor and the sandalwood trade began.

Many of them were part of the whaling fleets that began operating in the north-central Pacific Ocean, and Hawai'i became the preferred place for rest and provisioning. The first whaling ship visited the islands in 1820, and each decade their numbers doubled. Hilo was the third port they used, after Honolulu and Lahaina, and local farmers began raising more fruit and vegetables to feed the hungry sailors. The strong presence of strict missionaries here is said to have restricted the large-scale alcohol and prostitution activities that occurred in other ports. At its peak during the 1850s, more than 500 whaling ships visited Hawai'i annually until the trade ended after the Civil War. In 1863, a landing wharf was built at the foot of Wai'ānuenue Street and the northern side of the bay became the focal point for the community's trade and commerce.

Interisland travel was another major use for the new passenger landing. By the 1870s, Hilo had grown into the second-largest population center in the islands and a major center for sugarcane production and export due to its fertile lands and abundant water. The Reciprocity Treaty with the United States served to dramatically increase the sugar trade in Hawai'i. Improvements in the harbor were needed, prompting the decision to build a new harbor facility on the calmer Waiākea side. The new wharf was completed there around 1900. Hilo Bay was still unprotected, however, from high winds and storm surges, so in 1908 construction began on a breakwater along the shallow reef, beginning at the shoreline east of Kūhīo Bay. The breakwater was completed in 1929.

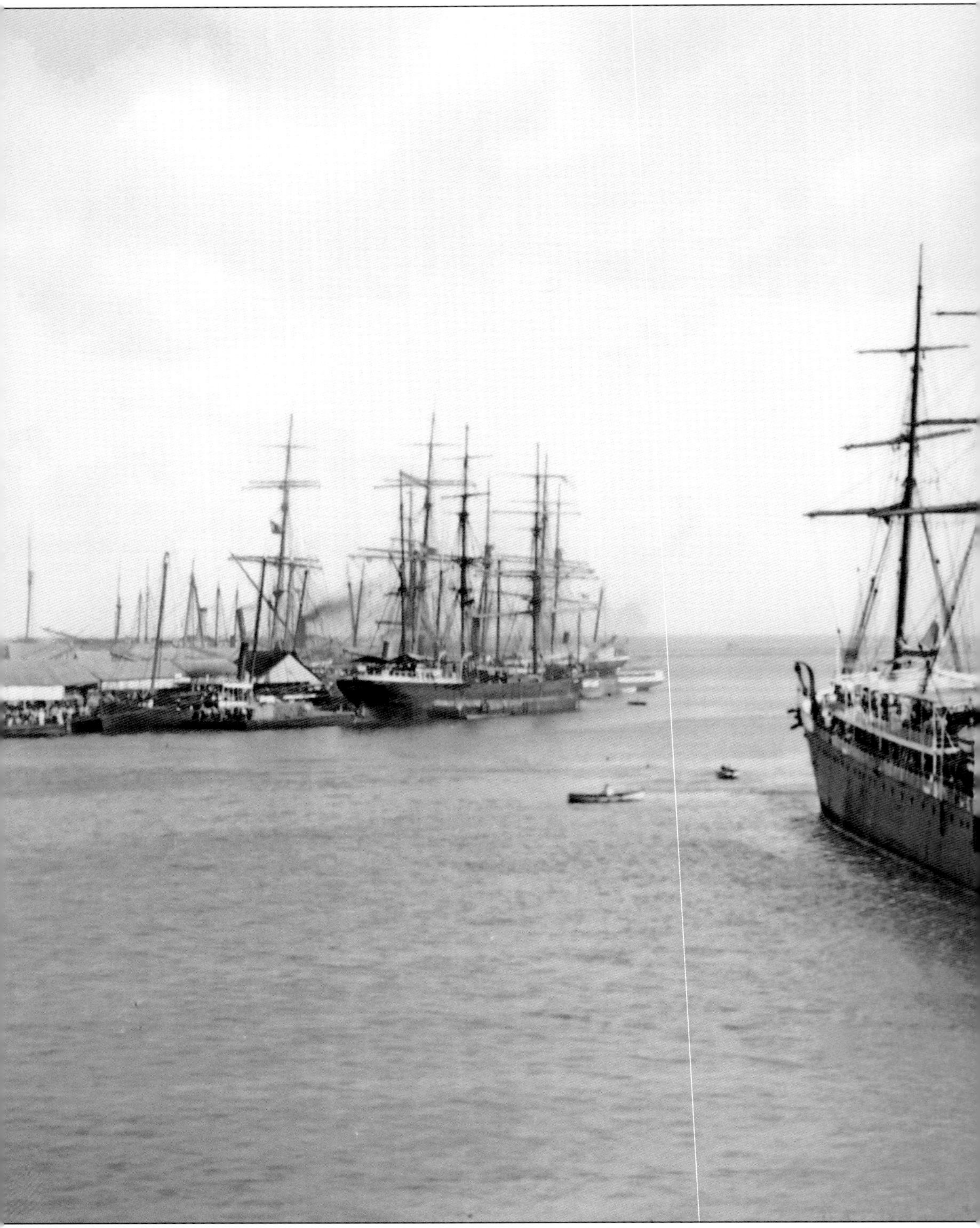

Ships of the same type that came to Hilo sit in Honolulu Harbor. A steamer with auxiliary sail leaves the harbor as schooners like those used in the whaling trade lie nearby. This photograph was taken by Brother Gabriel Bertram, an avid hobby photographer and the first director of Saint

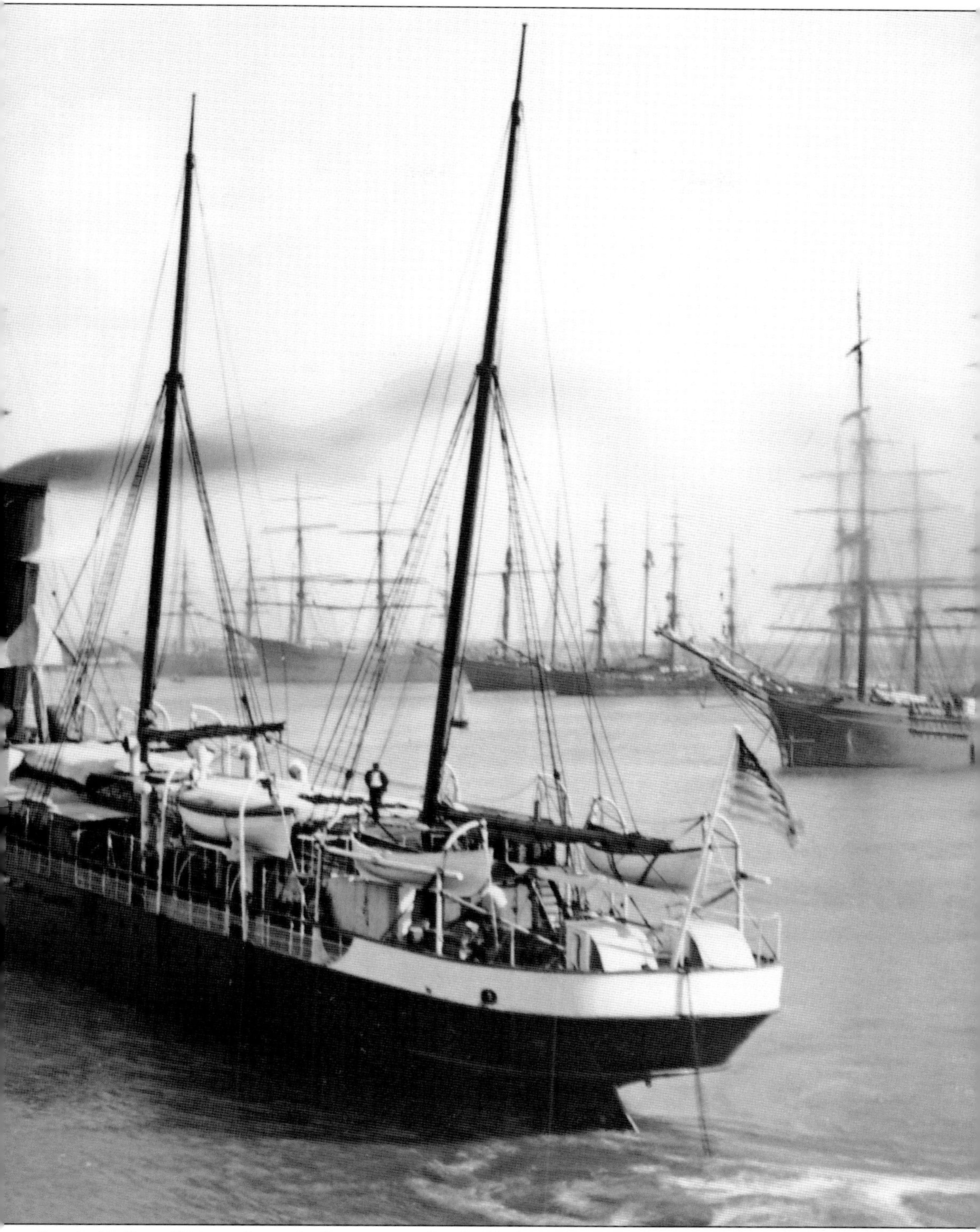

Louis College. Using a large, bulky camera that held glass photographic plates (used as negatives before photographic film), Brother Bertram chronicled life in Hawai'i from about 1885 to 1905. His favorite subjects were said to be ships and volcanoes. (Courtesy of Hawai'i State Archives.)

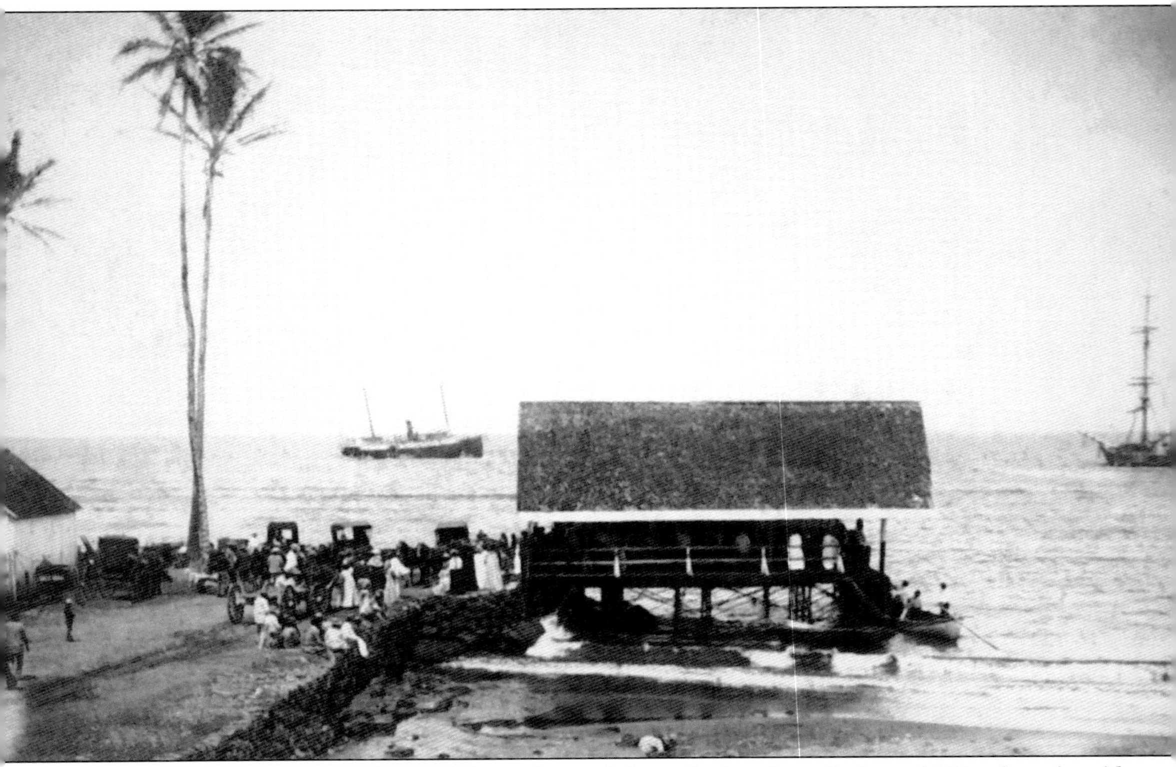

Passengers and cargo landed at Hilo in the surf along the beach until about 1863, when the old Hilo Wharf was constructed at the base of present-day Wai'ānuenue Street. This photograph shows passengers waiting to be taken in lighters or rowboats out to the waiting ship. (Courtesy of Hawai'i State Archives.)

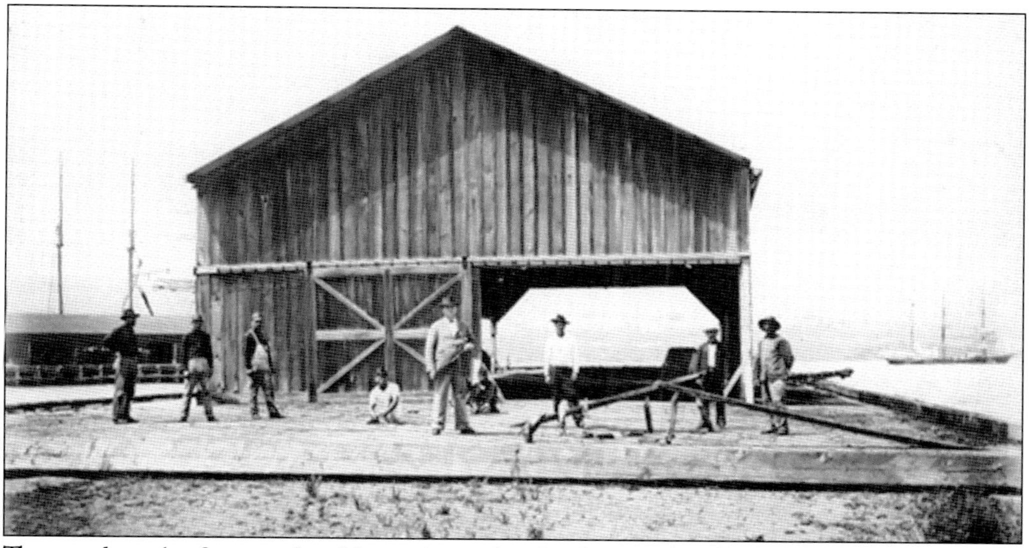

The wooden wharf was replaced by an iron pile wharf in 1865 and was extended around 1890. Raw sugar came by interisland steamships from the Hāmākua coast to Hilo before being shipped overseas. (Courtesy Hawai'i State Archives.)

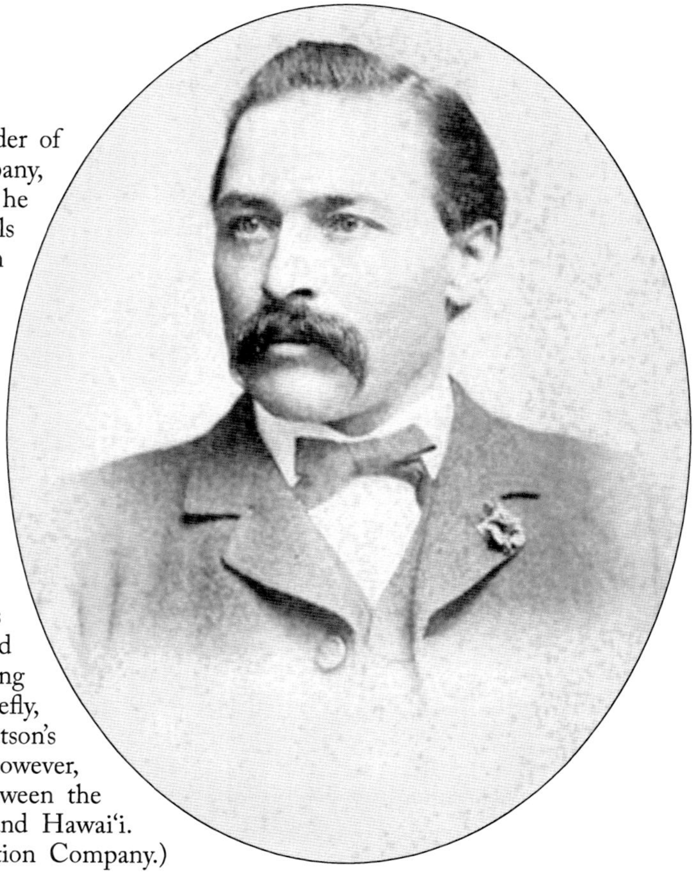

Capt. William Matson, founder of Matson Navigation Company, started in San Francisco, where he was hired by the J.D. Spreckels family to serve as skipper on their yacht, *Lurline*. The family later assisted Captain Matson in obtaining his first ship, the *Emma Claudina*. He sailed it to Hawai'i and thus launched the company that became, and is to this day, the primary transporter of cargo between the mainland and Hawai'i. Matson Navigation Company has since been involved in such diversified interests as oil exploration, hotels and tourism, military service during two world wars, and even, briefly, the airline business. Matson's primary interest throughout, however, has been carrying freight between the United States' Pacific coast and Hawai'i. (Courtesy of Matson Navigation Company.)

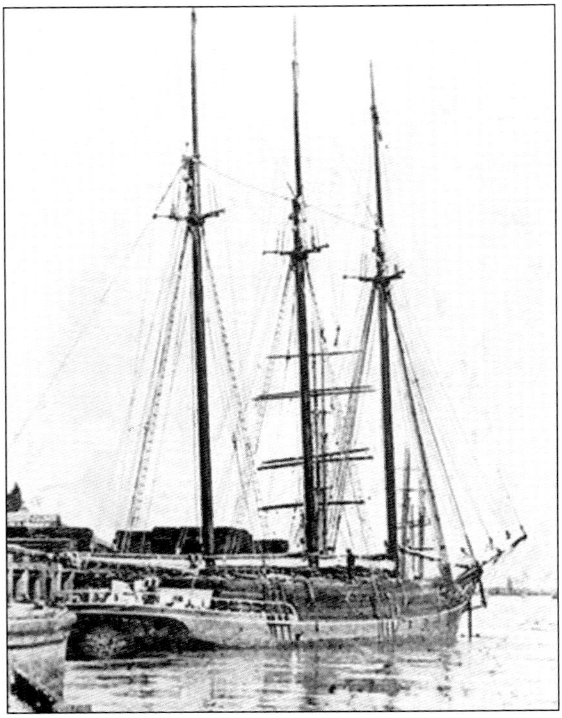

Gliding into Hilo Bay in the early dawn of April 23, 1882, was the three-masted schooner *Emma Claudina*, 13 days out of San Francisco under Capt. William Matson. The ship carried 300 tons of food, plantation supplies, and general merchandise. Another story involving Hilo was the wreck of the brigantine *Selena* in 1887, with Matson as captain. Carrying a full load of cargo and passengers coming from San Francisco into Hilo Bay, it crashed in a storm near the Wainaku Sugar Mill, becoming one of Hilo's shipwrecks. The townspeople helped, and all passengers were saved. (Courtesy of Matson Navigation Company.)

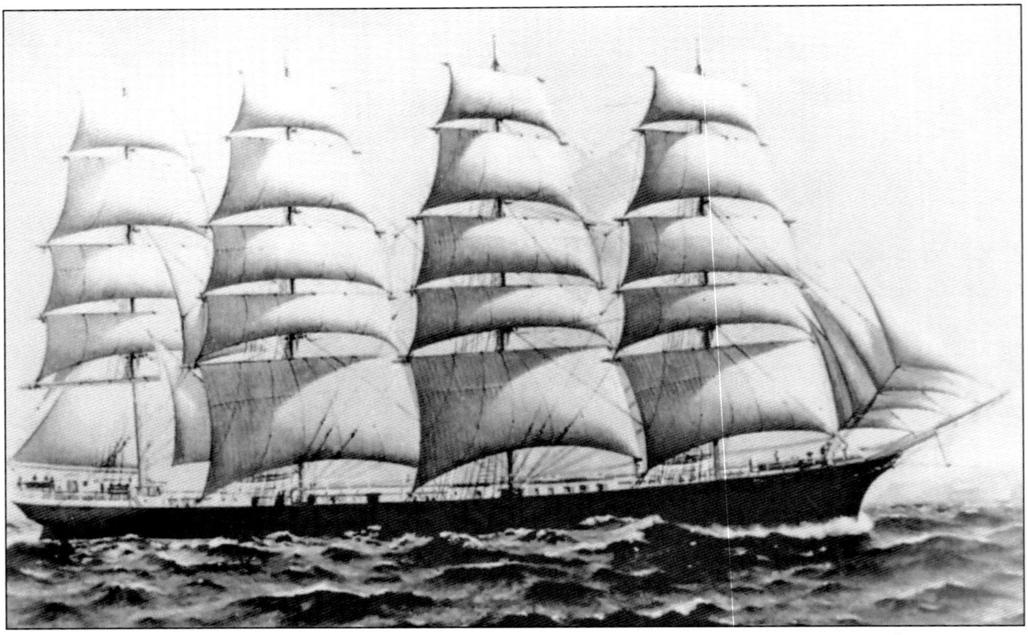

Matson Navigation Company's *Falls of Clyde*, shown here under full sail, carried passengers and was involved in the Hawaiian transpacific sugar trade. Just as modern Matson ships bring in assorted cargoes that fill a variety of shelves across the islands, the *Falls of Clyde* supplied Hawai'i with various goods and often sailed to Hilo. After modifications, she carried sugar from Hilo to San Francisco until 1906, when she was sold and converted into a sailing oil tanker. In the end, the *Falls of Clyde* became a floating museum in Honolulu. (Courtesy Matson Navigation Company.)

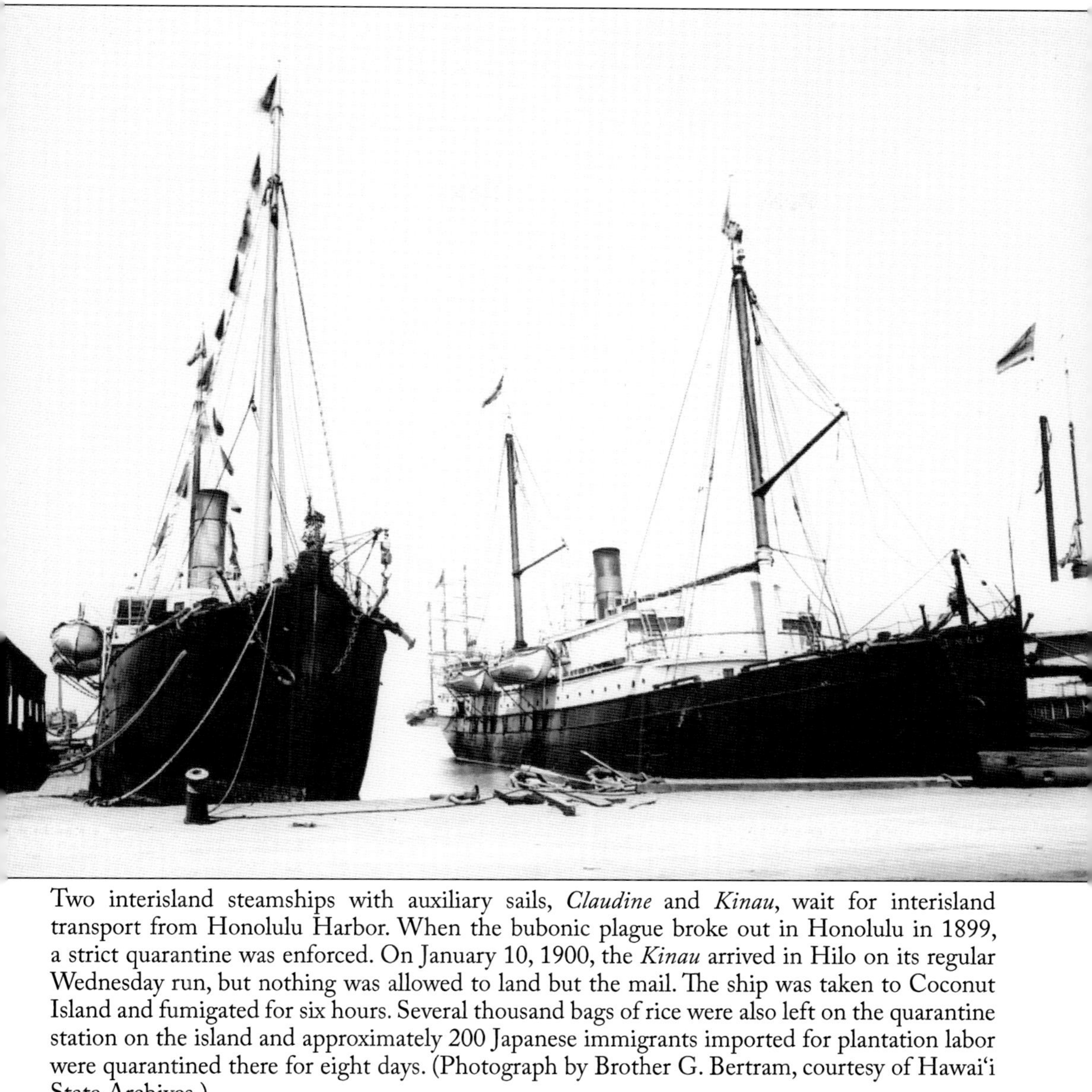

Two interisland steamships with auxiliary sails, *Claudine* and *Kinau*, wait for interisland transport from Honolulu Harbor. When the bubonic plague broke out in Honolulu in 1899, a strict quarantine was enforced. On January 10, 1900, the *Kinau* arrived in Hilo on its regular Wednesday run, but nothing was allowed to land but the mail. The ship was taken to Coconut Island and fumigated for six hours. Several thousand bags of rice were also left on the quarantine station on the island and approximately 200 Japanese immigrants imported for plantation labor were quarantined there for eight days. (Photograph by Brother G. Bertram, courtesy of Hawai'i State Archives.)

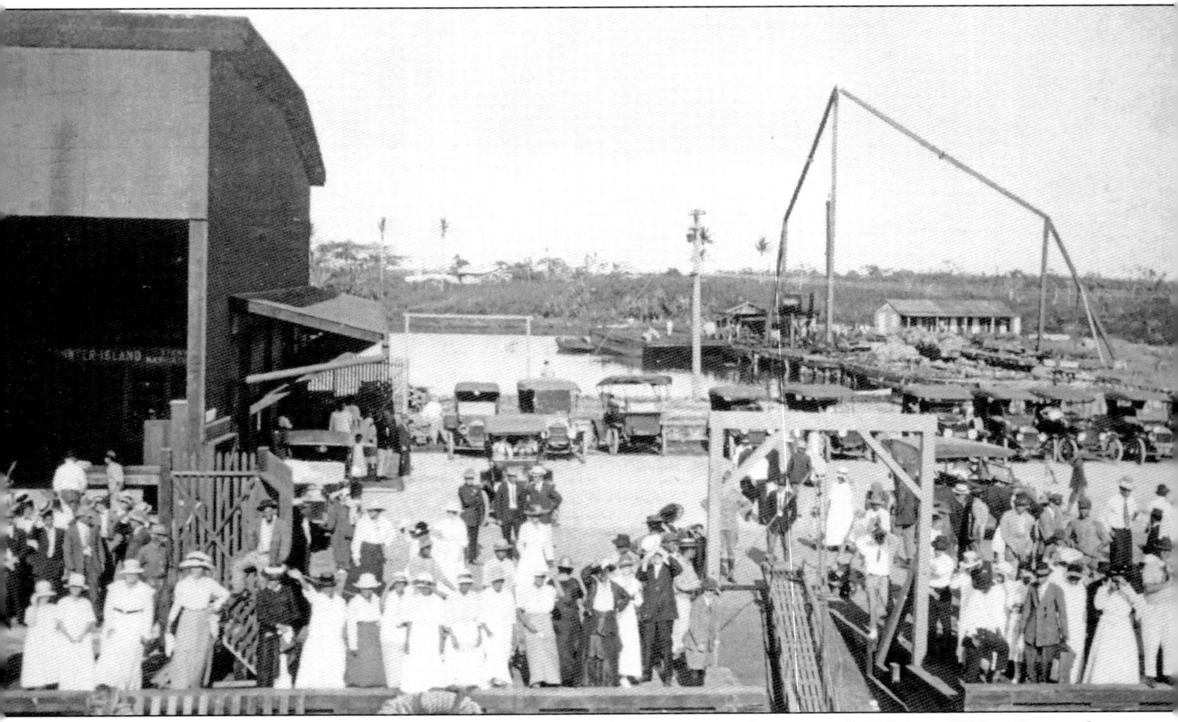

People and cars assemble on the new pier in this c. 1900 photograph. Kūhiō Wharf was first constructed around 1900. In 1912, the harbor was dredged and railroad track was laid coming into the new harbor facility. Pier 1, completed in 1916, was a 1,400-foot-long wharf with a wooden storage shed. The next year, a mechanical conveyor for bagged sugar with derricks for loading ships was built. In 1923, Pier 2 was constructed and additional dredging was done. By 1927, Pier 3 was added on the west side of Pier 2. The 1946 tsunami seriously damaged the structures. (Courtesy of Hawai'i State Archives.)

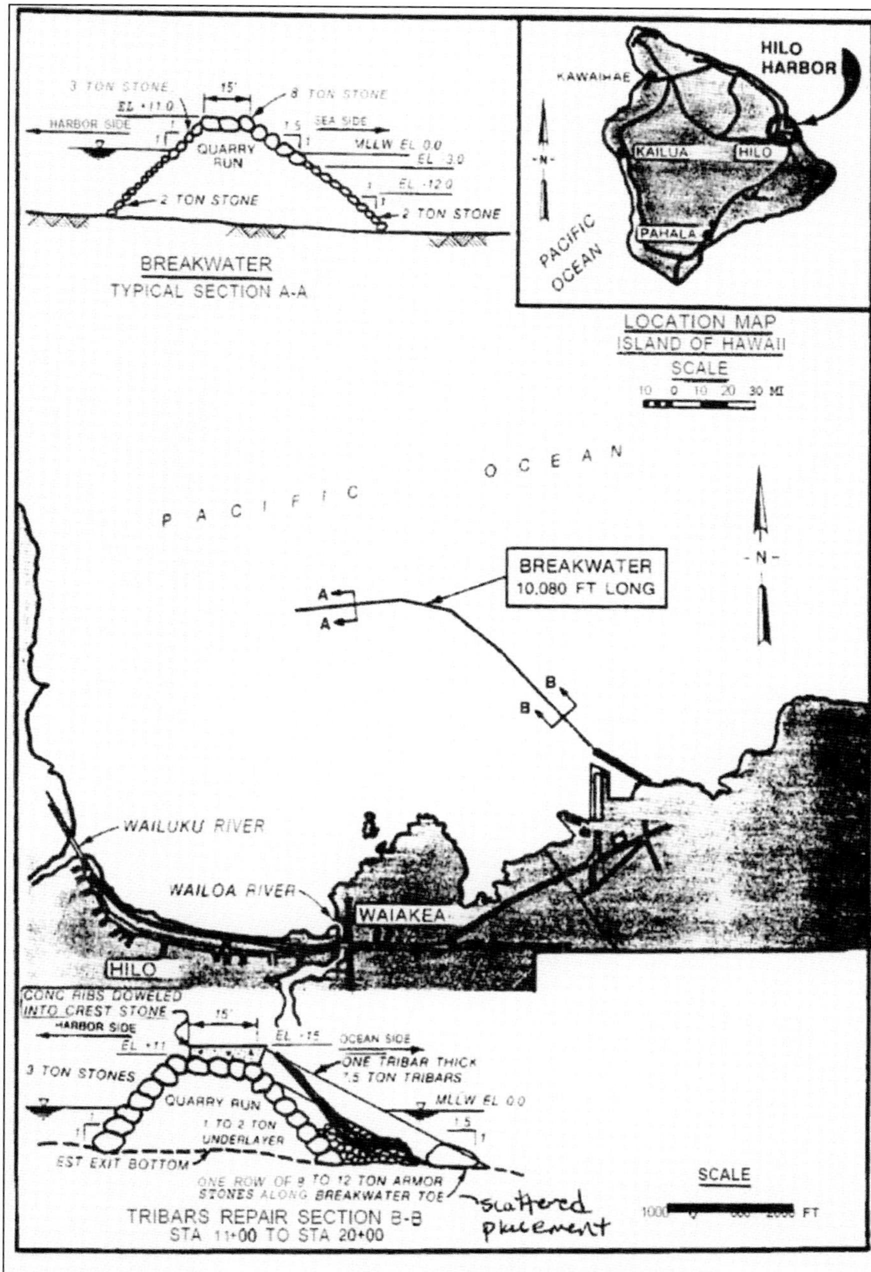

Hilo Harbor, Hawaii, Hawaii

In 1905, the US government appropriated an initial $400,000 to build the Hilo Breakwater. This is the US Army Corps of Engineers construction layout. The breakwater was built in stages, and construction included five contracts with different companies. Work commenced in 1908 on the substructure and superstructure of the first section. A total of three sections were completed in 1910, 1911, and 1929—achieving a total length of 10,070 feet, or 1.9 miles. Some 951,273 tons of rock were used in the construction. Sections on the plan show the layout for placement of different sizes of stone to make a wall 11 feet above the existing reef. In the end, the cost was nearly $1.4 million. Many challenges were faced with finding the right equipment, building special barges and equipment, and battling sea conditions, as well as mishaps along the way.

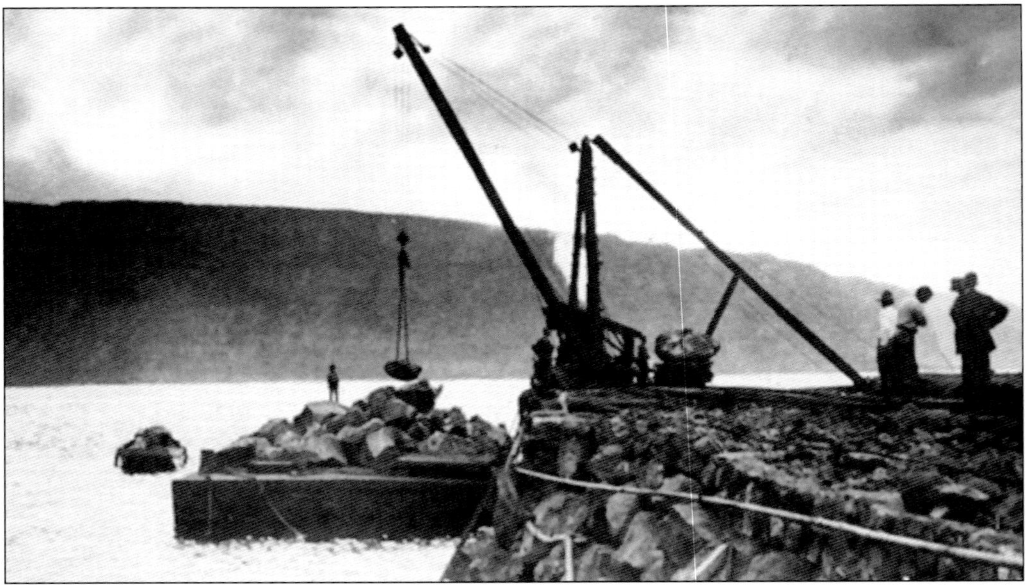

Railroad track was laid along the top of the wall and stretched two miles from the Hilo Railroad line to carry equipment, such as this crane and rock from the Waiākea Quarry. Stone later came from Kapoho and Waipio, where it was hauled on special steel barges built for the project. Some barges could hold up to 650 tons of rock. Here, a derrick lifts boulders from a barge. (Courtesy of Hawai'i State Archives.)

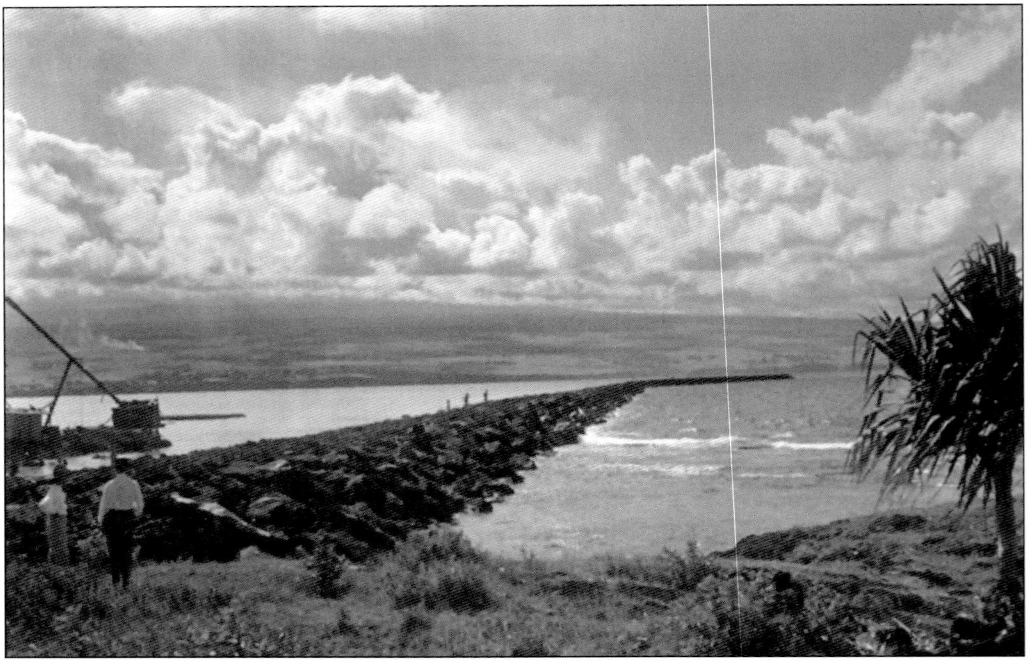

The two-mile-long Hilo Breakwater is complete in this image. The railroad tracks stayed in place for a time, and people enjoyed taking a ride along the wall. (Courtesy of Hawai'i State Archives.)

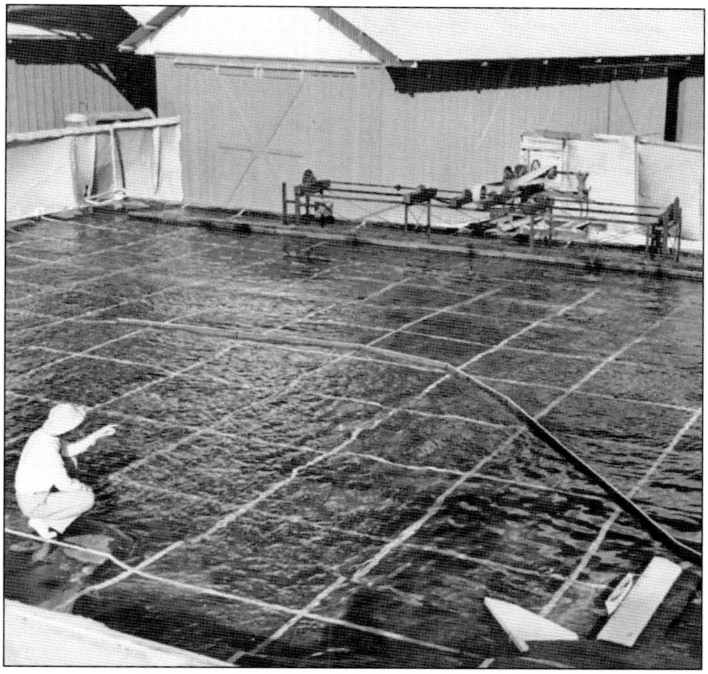

In 1938, the US Army Corps of Engineers in Honolulu built a scale model of Hilo Harbor and the breakwater. Using a wave-making machine, seen in the background, engineer Charles B. Jones is shown here conducting various tests. In 1946, a tsunami tore away sections compromising 80 percent of the wall. Its repair by the Army Corps of Engineers cost $1.14 million. The wall was never planned to be protection against tsunami waves, only normal sea conditions. (Photograph by Pan-Pacific Press Bureau, courtesy of Hawai'i State Archives.)

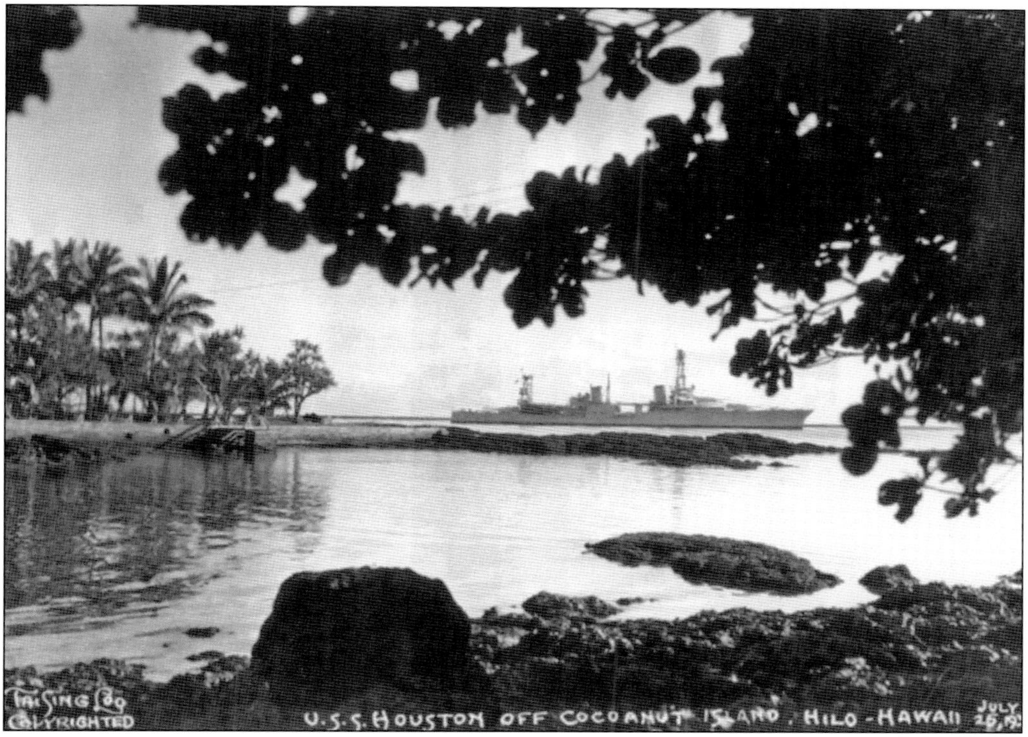

The USS *Houston* battleship lies off Coconut Island in 1934. During this era, Hawai'i was still a territory of the United States, with a territorial government. From 1941 to 1944, during World War II, the islands were placed under martial law. Civilian government was dissolved and a military governor was appointed. Coconut Island and Hilo Harbor were taken over by the military. (Courtesy of Library of Congress.)

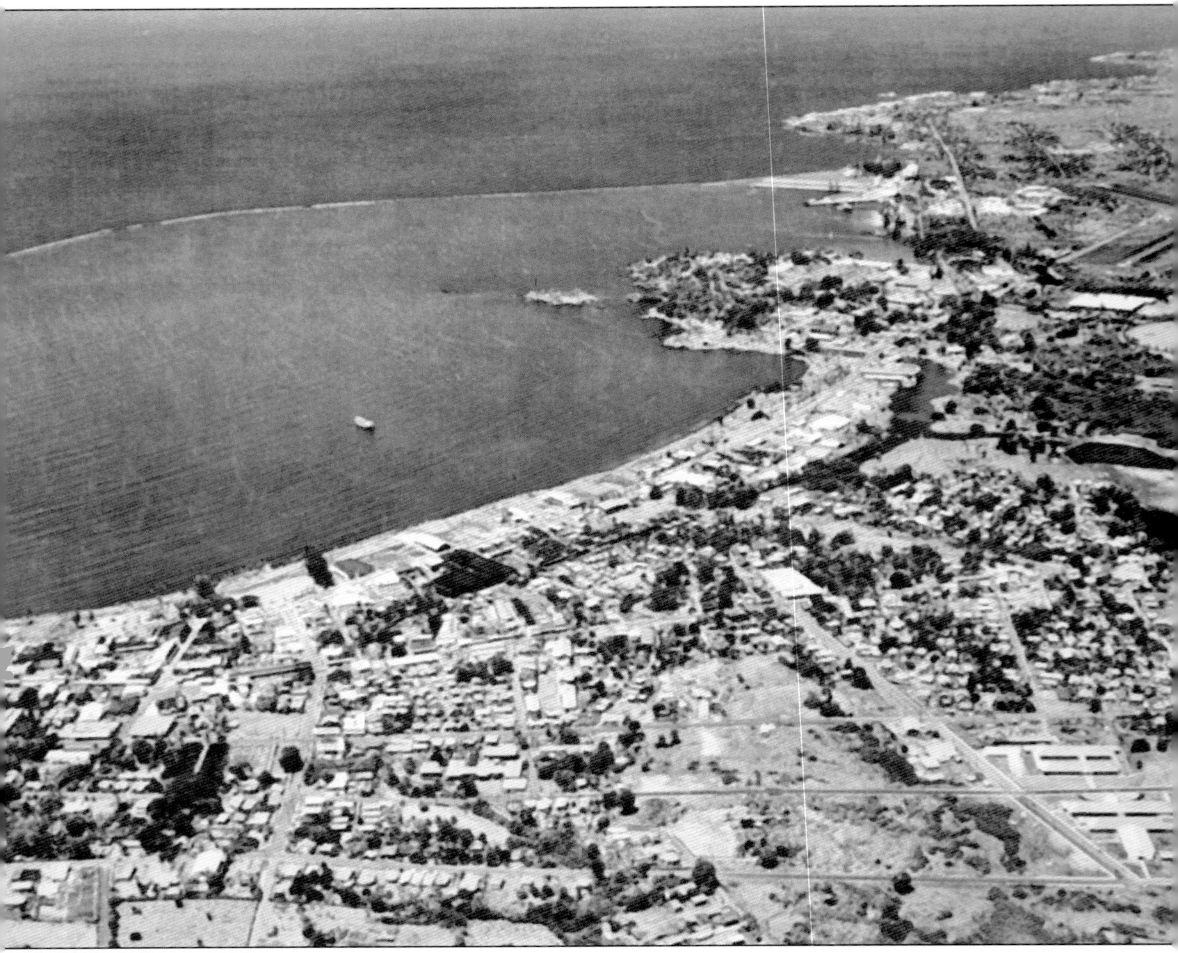

An aerial view of Hilo Harbor in the 1940s shows the entire harbor and the breakwater. The calmer water inside the breakwater has a lighter shade than the water beyond the seawall. (Courtesy of Hawai'i State Archives.)

Six

Hilo Town Grows Up

From the time of the missionaries until 1900, Hilo grew into a town, with named streets replacing meandering footpaths. The effect of the whaling trade and the new potential of sugarcane as a major cash crop gave local entrepreneurs (mostly Caucasian) the impetus to build businesses to supply them with everything they needed. General merchandise, machine shops, lumber mills, hardware stores, and chandlers built wooden stores with boardwalks in the center of town, along the bay shoreline. Grass houses, which had an average life span of four years, were being replaced with houses built of wood and traditional shingle roofs, some of which were handsome residences following mainland styles. Hawai'i's tropical climate, however, gave rise to the plantation style house, with large roof overhangs and covered lanais (verandas) to protect from sun and rain.

With the foresight of David and Sarah Lyman, Hilo Boarding School began graduating skilled carpenters, farriers, mechanics and tailors. The Hawaiian population, though increasingly educated in reading and writing, was declining due to disease while the Asian and European populations were increasing. In the end, they mixed together with the frequent intermarriage of races.

The laws allowing free simple ownership of land made perhaps the greatest impact. Large tracts of land were acquired for sugar plantations and ranches; by the 1880s, there were 17 sugar mills in operation in the area and 125 on the island. Individuals such as William H. Reed, Charles E. Richardson, and William H. Shipman shaped the destiny of Hilo. Reed built bridges (including the third and most substantial bridge across the Wailuku River), the first harbor, landing, and streets, while Richardson was involved in lumber, land leases, shipping, retailing, and ranching. Shipman operated Kapāpala Ranch in Ka'ū, acquired land in Kea'au (formerly Ola'a) that would become Waiākea Plantation, and for a time was involved in sugar. The three men created various partnerships among them. These names are still familiar today to people who visit Reed's Bay, Richardson's Beach Park, and the Shipman House Bed and Breakfast.

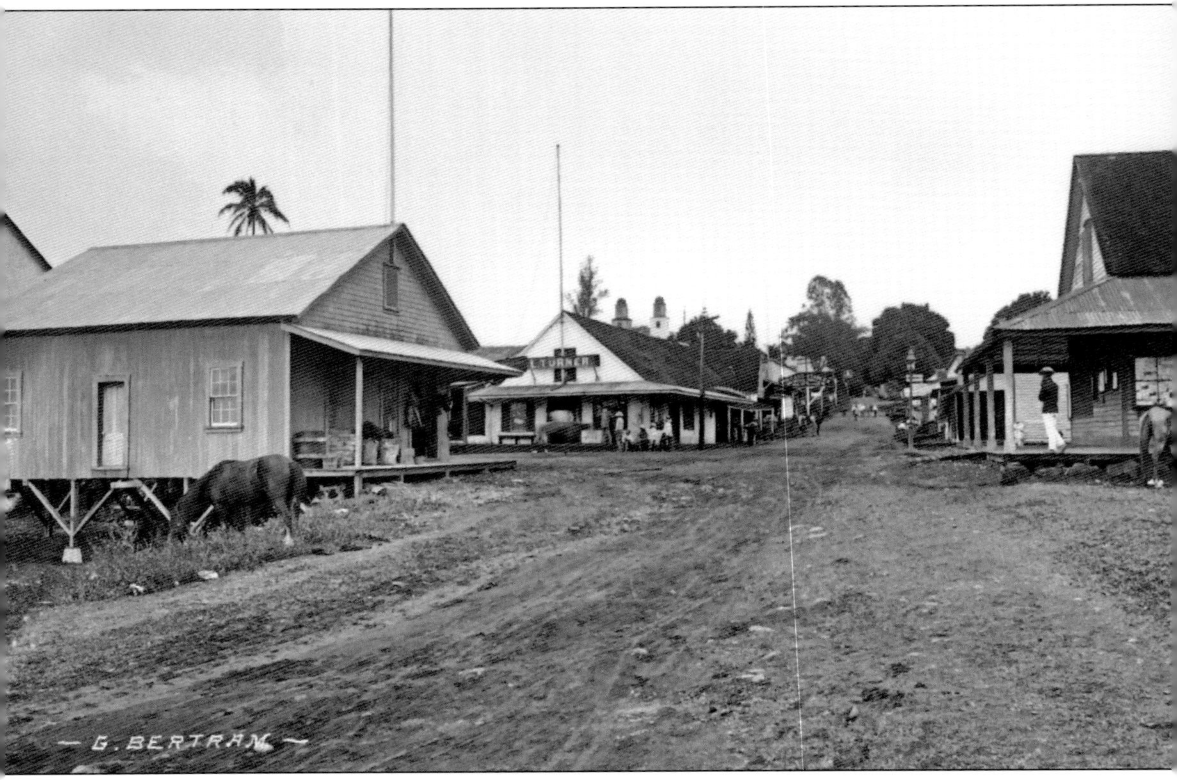

A beautifully preserved photograph of Wai'ānuenue Avenue shows the view looking mauka pre-electricity during the 1890s. The horse on the far right is tied up at the post office with a gas lamp in front. L. Turner's grain and feed store is on the left corner and up the street is Volcano Stables, which later established a taxicab company. (Photograph by Brother G. Bertram, courtesy of Hawai'i State Archives.)

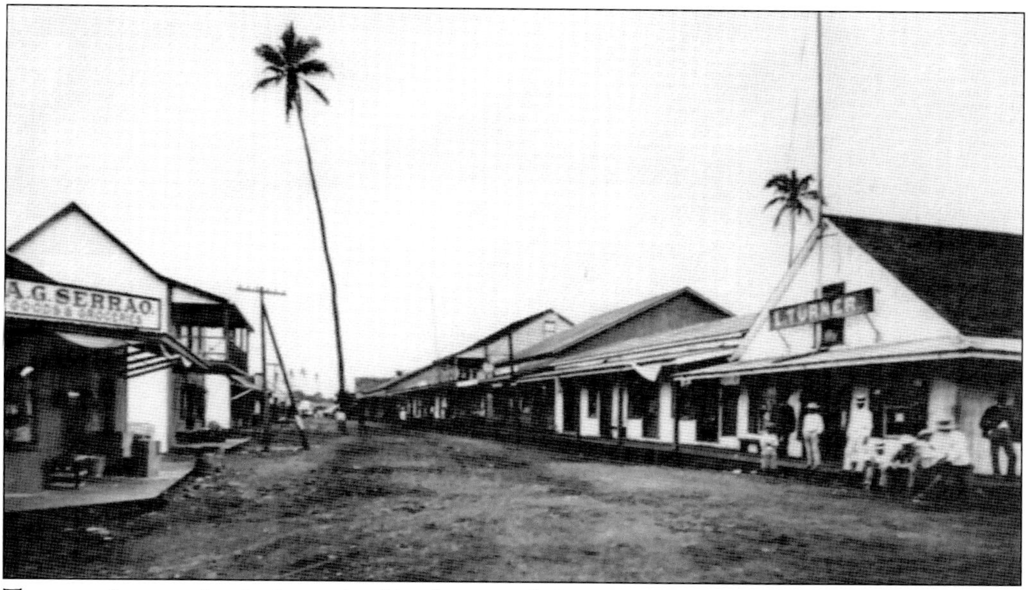

The same intersection is shown in this photograph from the 1880s, with a view looking east on Front Street, which later became Kamehameha Avenue. L. Turner's store is now on the right, and across the street is A.G. Serrao's general store. Mrs. Serrao contracted what was believed to be bubonic plague in 1900, and the store was ordered burned to the ground. Another Serrao brother, Jose, opened a winery and rum distillery in Hilo. (Courtesy of Hawai'i State Archives.)

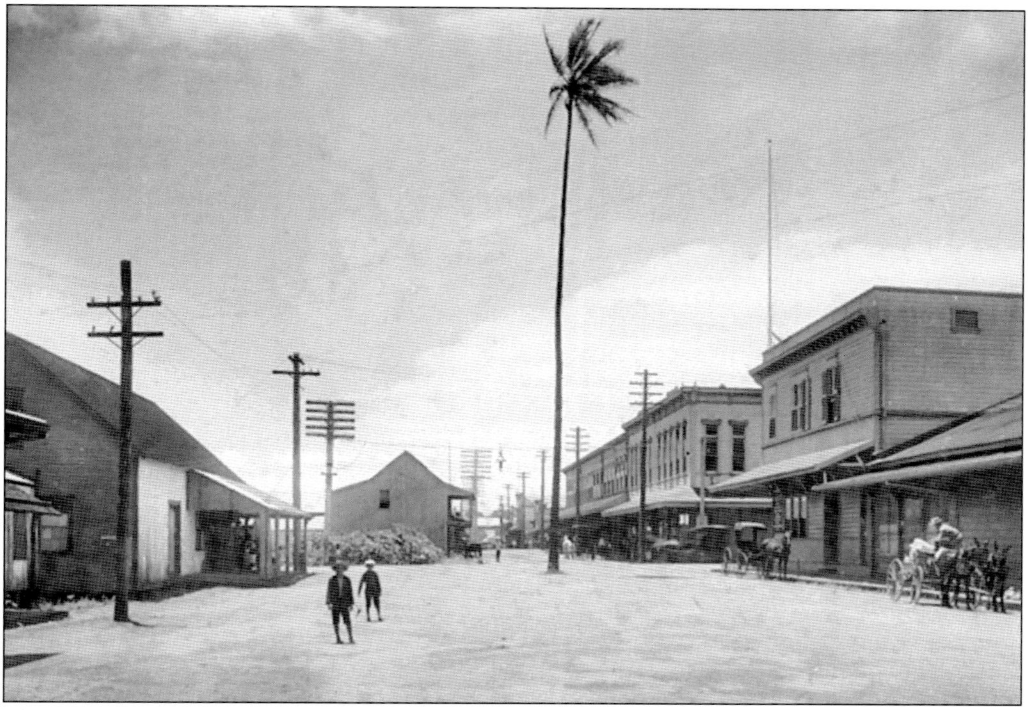

This view also looks east, and the same intersection is about halfway up the street. Notice that the Serrao store is gone, but the coconut tree remains in the middle of the street, making a handy hitching post. The Hilo Telephone Company was started in 1882 (notice the wires), and in 1894 the Hilo Electric Light Company was formed. (Courtesy of Hawai'i State Archives.)

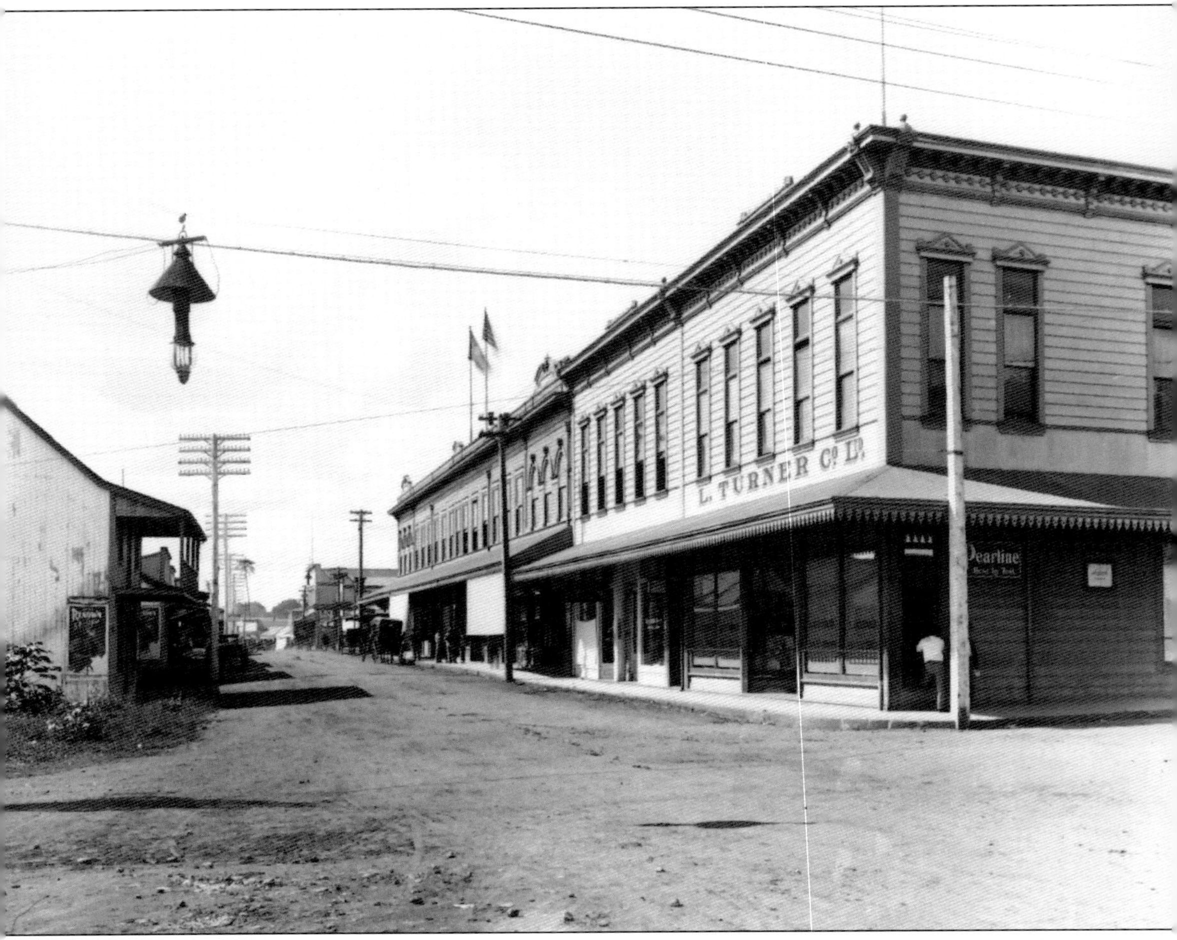

Here is another photograph by Brother Gabriel Bertram, taken around 1890, showing the same intersection. L. Turner's store has expanded and become a two-story building. Note the new electric streetlight. The first electricity in Hilo appeared in1890, when the operators of the Hilo Boarding School installed a water-driven dynamo on an irrigation ditch. After that, everyone wanted electricity. The new Hilo Electric Light Company started modestly with a small ice plant and a 500-light dynamo. (Courtesy of Hawai'i State Archives.)

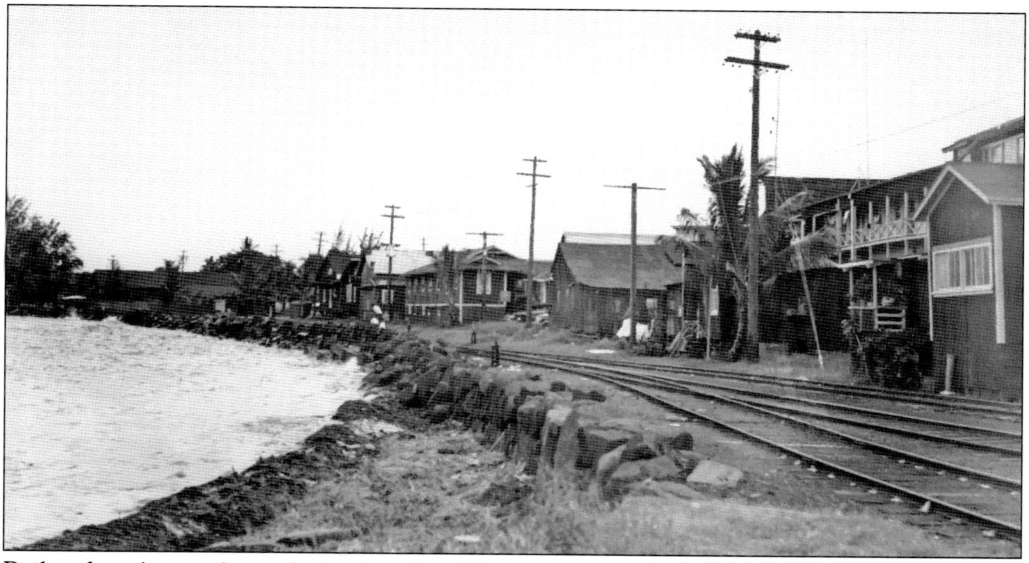

Railroad tracks ran alongside the shoreline. This photograph shows the backs of businesses facing Front Street near the train depot, which lies behind the photographer. Many of the owners of these stores were former plantation workers—primarily Japanese, Filipino, and Chinese immigrants—and they usually lived in back. These buildings were all destroyed in the tsunami of 1946. (Courtesy of Hawai'i State Archives.)

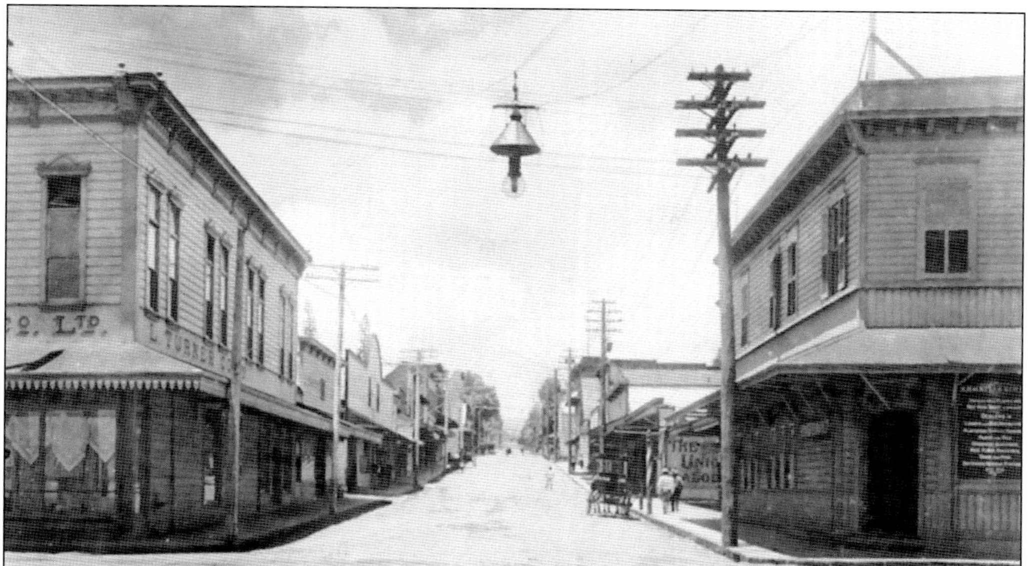

This is another image from the intersection of Front Street with a view that looks mauka on Wai'ānuenue Avenue; L. Turner Co. is on the left corner. On the same side is the *Hawai'i Herald* print shop, which started printing the newspaper of the same name in 1896. The year before, the *Hilo Tribune* had started publishing in English and Hawaiian. The two merged in 1914 as the *Hawai'i Tribune-Herald*. Across the street on the right is the Union Saloon, owned by Jose Serrao. On the right corner is an office of land development company H. Hackfeld & Co., owned by German immigrant Heinrich Hackfeld. It was an agent for sugar plantations and later became American Factors, one of the "Big Five" companies forming a sugar consortium in Hawai'i. (Courtesy of Hawai'i State Archives.)

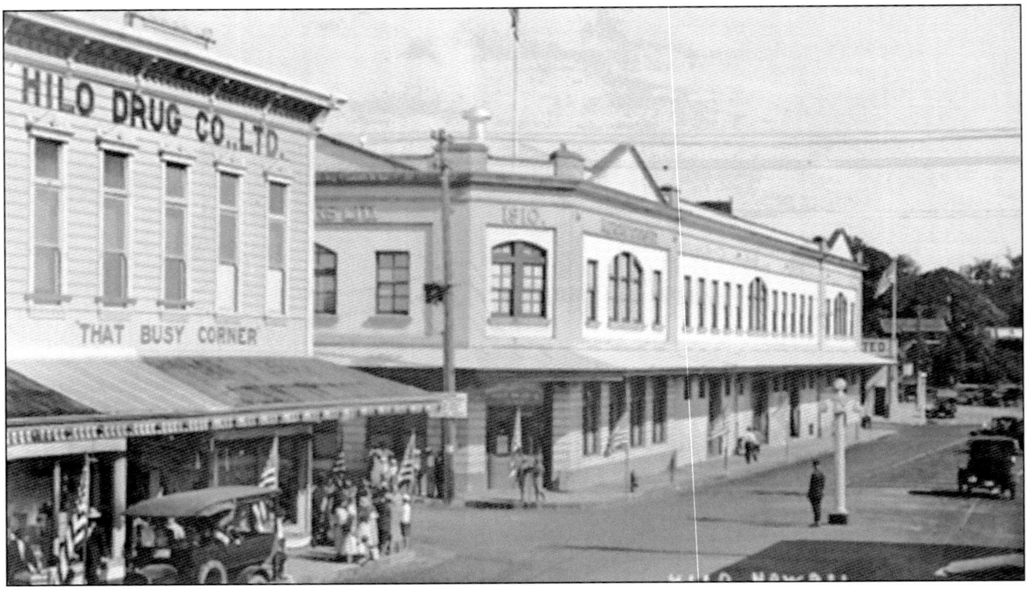

Here is the familiar intersection, with the view facing west toward the Wailuku River around 1928. The building that was once L. Turner Co. now houses Hilo Drug Store, Hilo's first drugstore, founded by missionary Dr. Charles Hinckley Wetmore, the island's first physician. During World War I, the Hackfeld Company was seized by the US government as an alien property because it was owned by a German. It was later sold to the consortium, or *hui*, of Hawai'i businessmen in 1918, who changed the name to American Factors, perhaps to emphasize its new American heritage. The building later became the home of Koehnen's Furniture. The streets are now paved and there is a policeman in the intersection, along with a "concrete policeman" light pole. (Courtesy of Hawai'i State Archives.)

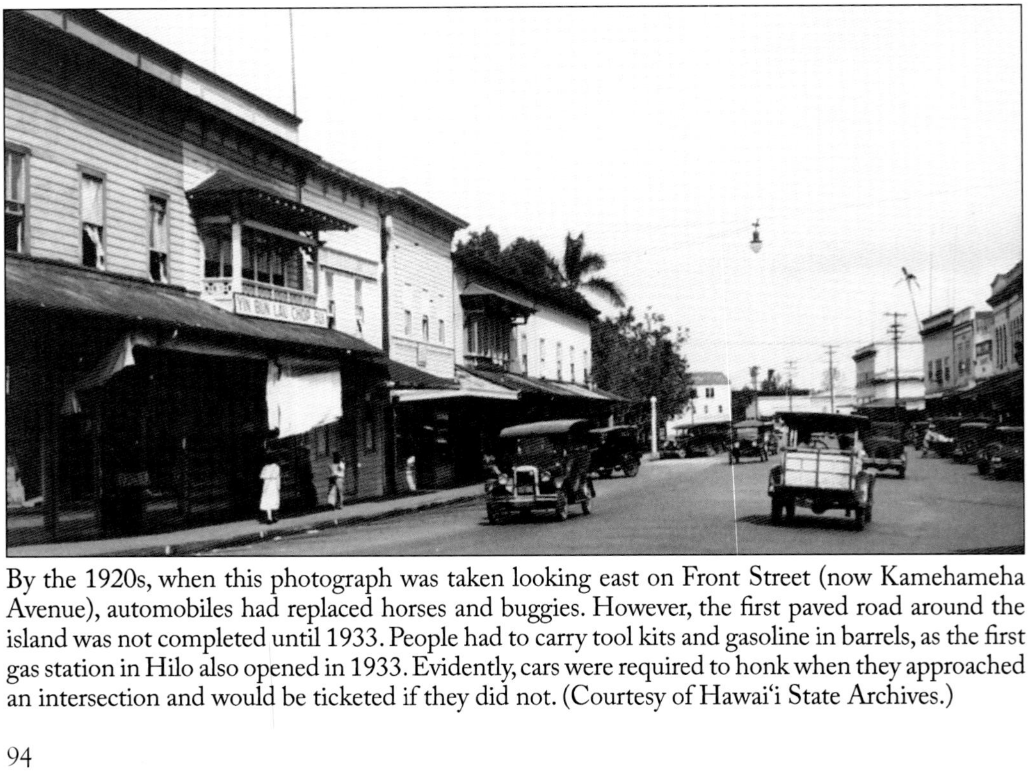

By the 1920s, when this photograph was taken looking east on Front Street (now Kamehameha Avenue), automobiles had replaced horses and buggies. However, the first paved road around the island was not completed until 1933. People had to carry tool kits and gasoline in barrels, as the first gas station in Hilo also opened in 1933. Evidently, cars were required to honk when they approached an intersection and would be ticketed if they did not. (Courtesy of Hawai'i State Archives.)

William H. Shipman was the son of early missionary William C. Shipman and Jane Shipman, who later married William H. Reed. A savvy businessman, ranching was the younger Shipman's main vocation. When the estate of the late King Kamehameha IV offered to sell the entire *ahupua'a* of Kea'au—a parcel of 64,275 acres—in 1881 to finance a rest home on O'ahu, Shipman, age 27, bought it with two other partners, Capt. J.E. Elderts and Samuel Damon, for $20,000. Within several years, the two other partners sold out to Shipman. Over the years, parcels were sold or leased to others such as Ola'a Sugar. He later founded the Hilo Meat Company, a cooperative of several ranches. (Courtesy of Shipman family.)

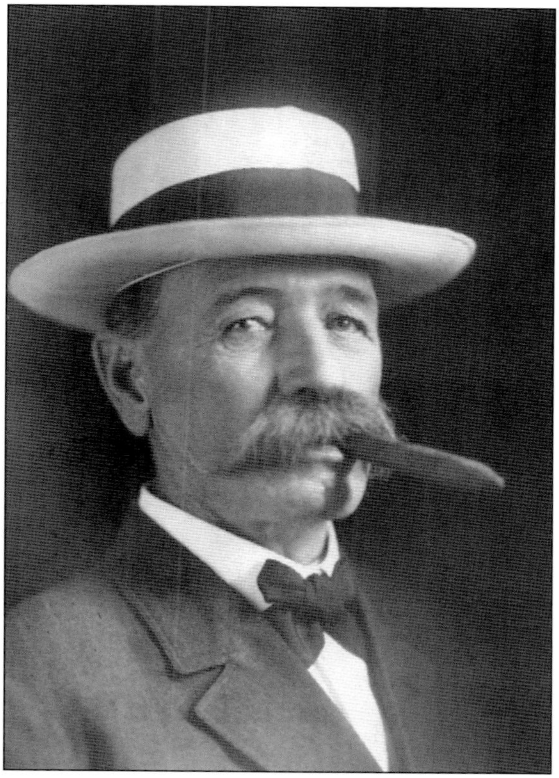

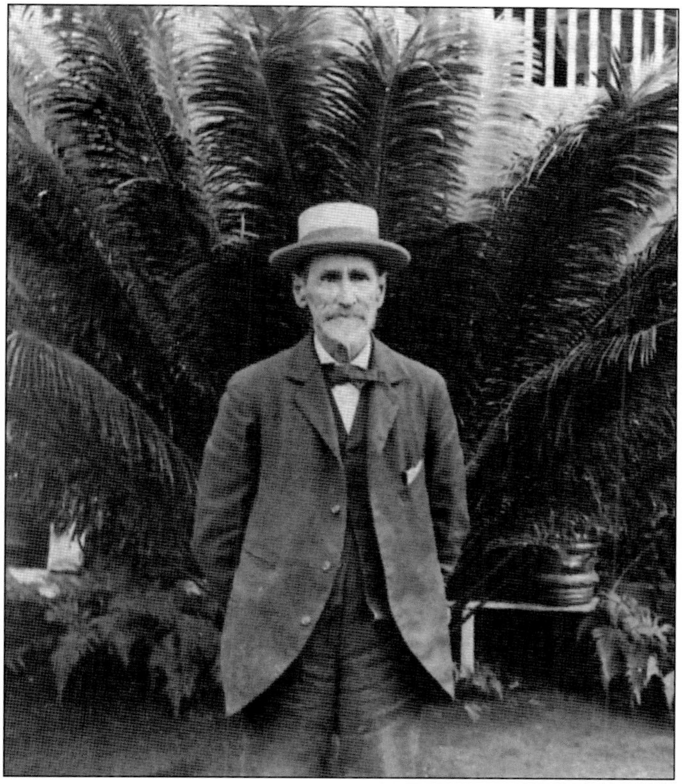

Charles E. Richardson, shown in this photograph as an elderly man, was a prominent Hilo businessman at the turn of the century. He had partnerships with both William H. Reed and William H. Shipman in different enterprises. (Courtesy of Lyman Museum.)

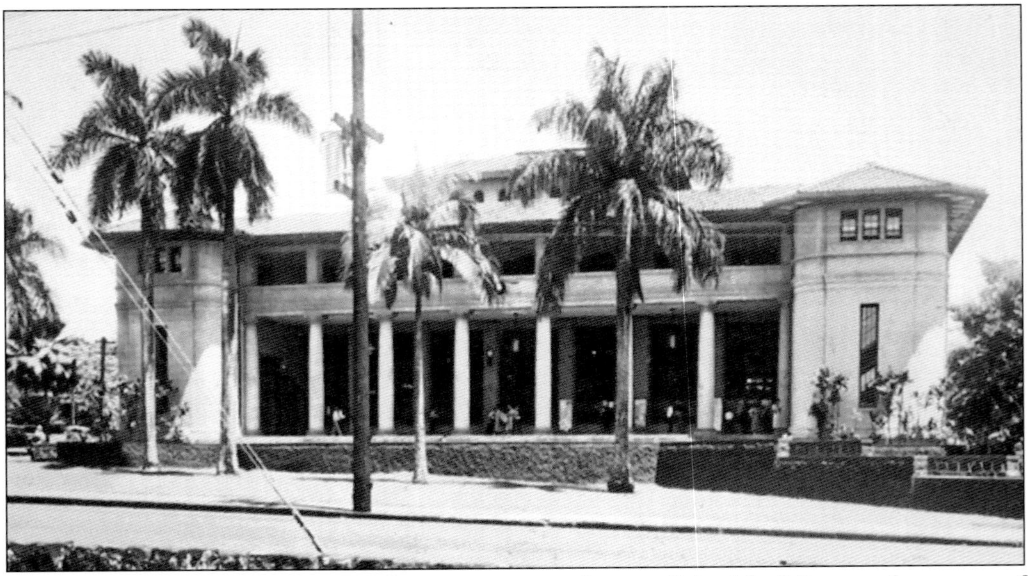

Federal funding of $200,000 paid for construction of a new federal building on the corner of Waiʻānuenue Avenue and Kinoʻole Street (changed from Pitman Street in 1916). Territorial government officials in 1913 had wanted both postal and court facilities expanded to better serve citizens and to reinforce the image of Hilo as an influential city. New York architect Henry Whitfield designed the reinforced concrete building in the Mediterranean Renaissance Revival style, which blends traditional classical architecture with features suited for a tropical climate, such as the open portico. Completed in 1817, it served as a courthouse, post office, and customs house. The above photograph was taken before new wings were added to the Hilo Federal Building and Post Office in 1938 to accommodate all tenants of the building. Louis A. Simon, supervising architect of the US Treasury, designed the wings in a style compatible with that of the original building, with a courtyard in the center. The Federal Building, US Post Office, and Courthouse was listed in the National Register of Historic Places in 1974. (Above, courtesy of Hawaiʻi State Archives; below, courtesy of Wikicommons.)

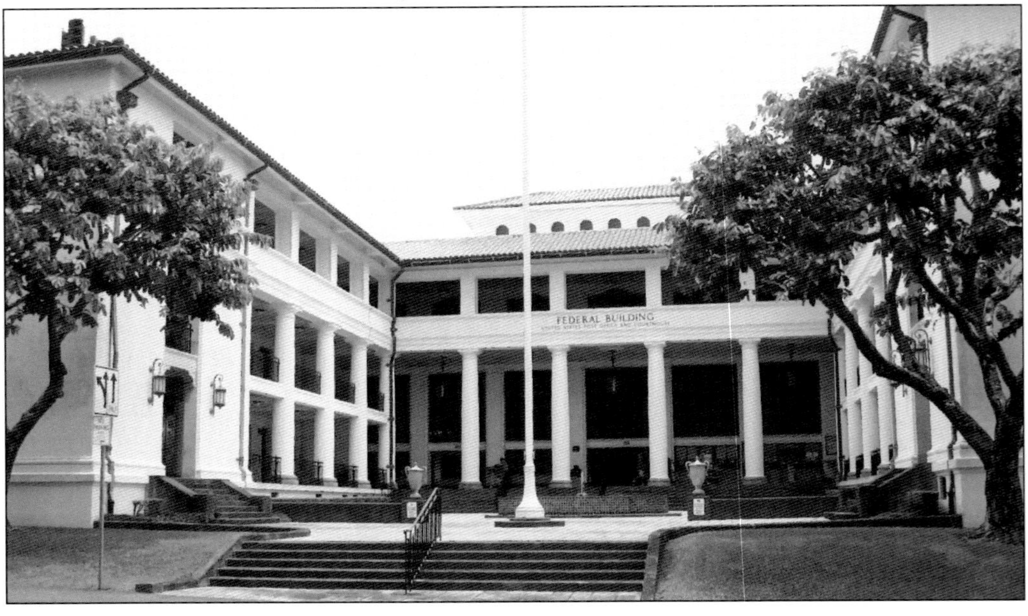

Seven

Sugar Sweetens Hilo's Economy

One industry has dominated Hilo and the entire state of Hawai'i. That industry was sugar, and it literally changed the character, landscape, and environment of the Hawaiian Islands for many decades to come, from the mid-1800s until the second half of the 20th century. It started in Kaua'i with the first commercially viable sugar plantation in 1835. Local Hilo businessmen became interested in the prospects of the new cash crop as a profitable use for the new lands they were buying. Because sugar requires an abundant water supply to manufacture, the Hilo area was particularly prime for plantations to thrive.

The sons of missionaries and other merchants and investors jumped on the bandwagon, and some of them became wealthy. Honolulu entrepreneurs were doing business throughout the islands, including Hawai'i Island. Some of the mills in Hilo and surrounding areas included Hilo Sugar Co., Waiākea Mill, Ola'a Sugar Co., Hilo Portuguese Sugar Co., Hawai'i Mill Co., Papaikou Sugar Co., Onomea Sugar Co., Pepeekeo Sugar Co., Honomū Sugar Co., and Hakalau Plantation. Various mergers and acquisitions changed the ownership throughout the era. C. Brewer & Co. was a major company that secured controlling interest in many of the local mills, including Hilo Sugar Co. Eventually, all plantations in Hawai'i were consolidated under five companies statewide. Called the Big Five, they included Castle & Cooke, Alexander & Baldwin, C. Brewer & Co., American Factors, and Theo H. Davies & Co. Their influence overthrew a monarchy and invited the United States to annex Hawai'i in the interest of improved business dealings. They promoted the 1876 Reciprocity Treaty between Hawai'i and the United States, which allowed duty-free sales of Hawai'i sugar to the United States. After that, sugar exports from Hawai'i to the United States soared, rising from 21 million pounds in 1876, to 114 million pounds in 1883, and to 224.5 million pounds in 1890.

The effect on Hilo was increased population, increased economy, employment, and expansion of the town into a city, with all of its features and functions. The sugar industry launched a railroad and instigated the expansion of Hilo Harbor's shipping facilities.

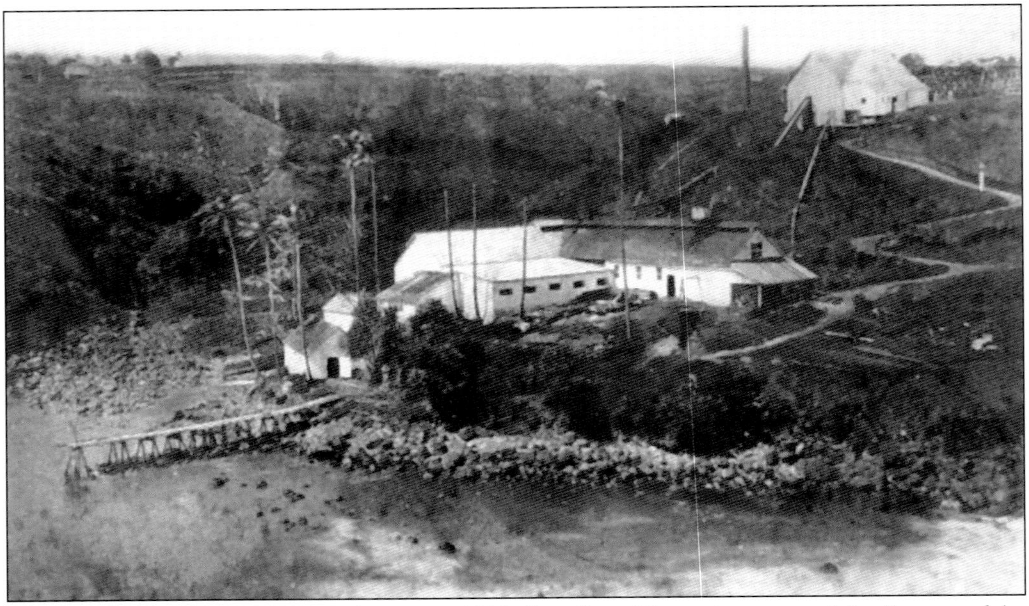

The sugar mill at Papaikou is shown in 1888. Papaikou Plantation was originally owned by Charles Whetmore and E.G. Hitchcock and later became consolidated into Onomea Sugar Company. Its location at the base of a gulch at the ocean level made shipping efficient. A metal waterwheel and boiler were shipped from Scotland in 1862. Water from flumes provided power to turn the wheel, which in turn moved the sugarcane crusher. The mill was eventually connected by rail to one of the best landing and loading devices on the coast.

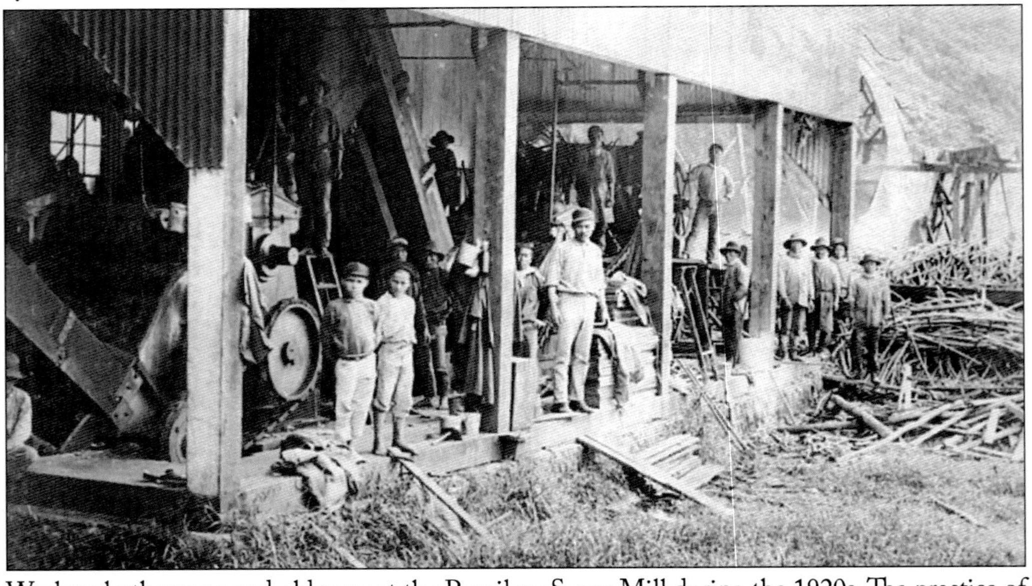

Workers both young and old pose at the Papaikou Sugar Mill during the 1920s. The practice of hiring children began with the Kingdom of Hawaii's Masters and Servants Act of 1850, which codified contract labor and provided the legal framework within which Hawai'i would receive immigrant apprentices under a contract with a specified term. Parents could sign on children as young as age 10. Until the mid-1930s, many worked to help support their families. The US Fair Labor Standards Act in 1938 banned the hiring of anyone under age 16. (Photograph by T. Ishii, courtesy of Memories of Hawai'i–Big Island.)

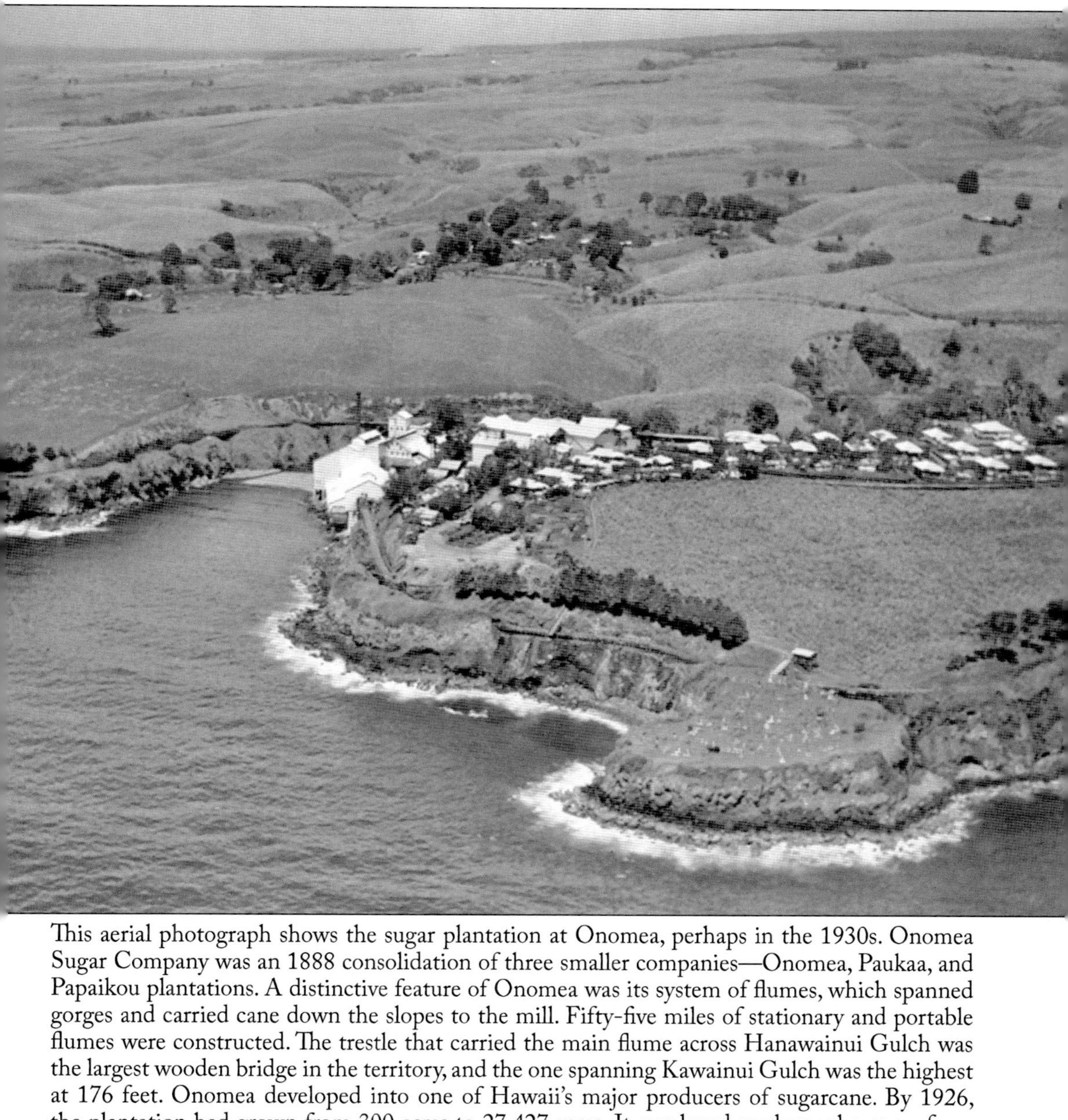

This aerial photograph shows the sugar plantation at Onomea, perhaps in the 1930s. Onomea Sugar Company was an 1888 consolidation of three smaller companies—Onomea, Paukaa, and Papaikou plantations. A distinctive feature of Onomea was its system of flumes, which spanned gorges and carried cane down the slopes to the mill. Fifty-five miles of stationary and portable flumes were constructed. The trestle that carried the main flume across Hanawainui Gulch was the largest wooden bridge in the territory, and the one spanning Kawainui Gulch was the highest at 176 feet. Onomea developed into one of Hawaii's major producers of sugarcane. By 1926, the plantation had grown from 300 acres to 27,427 acres. It employed workers who came from China, Japan, Portugal, the Philippines, Puerto Rico, and other countries. By 1941, over 3,000 men, women, and children were living in six villages on the plantation. There were 450 company-owned houses, which included garden space. Free medical services were also provided. Over the course of time, C. Brewer & Co. acquired controlling interest in the company and it merged with Hilo Sugar Co. into a single C. Brewer subsidiary called Mauna Kea Sugar Co. (Photograph by *Pan Pacific Press*; courtesy of Hawai'i State Archives.)

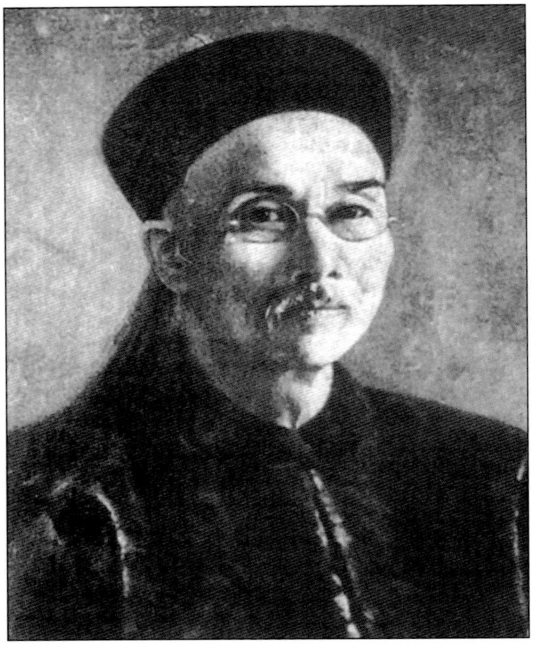

Many people do not know that the first two sugar mills in Hawai'i were owned and operated by Chinese businessmen. In fact, the Chinese were the first sugar makers and were experienced in all phases of the industry, from planting to marketing and management. Hilo-area plantation-owner Chun Afong was Hawai'i's first Chinese millionaire and was nicknamed the "Merchant Prince of the Sandalwood Mountains." At one time he owned 9,100 acres on the Hamakua Coast, including Pepeekeo Plantation. Fong's daughter married a local plantation manager and his family life is fictionalized in Jack London's famous short story *Chun Ah Chun*. (Courtesy of Zhuhai Museum, China.)

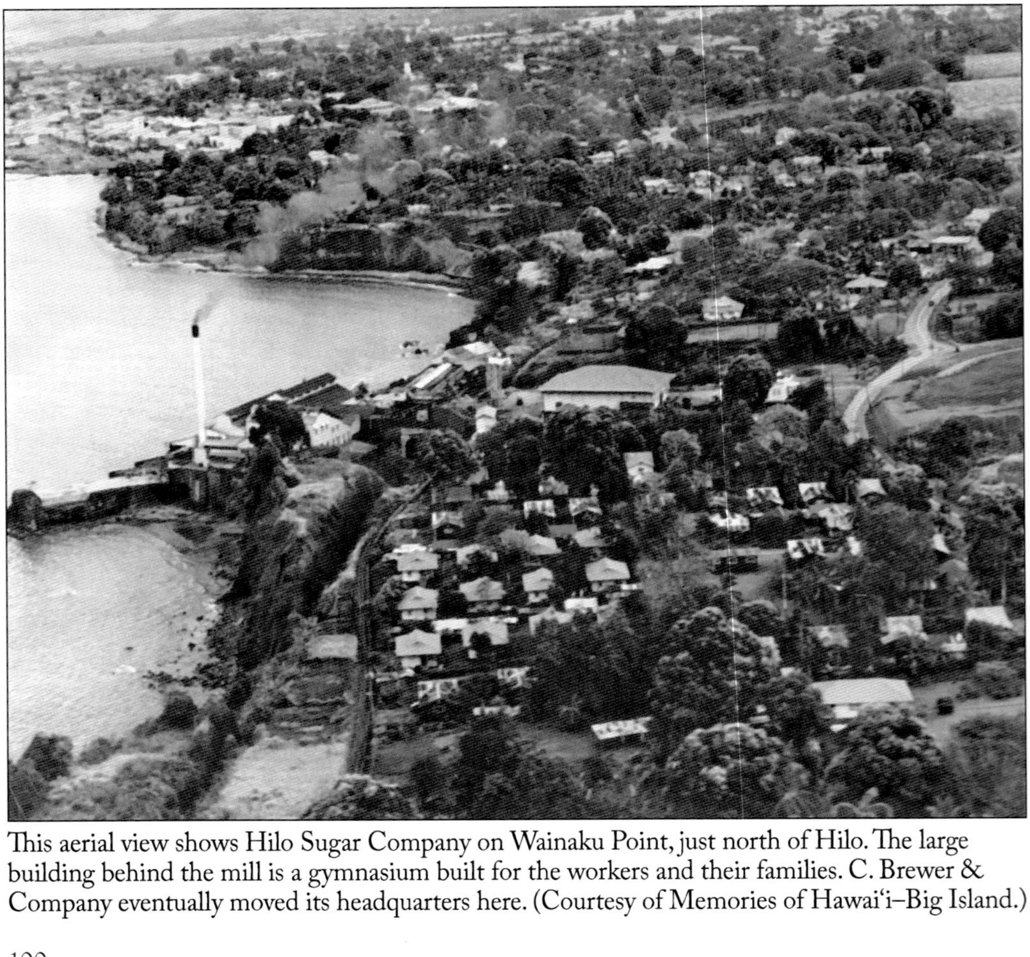

This aerial view shows Hilo Sugar Company on Wainaku Point, just north of Hilo. The large building behind the mill is a gymnasium built for the workers and their families. C. Brewer & Company eventually moved its headquarters here. (Courtesy of Memories of Hawai'i–Big Island.)

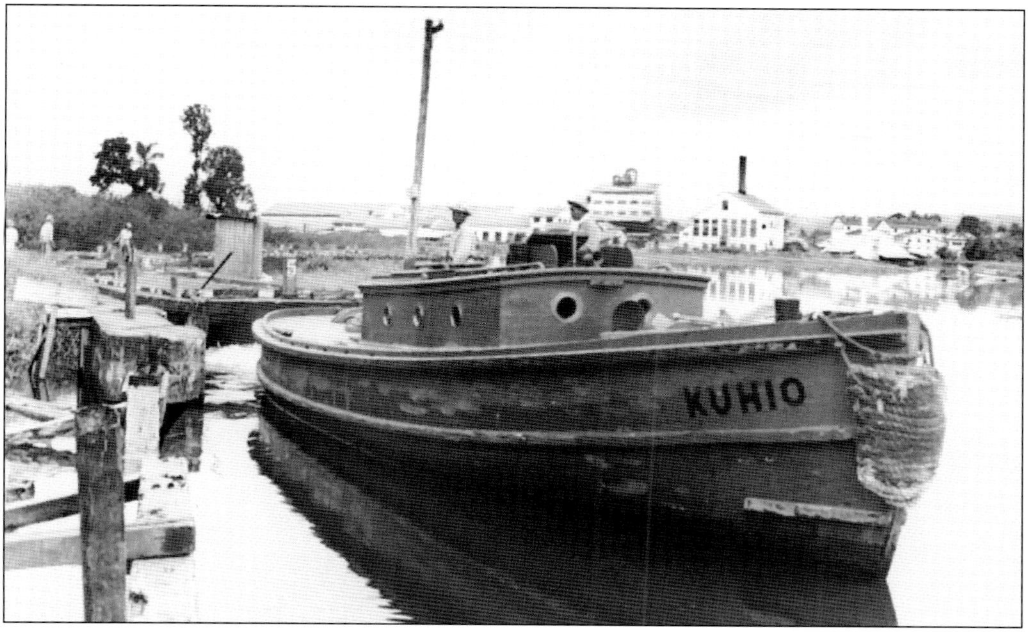

Barges were used to tow sugar from Waiākea Mill, seen in the background, along the Wailoa River to the Hilo docks. This area was known as UpGates. Waste from sugar processing, called bagasse, was sent from Waiākea Sugar Mill to the Canec plant, which pressed it into a kind of drywall for ceilings. Many homes still have these, though they contain asbestos. (Photograph by K. Padgett, courtesy of Memories of Hawai'i–Big Island.)

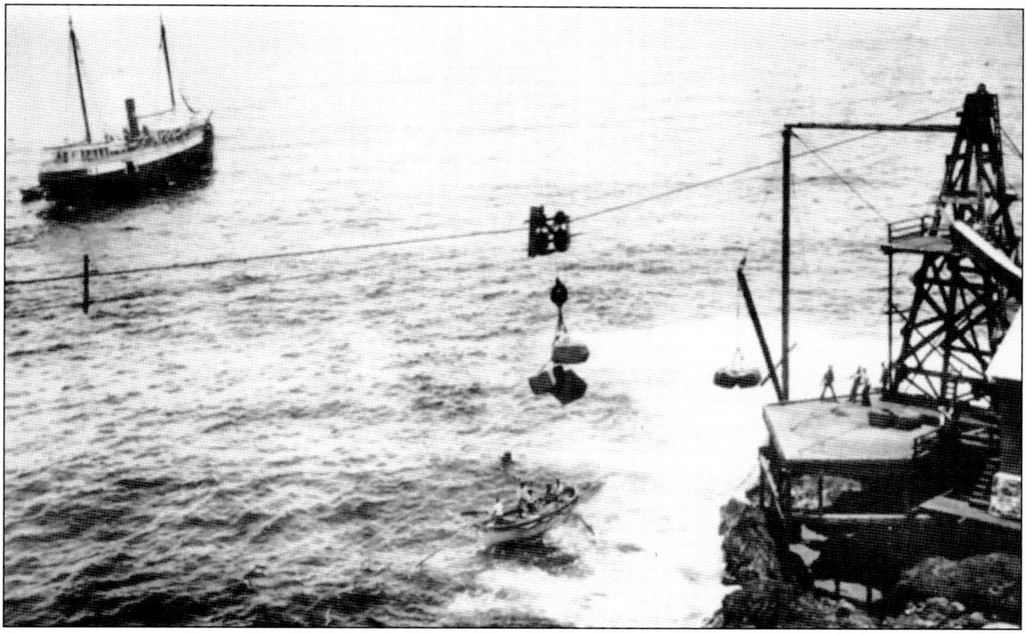

A steamship, such as the SS *Hawai'i*, based in Hilo Harbor, would carry supplies out to the sugar plantations along the Hamakua Coast, a coastline made up of cliffs from 100 to 400 feet high. Loading and unloading was a challenge, so they devised a system using derricks, winches, wires, and a running block to unload supplies and load sugar onto the ship, which was secured to moorings, for the return trip to Hilo. (Courtesy of Hawai'i State Archives.)

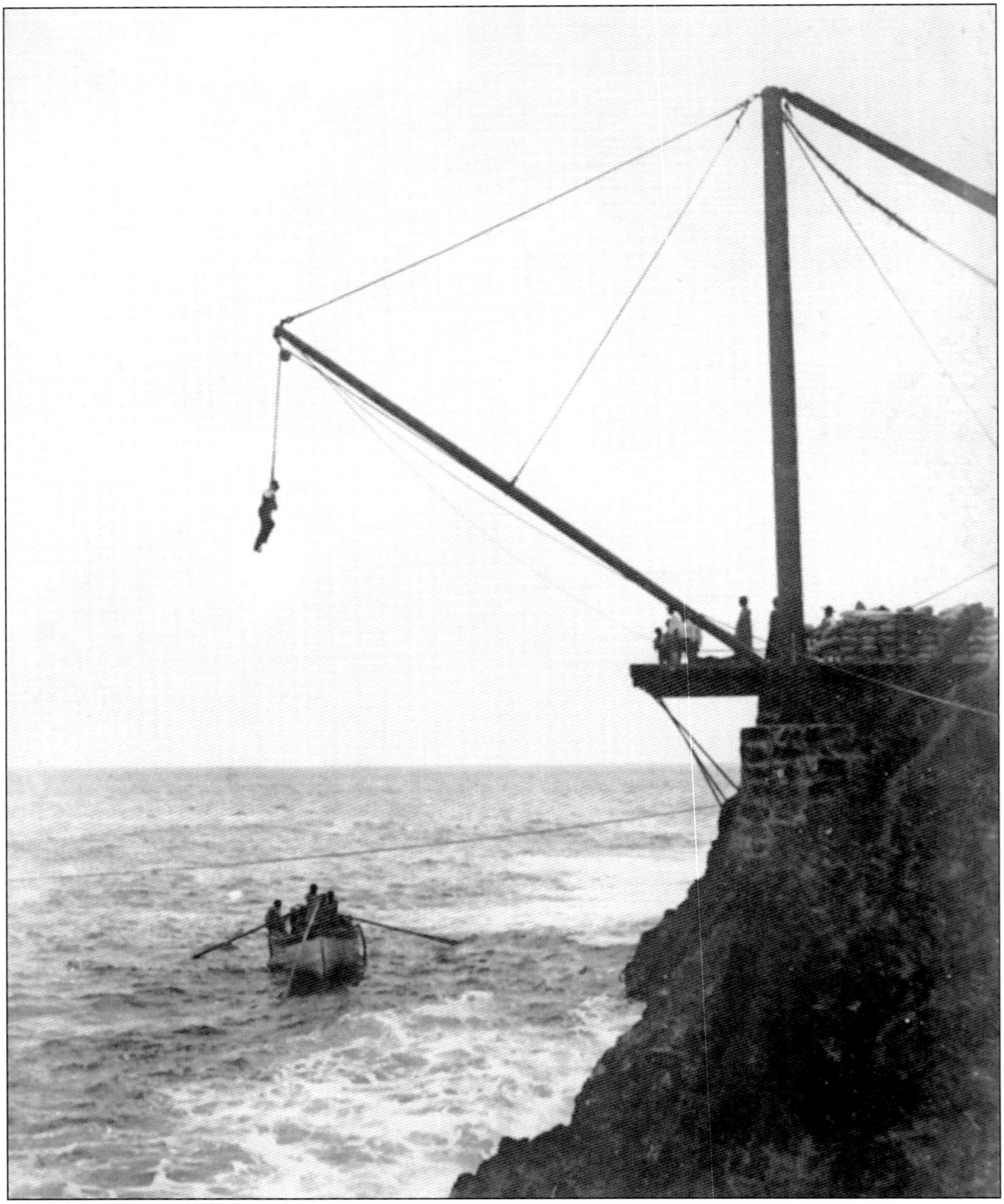

Passengers from along the Hamakua Coast could also be lowered with cable hoist into waiting rowboats that would then take them out to the steamer. (Courtesy of Hawai'i State Archives.)

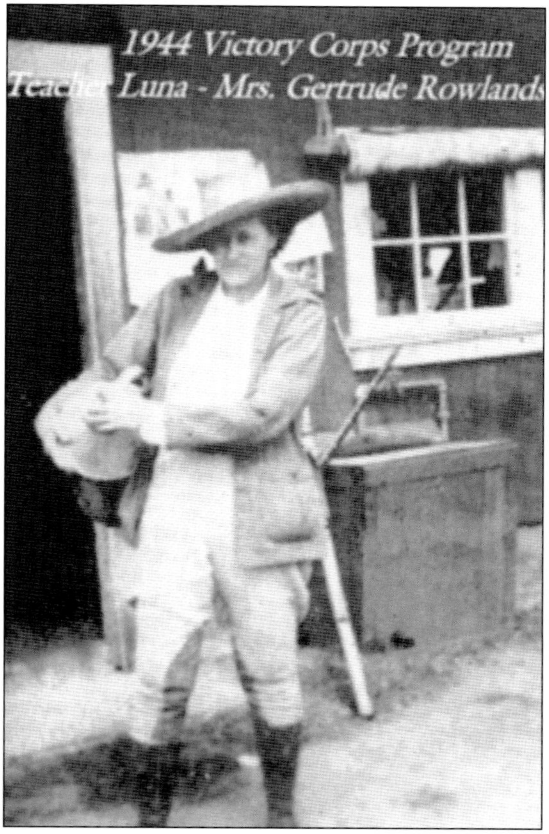

During World War II, the 1944 Victory Corps Program allowed Hilo High School students to volunteer to work on the plantation for Hilo Sugar Company after it suffered a labor shortage due to World War II enlistment of plantation workers. Hilo High School cooperated with a four-day school week, allowing Fridays to be used for plantation work. Teachers such as Gena Rowlands, pictured at right, were assigned as plantation boss, or *luna*. (Both, courtesy of Memories of Hawai'i–Big Island.)

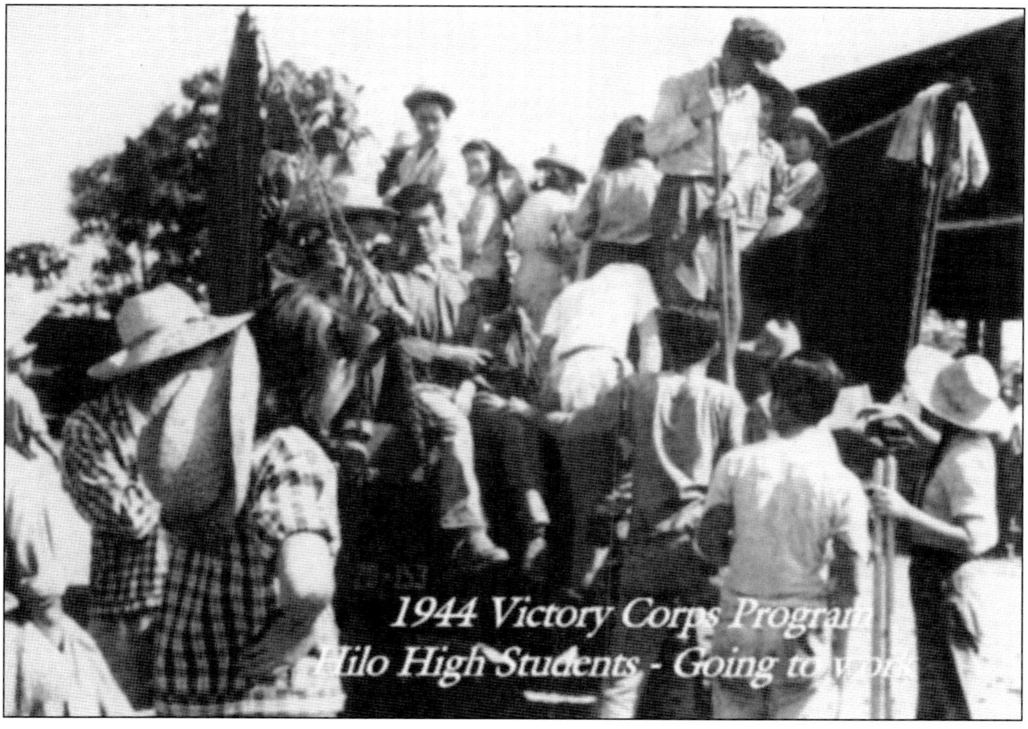

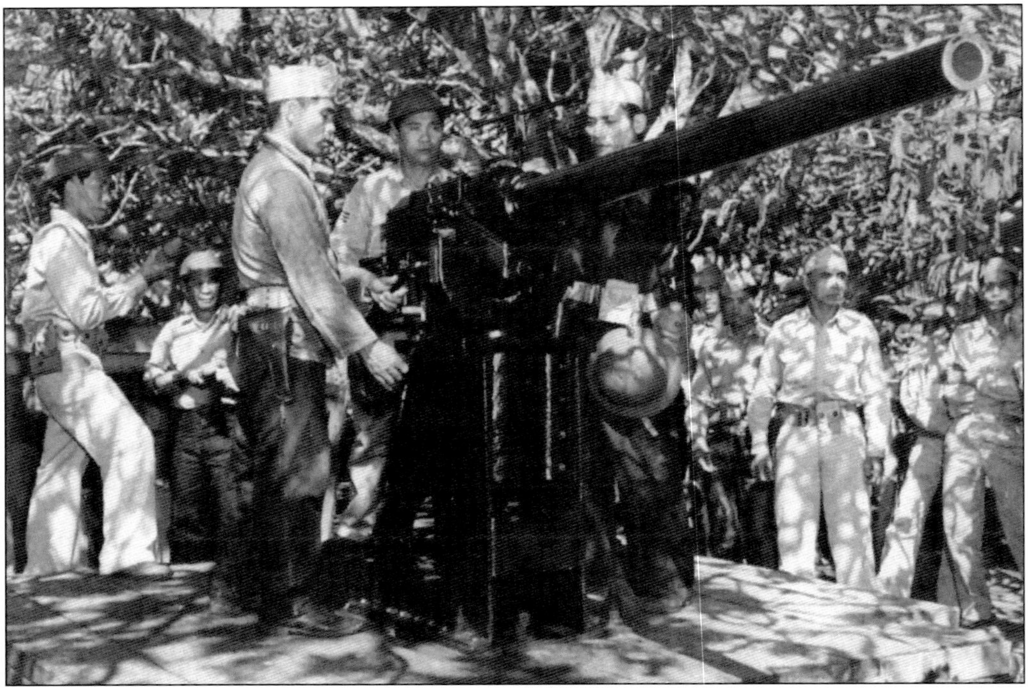

Almost every plantation on the island had a unit of the Hawai'i Rifles, a volunteer home guard formed in 1942 during World War II. In 1944, this group of men of Hawai'i Rifles checks out a four-inch coastal-defense gun hidden in a grove of trees. (Courtesy of Memories of Hawai'i–Big Island.)

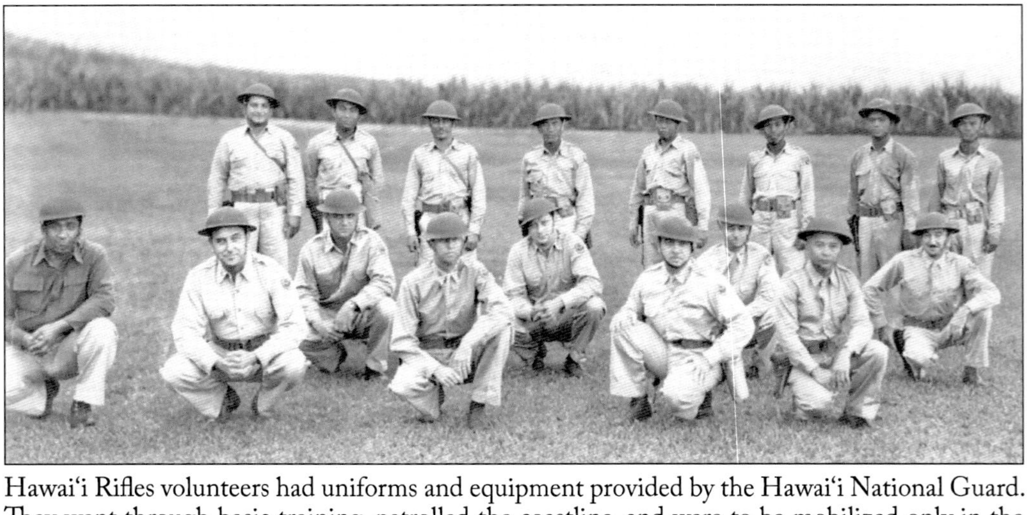

Hawai'i Rifles volunteers had uniforms and equipment provided by the Hawai'i National Guard. They went through basic training, patrolled the coastline, and were to be mobilized only in the event of a Japanese invasion or if all other military were taken off the island. These are members of the First Regiment, Ola'a Sugar Division. (Courtesy of Memories of Hawai'i–Big Island.)

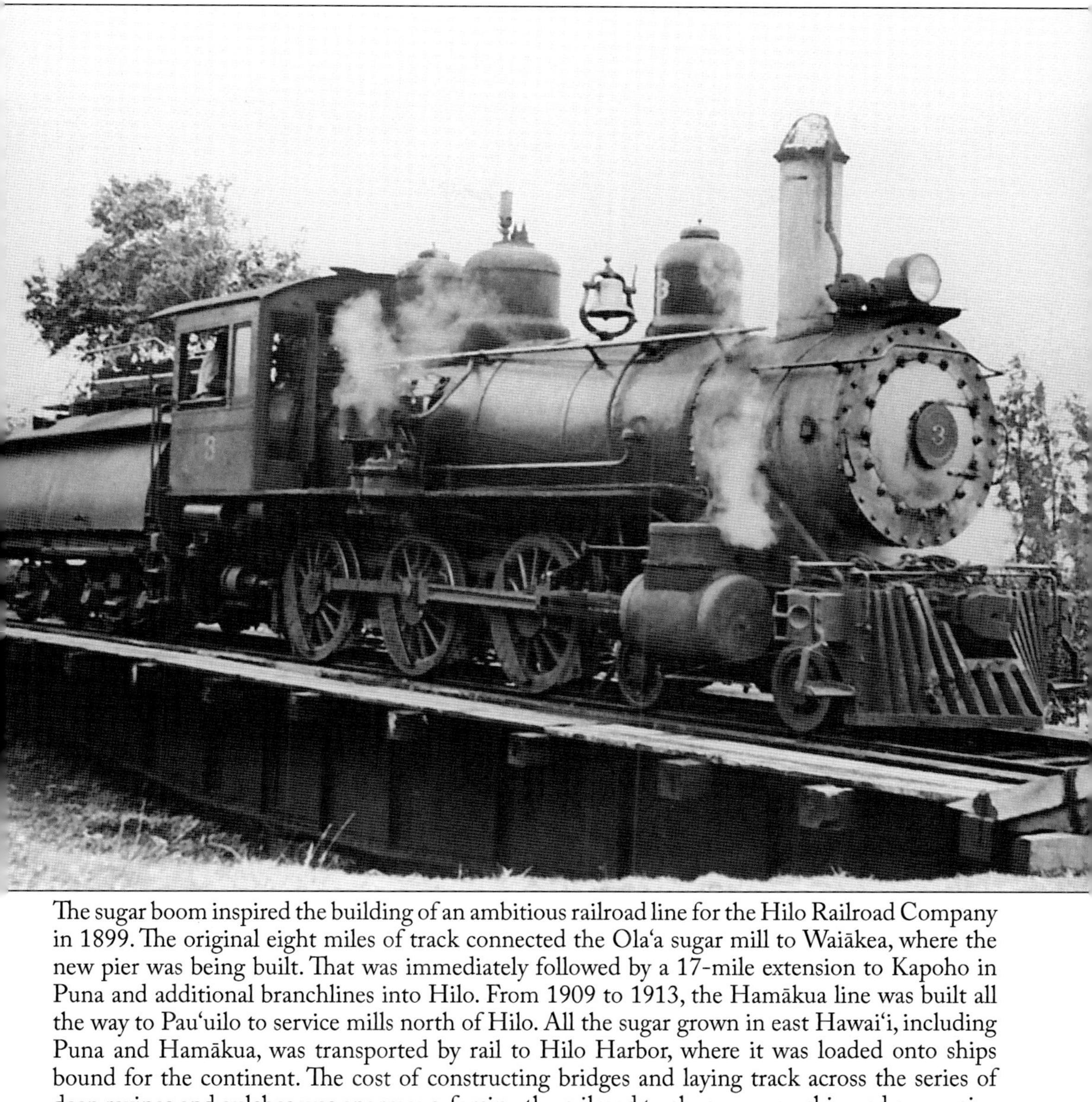

The sugar boom inspired the building of an ambitious railroad line for the Hilo Railroad Company in 1899. The original eight miles of track connected the Olaʻa sugar mill to Waiākea, where the new pier was being built. That was immediately followed by a 17-mile extension to Kapoho in Puna and additional branchlines into Hilo. From 1909 to 1913, the Hamākua line was built all the way to Pauʻuilo to service mills north of Hilo. All the sugar grown in east Hawaiʻi, including Puna and Hamākua, was transported by rail to Hilo Harbor, where it was loaded onto ships bound for the continent. The cost of constructing bridges and laying track across the series of deep ravines and gulches was enormous, forcing the railroad to change ownership and reorganize as the Hawaiʻi Consolidated Railway (HCR). Here, engine No. 3 is on the turntable at the end of the line in Pauʻuilo. Hilo also had a turntable that was located near the bridge across the Wailuku River. (Courtesy of Lyman Museum.)

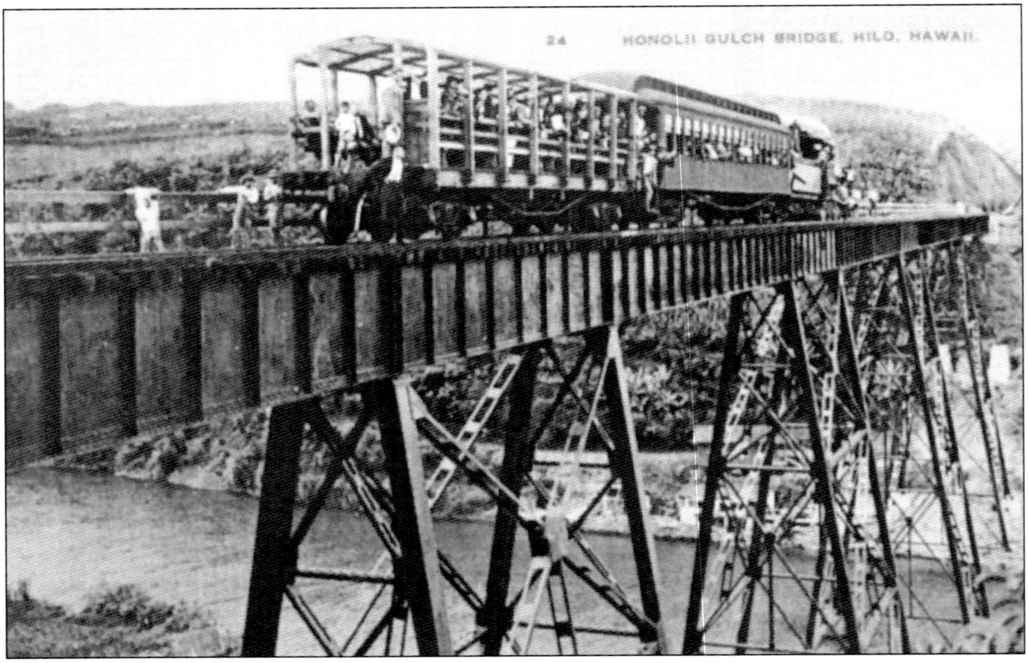

In addition to sugar and other freight, the railroad carried passengers. Targeting tourists to augment its business, the HCR ran sightseeing specials under the name Scenic Express. Not for the faint of heart, these trips included a stop on the trestles, where passengers disembarked to admire the outstanding scenery. This sightseeing train crossed Honoli'i Gulch Bridge. The entire rail line crossed over 12,000 feet in bridges, 211 water openings under the tracks, and individual steel spans of up to 1,006 feet long and 230 feet high. Some of the biggest were those over Maulua, Laupahoehoe, and Honoli'i Gulches and the Wailuku River. Over 3,100 feet of tunnels were constructed, one of which, the Maulua Tunnel, was more than a half mile in length. (Courtesy of Memories of Hawai'i–Big Island.)

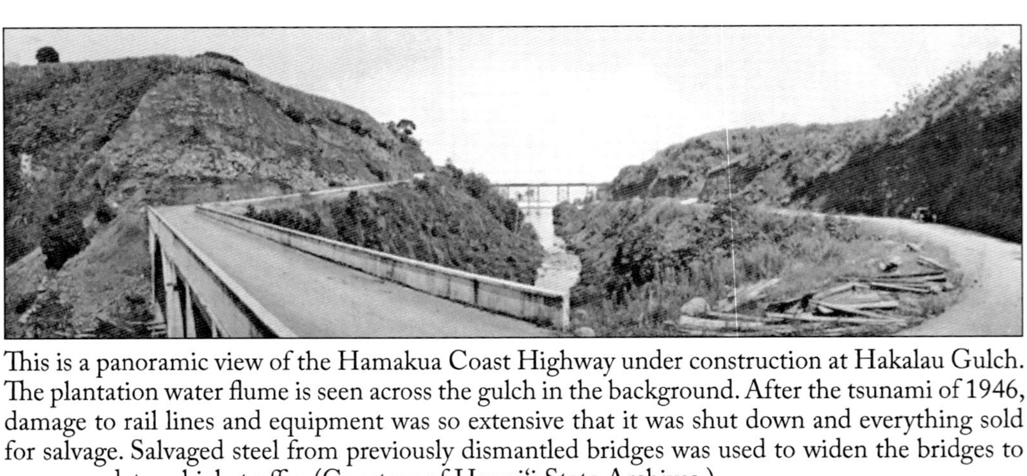

This is a panoramic view of the Hamakua Coast Highway under construction at Hakalau Gulch. The plantation water flume is seen across the gulch in the background. After the tsunami of 1946, damage to rail lines and equipment was so extensive that it was shut down and everything sold for salvage. Salvaged steel from previously dismantled bridges was used to widen the bridges to accommodate vehicle traffic. (Courtesy of Hawai'i State Archives.)

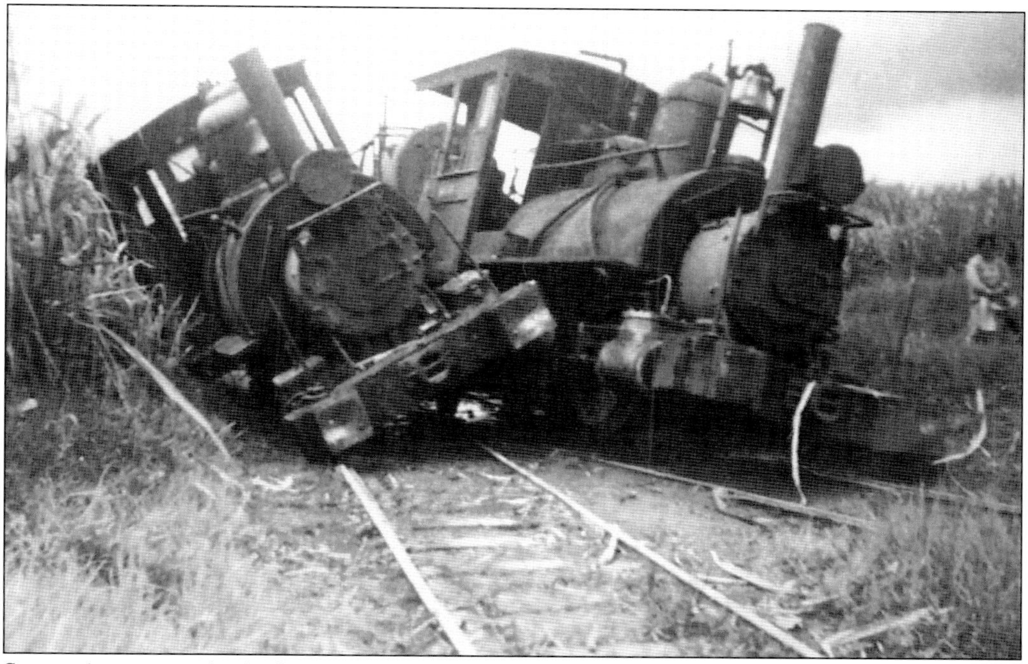

Sugar plantations also had their own trains. Here, two sugar plantation trains from the Waiākea and Portuguese Sugar Mills have collided. (Courtesy of Memories of Hawai'i–Big Island.)

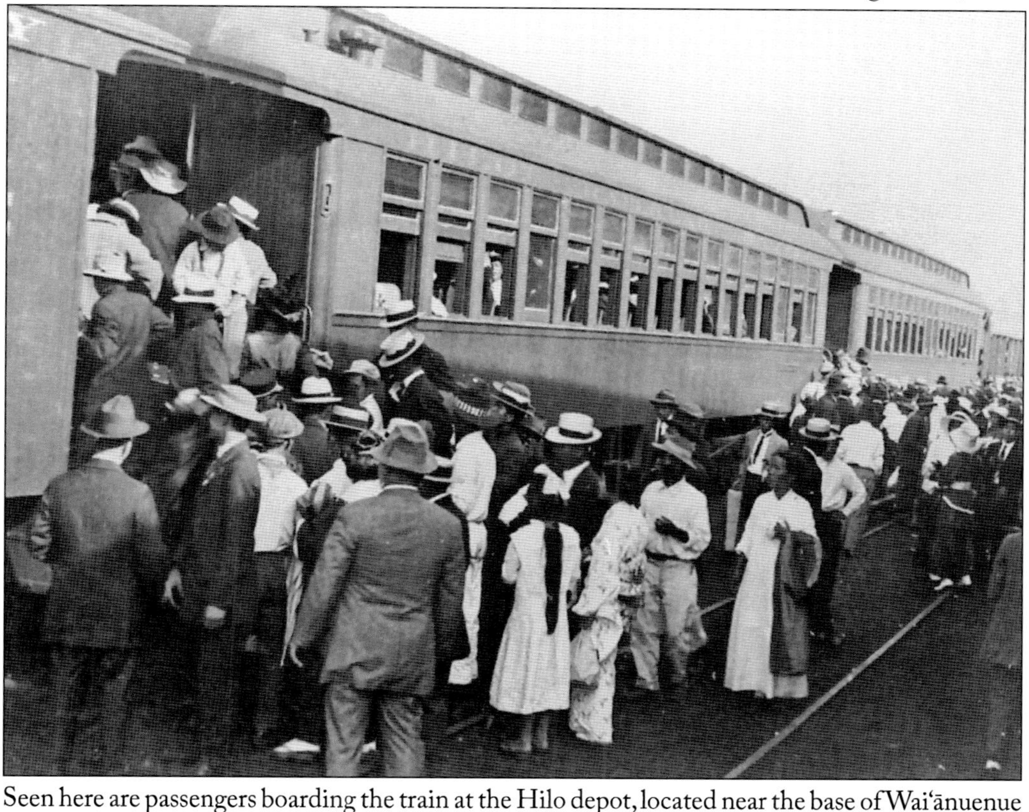

Seen here are passengers boarding the train at the Hilo depot, located near the base of Wai'ānuenue Avenue, on the Fourth of July in 1927. (Courtesy of Lyman Museum.)

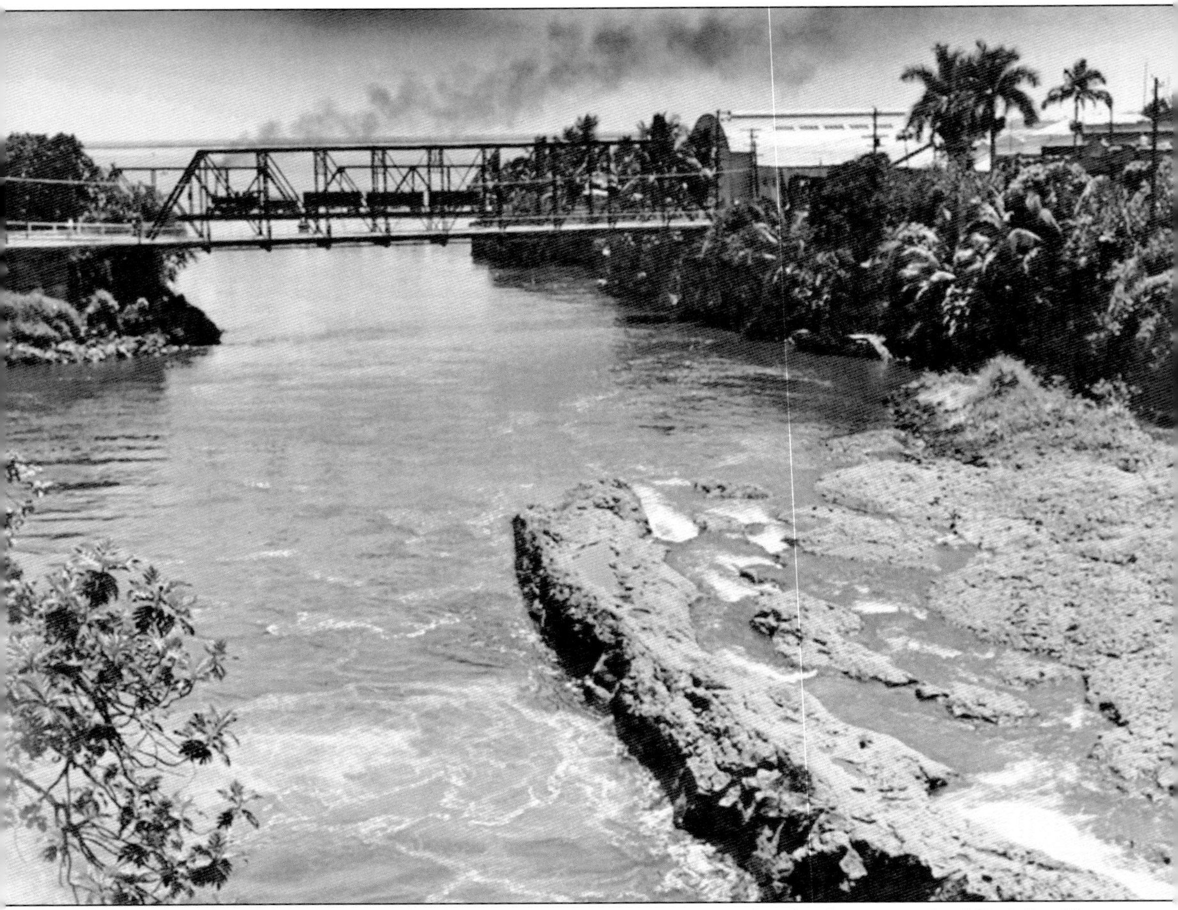

It appears in this photograph as if a small train is crossing this bridge over the Wailuku River from Hilo to Pu'ueo. In fact, there are two bridges, one for vehicles in the front and a railroad bridge behind it. In the foreground is a lava formation known as Maui's Canoe. In legend, the demigod Maui visited his mother, Hina, who lived at the base of Rainbow Falls, which is up the river several miles. One day, a large lizard, or *mo'o*, named Mo'o Kuna was creating mischief during a storm in which huge torrents of water and boulders were cascading over the falls. The mo'o moved a huge boulder over the falls and into the river, where it fit perfectly and prevented water from flowing farther. As the water level beneath the falls began to rise, Hina, realizing her danger, signaled her son. With two powerful strokes, he paddled his canoe from Maui to the mouth of the Wailuku. He rushed upstream and split the damming boulder with a single blow, thereby saving his mother. Maui did battle with the mo'o, and called upon Pele to send lava into the river to drive out the mo'o and kill it. Maui's canoe is part of a lava channel within the river, many other sections of which are also visible. (Courtesy of Hawai'i State Archives.)

Eight

Immigrants Change the Face of Hilo

The demand for labor in the booming sugar industry was larger than both the Hawaiian and foreign populations could provide in the mid-1800s. Native Hawaiians had succumbed to disease and their population declined dramatically statewide, from 800,000 in 1778 to 40,000 in 1878. Plantation owners petitioned the government to enable immigration from other countries. The Hawai'i government responded to labor shortages by allowing sugar planters to bring in overseas contract laborers bound to serve at fixed wages for three-to-five-year periods. Hawaiian Sugar Planters' Association coordinated efforts of plantations to import labor. The enormous increase in the plantation workforce consisted of first Chinese, then Japanese, then Portuguese contract laborers. The following years saw plantation employment rising from 3,921 in 1872, to 10,243 in 1882, to 20,536 in 1892. Beyond just employment, however, the multicultural transformation that took place in Hawai'i, including Hawai'i Island, was phenomenal.

Each immigrant group came with a different set of cultural values and language, diet, religion, and social traditions. Plantation owners recognized the value in keeping workers of the same nationality among friends. This resulted in what came to be called camps. In each plantation, there was a Japanese camp, a Filipino camp, a Portuguese camp, and so forth. Soon, they were sharing among each other and everyone learned something about other cultures. Since they had to work together, a unique form of language developed that remains today, called Hawaiian Pidgin. It combines words from different languages, including Hawaiian, and it created its own cadence as well. Plantations furnished everything for the workers, from housing and a plot of land to health care, recreational facilities, stores, and more. The plantations even had their own hospitals.

Many towns on the island were created as plantation towns that did not exist before this era. Problems developed and conditions were not perfect, of course. The percentage of men was much higher than women, and the government realized the advantage of bringing women over as picture brides. Labor unrest arose and unions were organized in 1944. Many workers went back home at the end of their contract period, but others stayed to make their homes here, creating their own coffee farms and opening their own stores. A trip around the island will show historic stores with Japanese names on them, still in the family after 100 years. Immigrants entered politics and became doctors, lawyers, mayors, governors, and US senators.

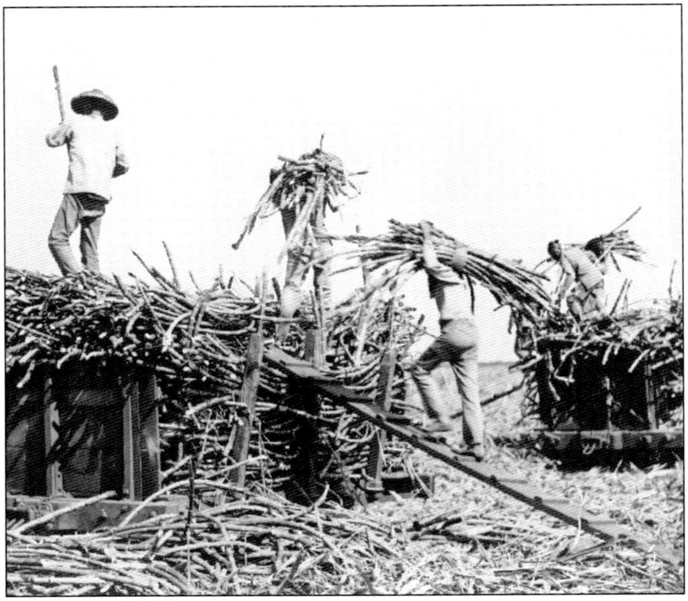

It is estimated that more than 46,000 Chinese were brought to Hawai'i as laborers in the late 1800s. This mass immigration of the Chinese into Hawai'i came to a close in the 1900s. When Hawai'i became a US territory, it was subject to US laws such as the Chinese Exclusion Act, passed due to California discrimination. In Hawai'i, it meant the legal end to large-scale Chinese immigration and forced plantations to seek workers from elsewhere. Here, Chinese laborers are shown loading sugarcane onto carts. (Courtesy of Hawai'i State Archives.)

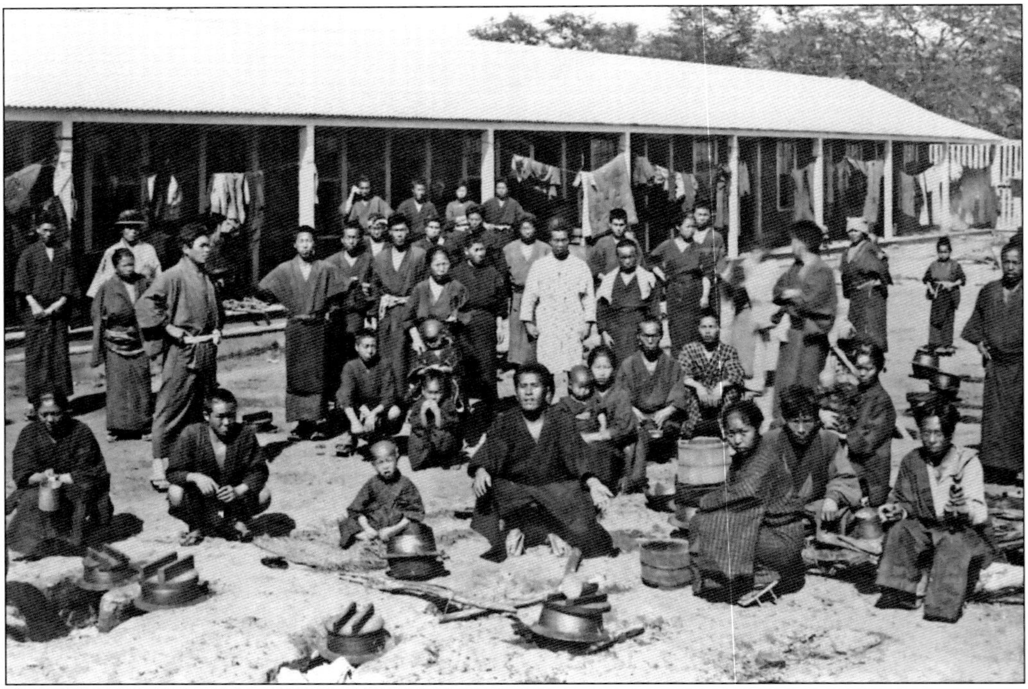

Japanese immigration to the Hawaiian Islands began in 1868, but the systematic immigration of contract workers did not begin until 1884, when the Japanese government finally approved it. King Kalākaua visited Japan and a Treaty of Commerce and Friendship was signed in 1871. Earlier contracts with the workers were improved by new, three-year contracts with free passage, improved wages, food allowance, lodging, medical care, fuel, and low-cost rice. Plantations were told that cleanliness was important to Japanese, so they were given five gallons of hot water daily for washing. In the camps, communal baths were set up. This c. 1886 photograph shows a group of Japanese immigrants wearing kimonos and perhaps preparing a communal meal. (Courtesy of Lyman Museum.)

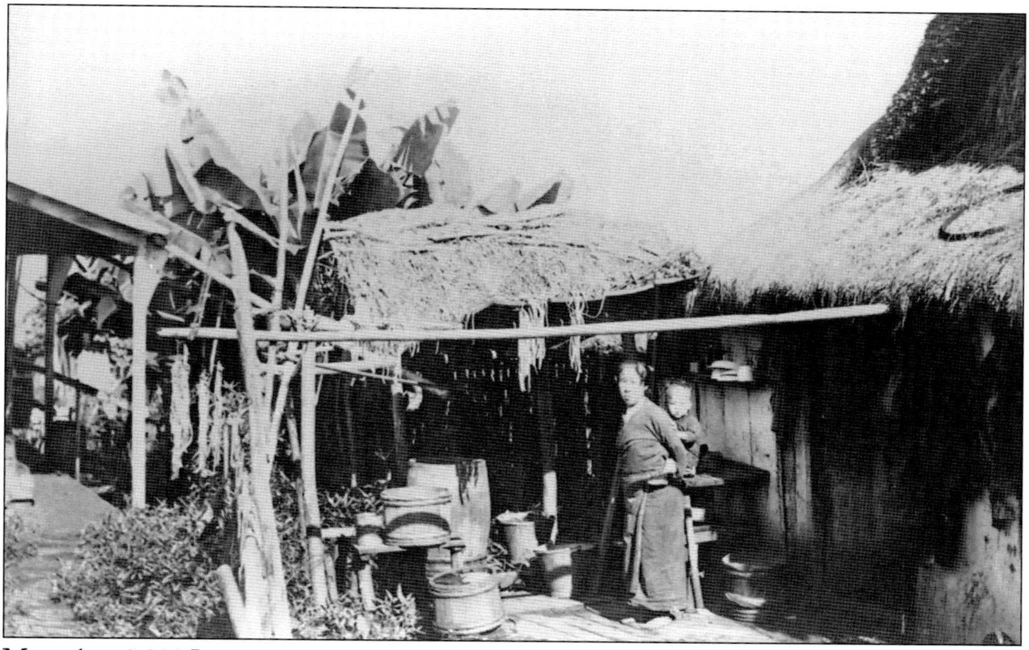

More than 9,000 Japanese contract workers and farmers came to the islands from 1885 to 1886. The first Japanese immigrants lived in unstable huts that they had to build themselves when they arrived. This photograph shows a Japanese woman and her baby by their thatched house. (Courtesy of Lyman Museum.)

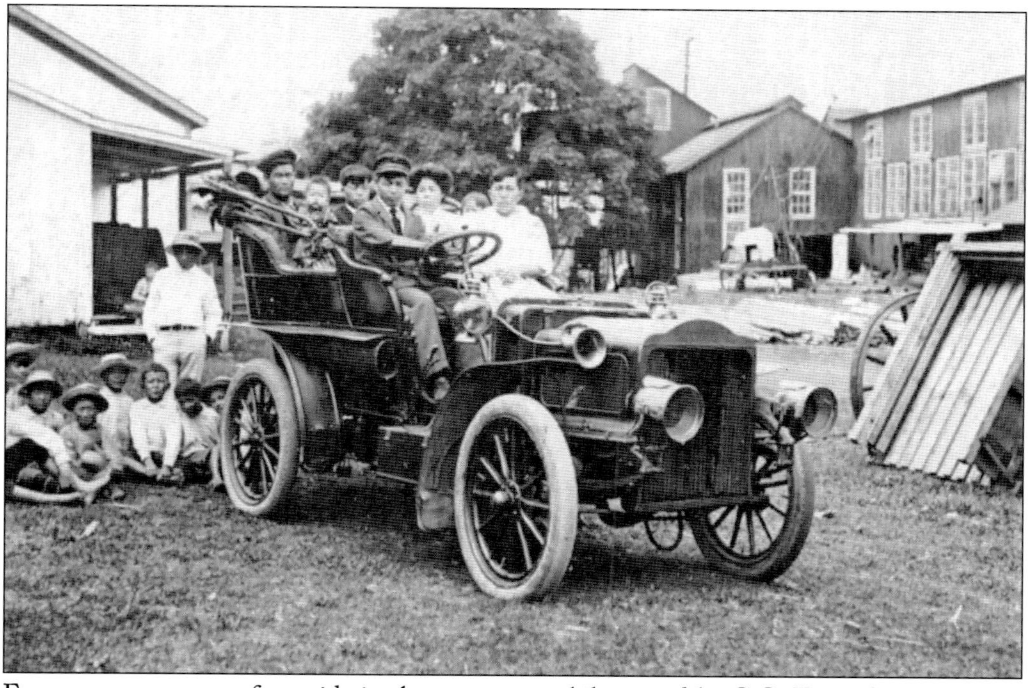

Everyone wants to go for a ride in the new automobile owned by C.C. Kennedy, manager of Waiākea Mill. His chauffeur, a Mr. Imanaka, takes family and friends for a ride in this White model around 1905. It was the second car registered on the island. (Photograph by T. Imanaka, courtesy of Memories of Hawai'i–Big Island.)

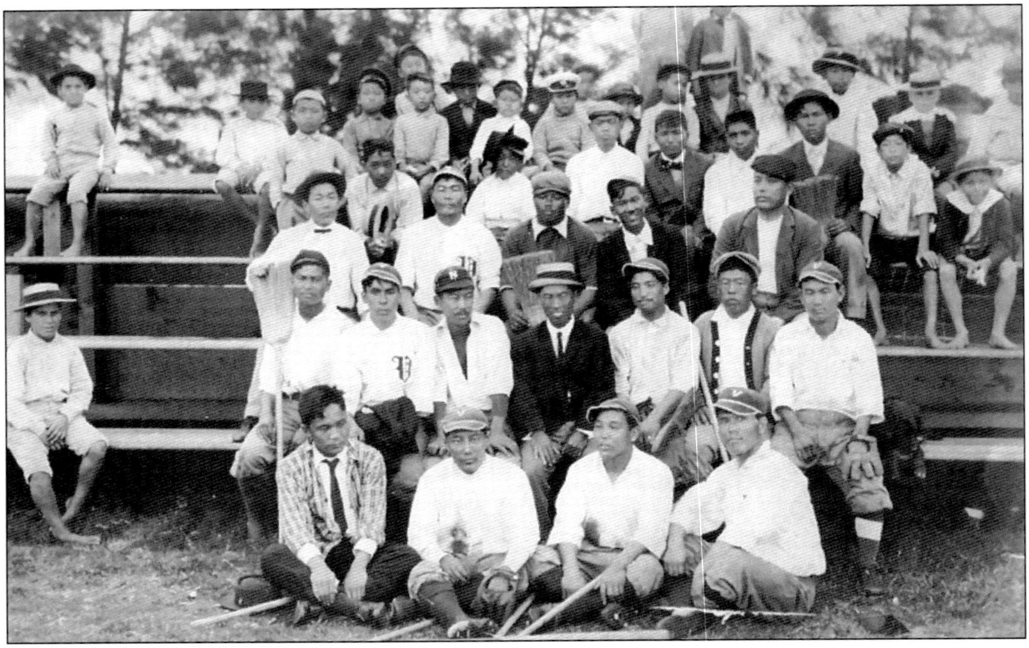

A baseball league was formed in 1919 by C. Brewer & Co.; games were played at Mo'oheau Park in Hilo. At first, teams were organized by ethnic groups, but later it was determined that mixed teams were better and each plantation had its own team. Here, a Japanese camp baseball team poses at Mo'oheau Park. Games were usually played on Sundays after church. (Courtesy of Memories of Hawai'i–Big Island.)

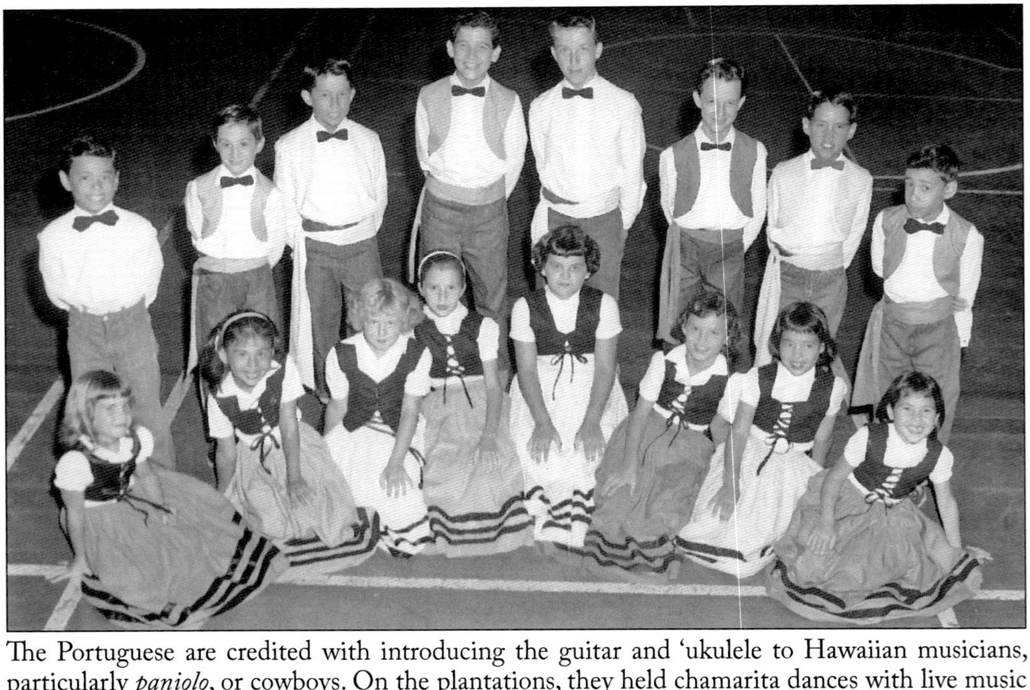

The Portuguese are credited with introducing the guitar and 'ukulele to Hawaiian musicians, particularly *paniolo*, or cowboys. On the plantations, they held chamarita dances with live music by the chamarita bands. These kids are all dressed up for the dance. (Courtesy of Memories of Hawai'i–Big Island.)

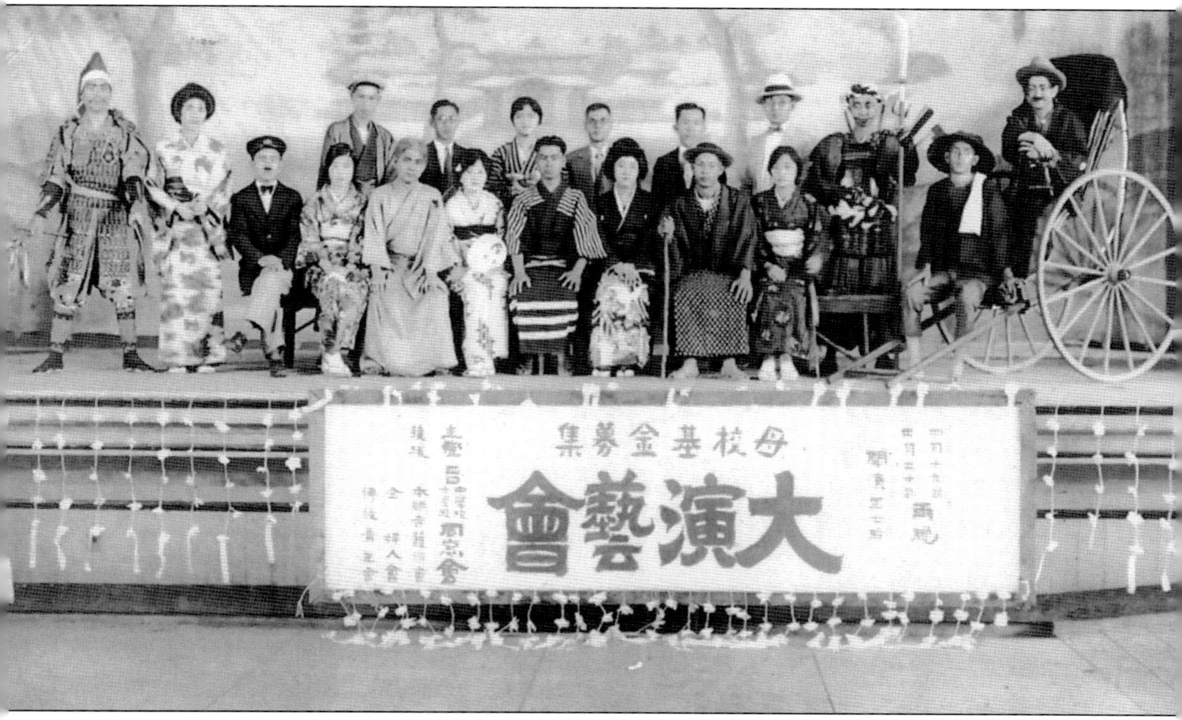

Japanese plantation workers created original melodrama productions called *shibai*, performed with original costumes, makeup, and props. It was a popular form of entertainment, usually held in plantation gyms or theaters around the island in the 1930s and 1940s. To advertise upcoming performances, they would drive around the camps in an old bus, pounding drums and yelling "Shibai!" while passing out leaflets. The word *shibai* has other meanings, too, including describing an action by a person who is disingenuous or "putting on an act." (Courtesy of Memories of Hawai'i–Big Island.)

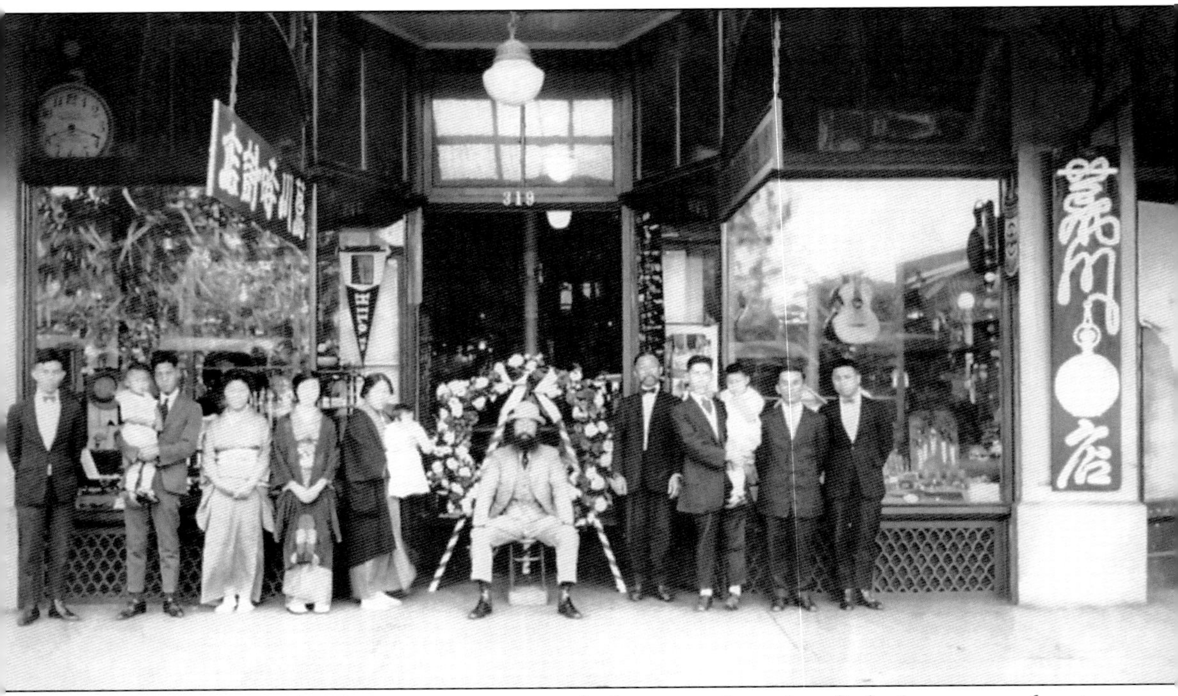

After completing his three-year contract with the sugar plantation, S. Arakawa opened a store on Hilo's Front Street in 1900. The business sold jewelry, radios, phonographs, optical goods, bicycles, guns, revolvers, and Hawaiian artifacts, and also repaired watches. In the 1940s, it became Arakawa Jewelers and survived two tsunamis, one in 1946 and the other in 1960. On either side were stores owned by Chinese merchants. (Courtesy of Memories of Hawai'i–Big Island.)

Nine

Social Life in Old Hilo

Before hotels were built on the island—and, in fact, throughout ancient Hawaiian times—the guesthouses of the day were people's homes. Hawaiians welcomed visiting missionaries into their homes with hospitality. Prominent families in Hilo welcomed visiting Hawaiian kings and queens, as well as famous writers and others seeking to enjoy the tropical ambience of the island. Kīlauea Volcano was a major attraction, and one could not visit Hilo without taking a tour to see the home of the goddess Pele. Of course, in the early days the journey was by horse and buggy and took two days, so a halfway house in Mountain View hosted travelers overnight. It was not until the 1930s that hotels began to be built on the Waiākea Peninsula along Banyan Drive. The banyans were planted with the idea that each one could be dedicated to a famous person, and they carry the names of Babe Ruth, Amelia Earhart, and others who were only visitors here at one time or another. Nearby Coconut Island, which had been used as a quarantine station in the early 1900s, became a place for fun, with a swimming pool, a water slide, and a diving tower being constructed. Families gathered for picnics among the coconut trees. The seashore has always attracted people seeking to relax, whether going for a stroll, swimming, boating, or fishing. After Hawai'i became a US territory, the Fourth of July became a focal point for celebrations that included parades and boat races.

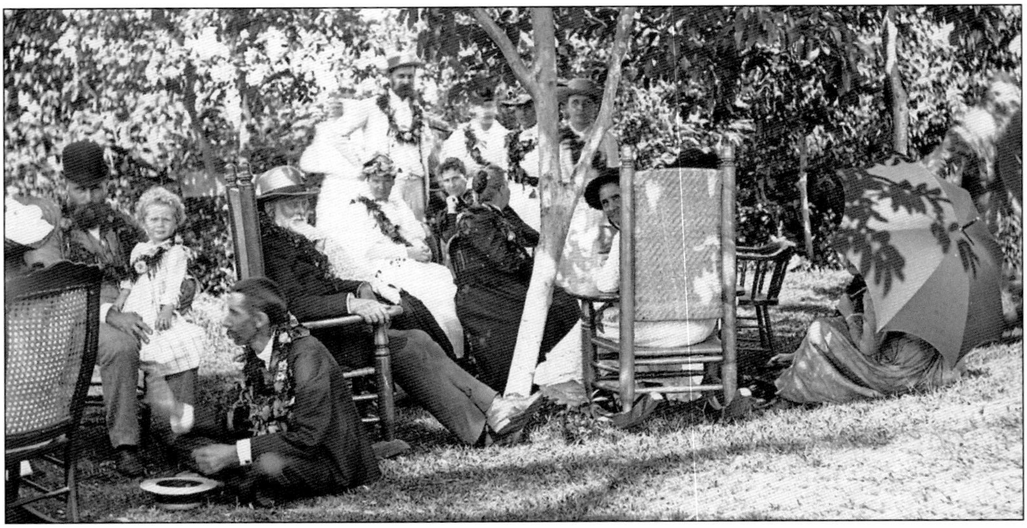

The family of David Howard Hitchcock, a prominent Hilo lawyer, is shown in a casual setting in an 1896 photograph taken from a glass plate negative. Hitchcock, who had a Hilo law practice that later became the Carlsmith firm, is shown seated in the rocking chair. He is age 65 at the time of the picture. Hitchcock also served in the Hawai'i Legislature and as sheriff in Hilo. Others identified in the photograph are John Scott and his daughter, at left, and a Mrs. Townsend in the other rocking chair. The rest are unidentified. (Courtesy of Lyman Museum.)

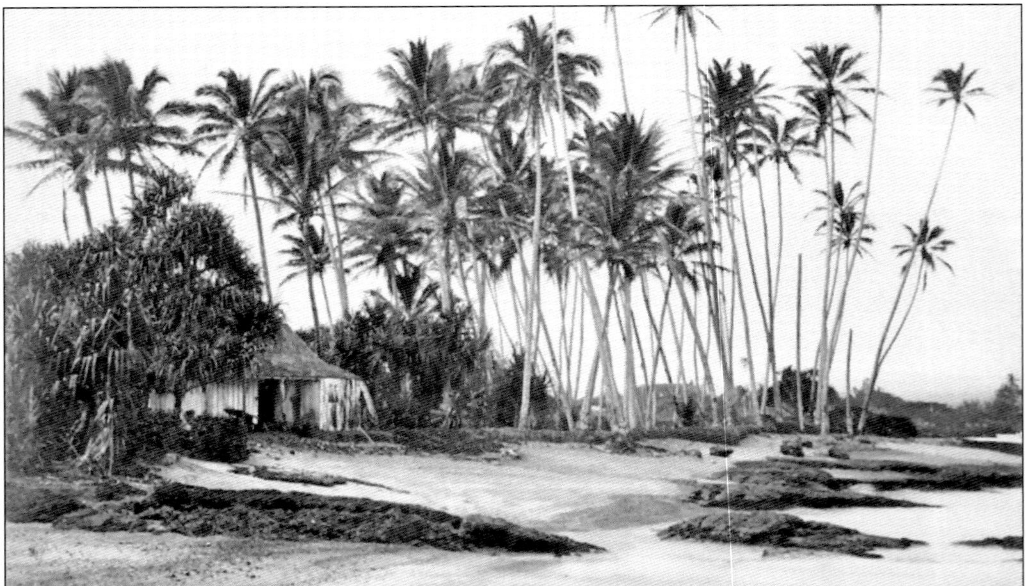

Coconut Island, or Moku Ola ("healing island" in Hawaiian), was known as a *pu'uhonua*, a place of refuge or a place of healing. All islands had pu'uhonua; they were also part of the penal system, serving as a place for judgment by a kāhuna. The 3.1-acre Moku Ola has been a social gathering place for the last century. Located just off the Waiākea Peninsula, it has been inundated by tsunamis numerous times, including a large one in 1877, which wiped it clean of its first structures. In 1880, a smallpox epidemic swept the islands, and Moku Ola was designated a quarantine station, with several buildings erected for that purpose. It was used again for the bubonic plague epidemic in 1900. After that, it became a recreational park. (Courtesy of Hawai'i State Archives.)

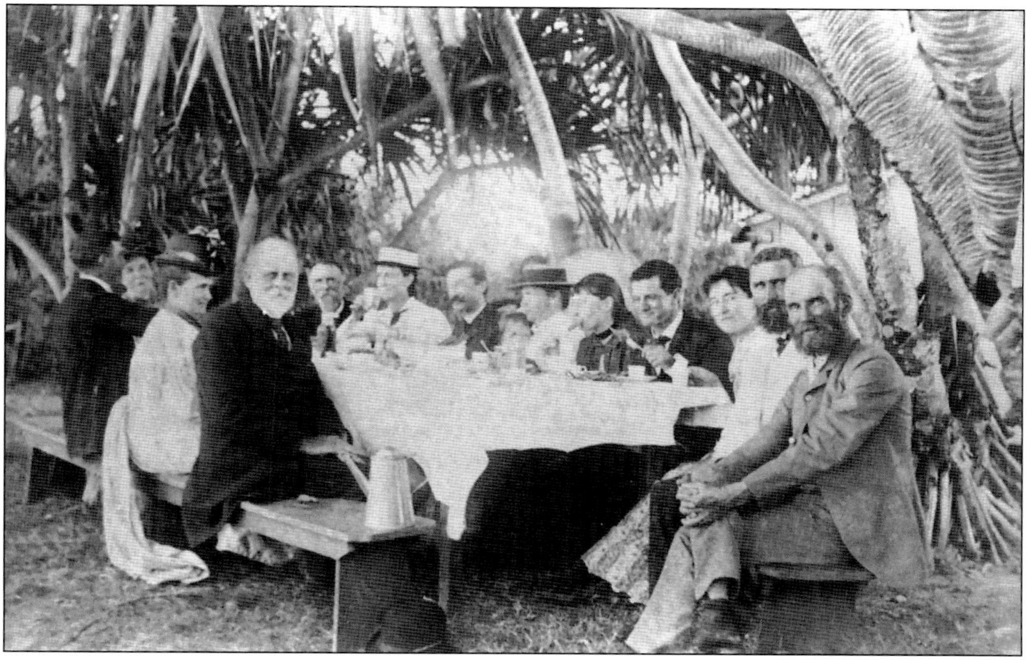

Coconut Island was a popular spot for family gatherings in the early days. People would cross over by canoe. Here, members of the Wetmore, Severance, and other prominent 19th-century Hilo families are shown at a picnic on Coconut Island on an unknown date. With their seating arrangement unspecified, members of the party include Dr. Charles Wetmore, Mrs. L. Severance, Hattie Coan, Gertrude Severance Sawyer, Mrs. L. Turner, Mrs. Herbert Austin, Helen Severance, and Dr. Wiggins. (Courtesy of Lyman Museum.)

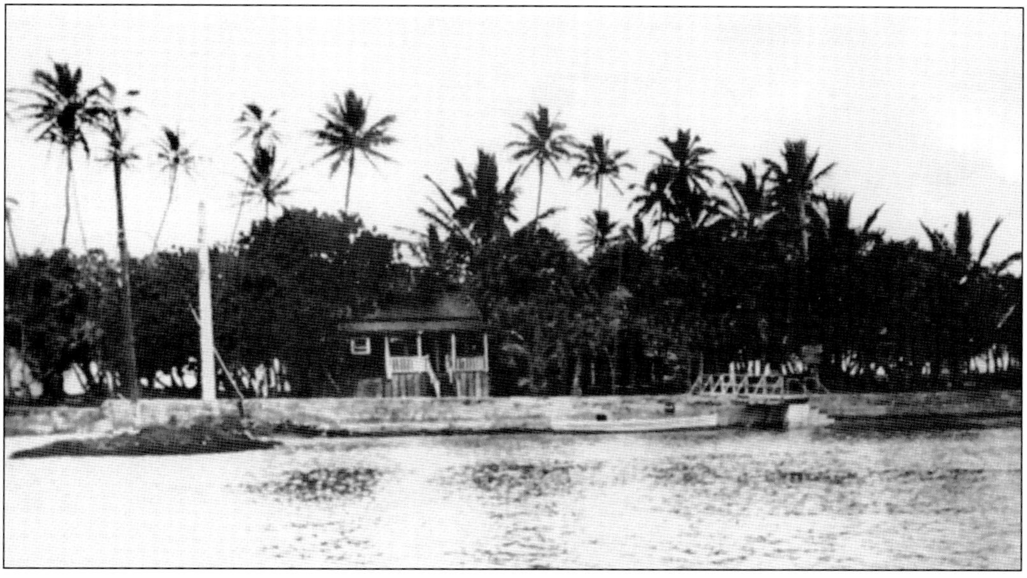

In 1909, Isaac K. Keliipio was hired as the official caretaker for Coconut Island. He was allowed to ferry visitors to the island in a boat, charging 10¢ for adults and 5¢ for children. This photograph shows Keliipio's house at Coconut Island, surrounded by the coconut trees for which the island was named. Caretaking duties on Coconut Island remained in the Keliipio family for many years, even after Isaac's death. (Courtesy of Memories of Hawai'i–Big Island.)

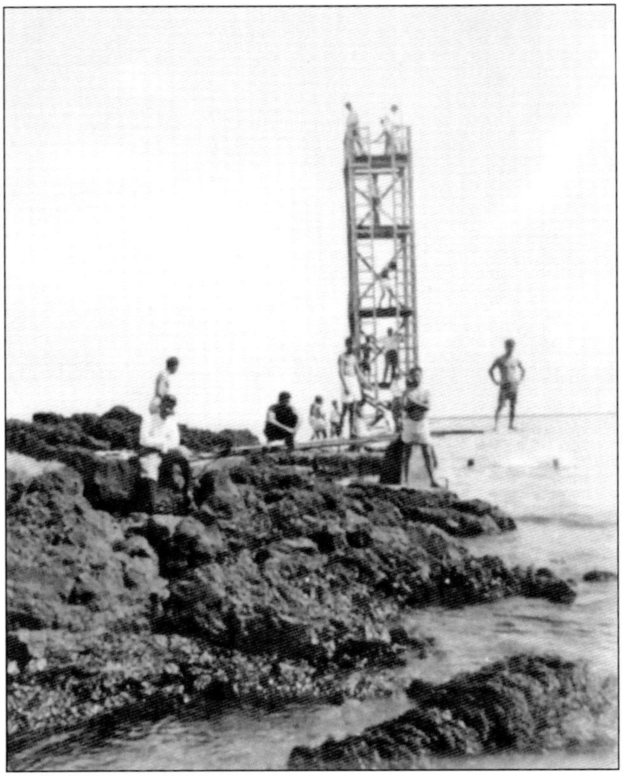

In 1900, the Hilo Swimming Club petitioned the government to designate Moku Ola (Coconut Island) as a recreation area for the first time. Swimming facilities including a bathhouse and diving boards were built. In 1910, a 30-foot-high wooden diving tower was built with platforms at 5-foot, 14-foot, and 30-foot levels. After it was destroyed in the tsunami of 1923, a stone tower was built with two levels, steps, springboards, and railings. At the beginning of World War II, the military took control of Coconut Island, and the Navy used this tower to train troops in amphibious warfare. (Courtesy of Memories of Hawai'i–Big Island.)

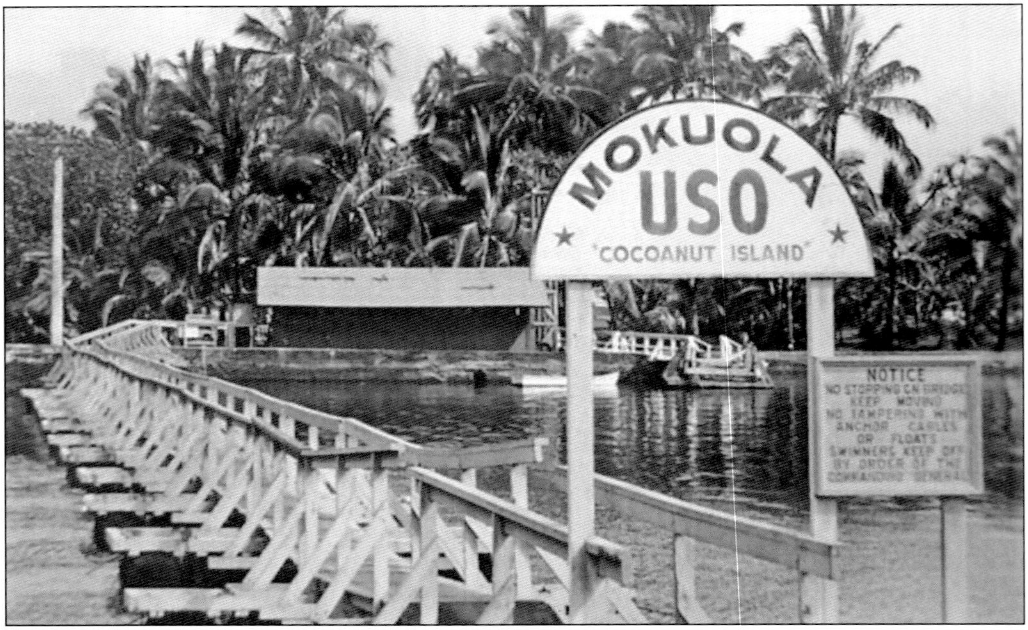

During the war, the island was restricted to military personnel. On two days per week, however, lady friends of servicemen were allowed to visit the USO, which was accessed by a pontoon bridge, the first bridge to the island. During the occupation, a new pavilion, showers, and restrooms were built. The military gave the island back to the county in 1945. (Courtesy of Memories of Hawai'i–Big Island.)

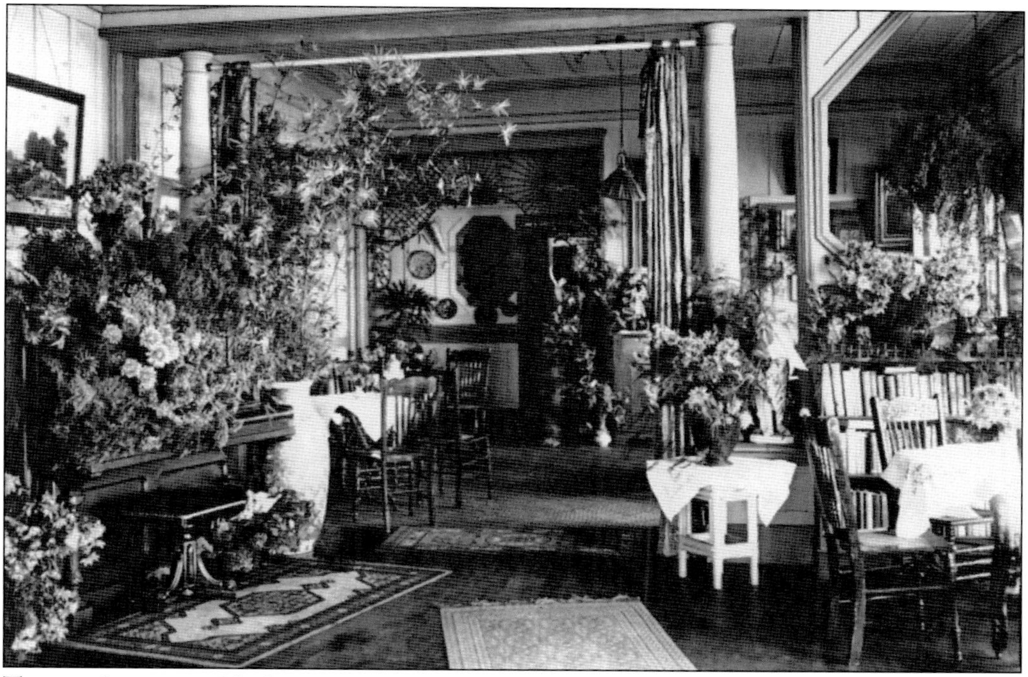

The grand interior of the home of Mr. and Mrs. Luther Severance is shown here. Severance served as Hilo's postmaster (1870–1884), sheriff, and various other civic appointments. Perhaps fittingly, his elegant home was located on the site of today's Federal Building and US Post Office. He and Mrs. Severance hosted prominent guests in their home and operated the house commercially as a "select boarding establishment" with "baths on the premises." (Courtesy of Lyman Museum.)

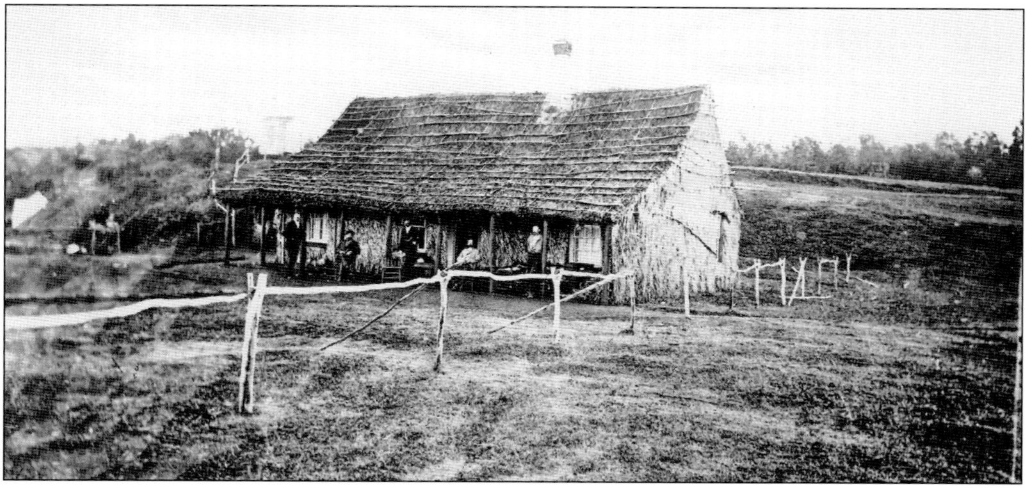

Enterprising Hilo businessman Benjamin Pitman built the first "hotel" on the island—on the rim of Kīlauea Volcano—in 1846. The earliest incarnation of today's Volcano House, it was only a one-room grass shelter, and the attraction of the volcano was its major draw. A more substantial wood-frame structure was built in 1866, with four bedrooms, parlor, and dining room. Mark Twain stayed here and wrote about his visit in the book *Roughing It*: "Neat, roomy, well furnished and a well kept hotel. The surprise of finding a good hotel at such an outlandish spot startled me, considerably more than the volcano did." It was not until 1916 that a national park was established. (Courtesy of Hawai'i State Archives.)

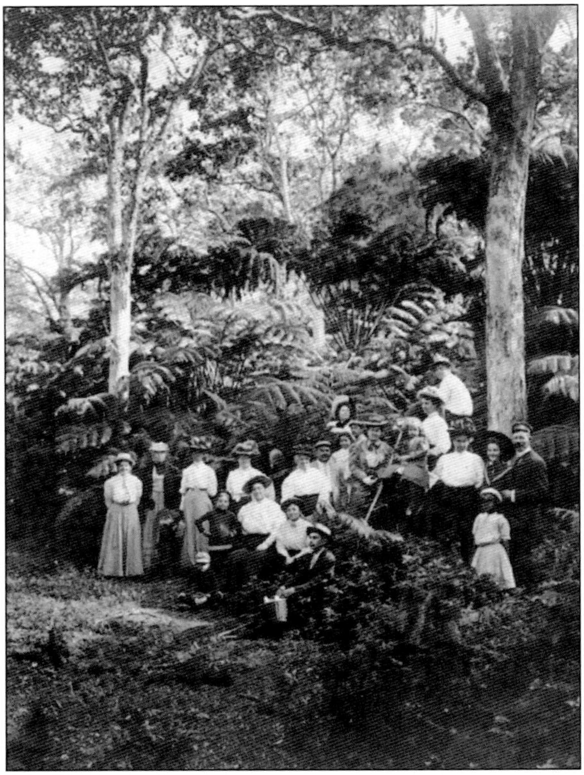

Several taxi businesses were started in Hilo to take people to see the volcano. The first was owned by John Maa, who billed himself as a "native volcano guide, expressman," with "first-class saddle horses and mules for ladies and gentlemen." Here, a group of tourists takes a rest in a grove of hapu'u tree ferns. (Courtesy of Hawai'i State Archives.)

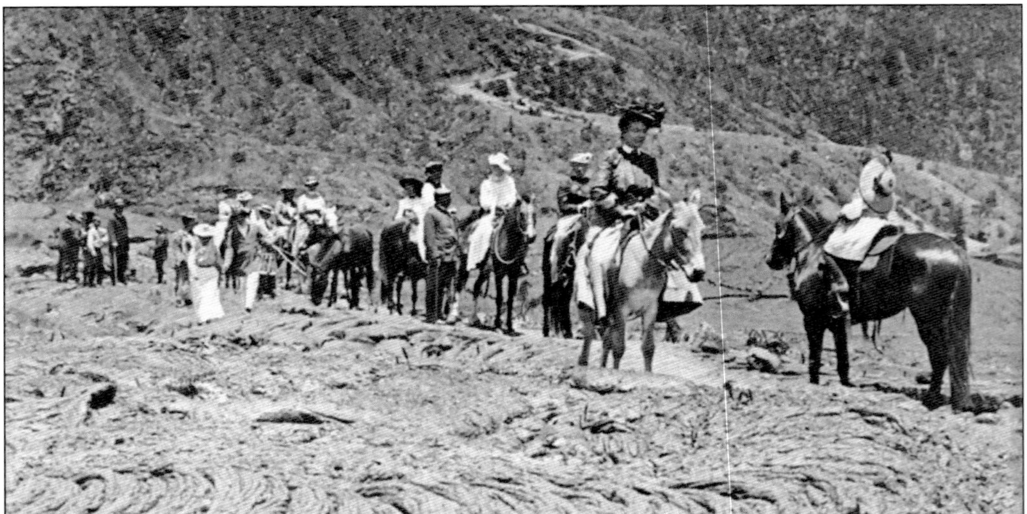

Kīlauea Volcano has always been the number one visitor attraction on Hawai'i Island. It was an adventure for tourists who rented horses and mules for the eight-hour ride from Hilo through dense 'ōhi'a and fern forests over a dirt road that was more often mud. The destination made it worth the trip, and many returned again and again, spreading the word to others. The missionary Titus Coan also described his many visits to the very active caldera during the late 1800s: "Its outer wall remains nearly the same from age to age, but all within the vast cauldron undergoes changes. I have visited it when there was but one small pool of fusion visible, and at another time I have counted 80 fires in the bottom of the crater." (Courtesy of Hawai'i State Archives.)

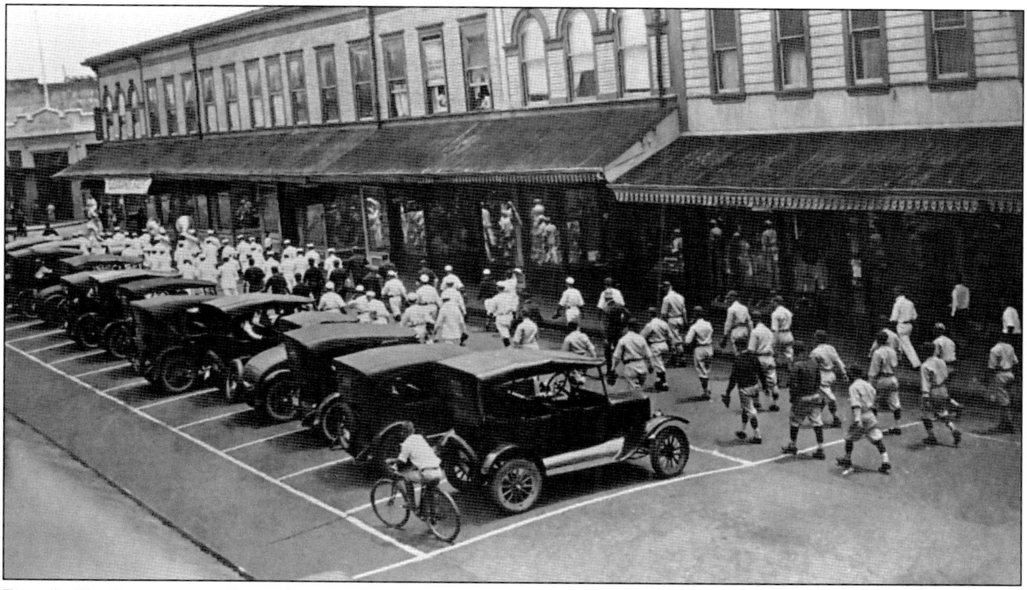

Baseball players march in front of buildings along Kamehameha Avenue with 1910–1920's cars in the foreground. In 1916, the names of streets in Hilo were changed by the Hawai'i County Board of Supervisors from names that identified businessmen or locations to new, Hawaiian names. For example, Front Street became Kamehameha Avenue, Volcano Street became Kīlauea Avenue, and Pitman Street was changed to Kino'ole Street. (Courtesy of Lyman Museum.)

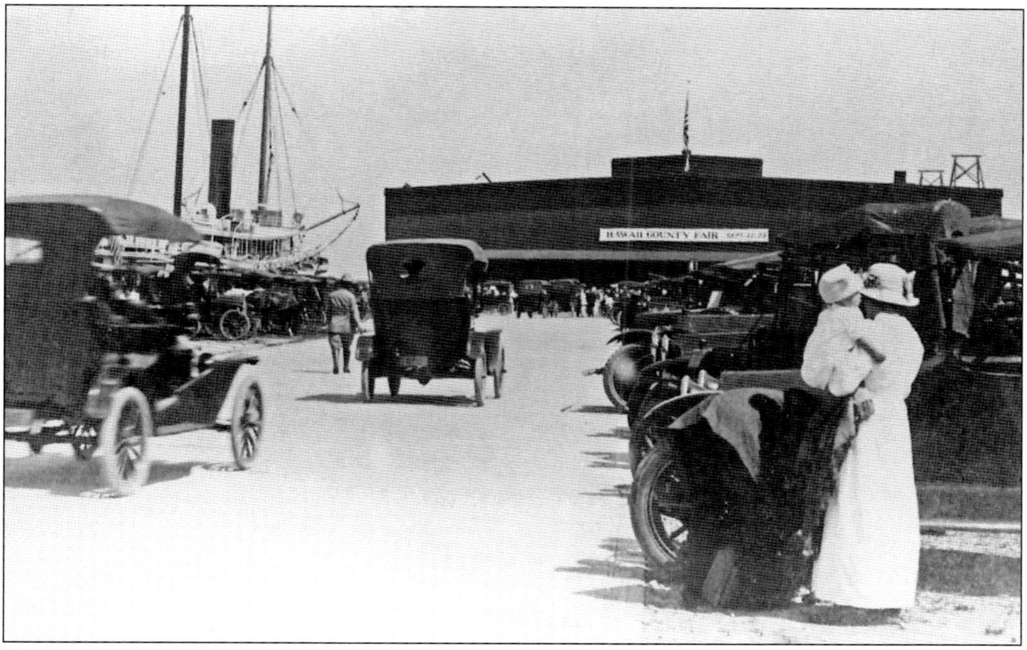

The first Hawai'i County Fair was held in 1914 at the Hilo Armory at Kūhiō Wharf with exhibits inside and out. Exhibits of agricultural equipment and new consumer products such as typewriters, sewing machines, and Victrolas were viewed by visitors from this island and others. Local farmers entered their animals and mothers entered their beautiful babies in the baby show. This photograph was taken in 1916 at the Hawai'i County Fair, held September 22 and 23. (Courtesy of Lyman Museum.)

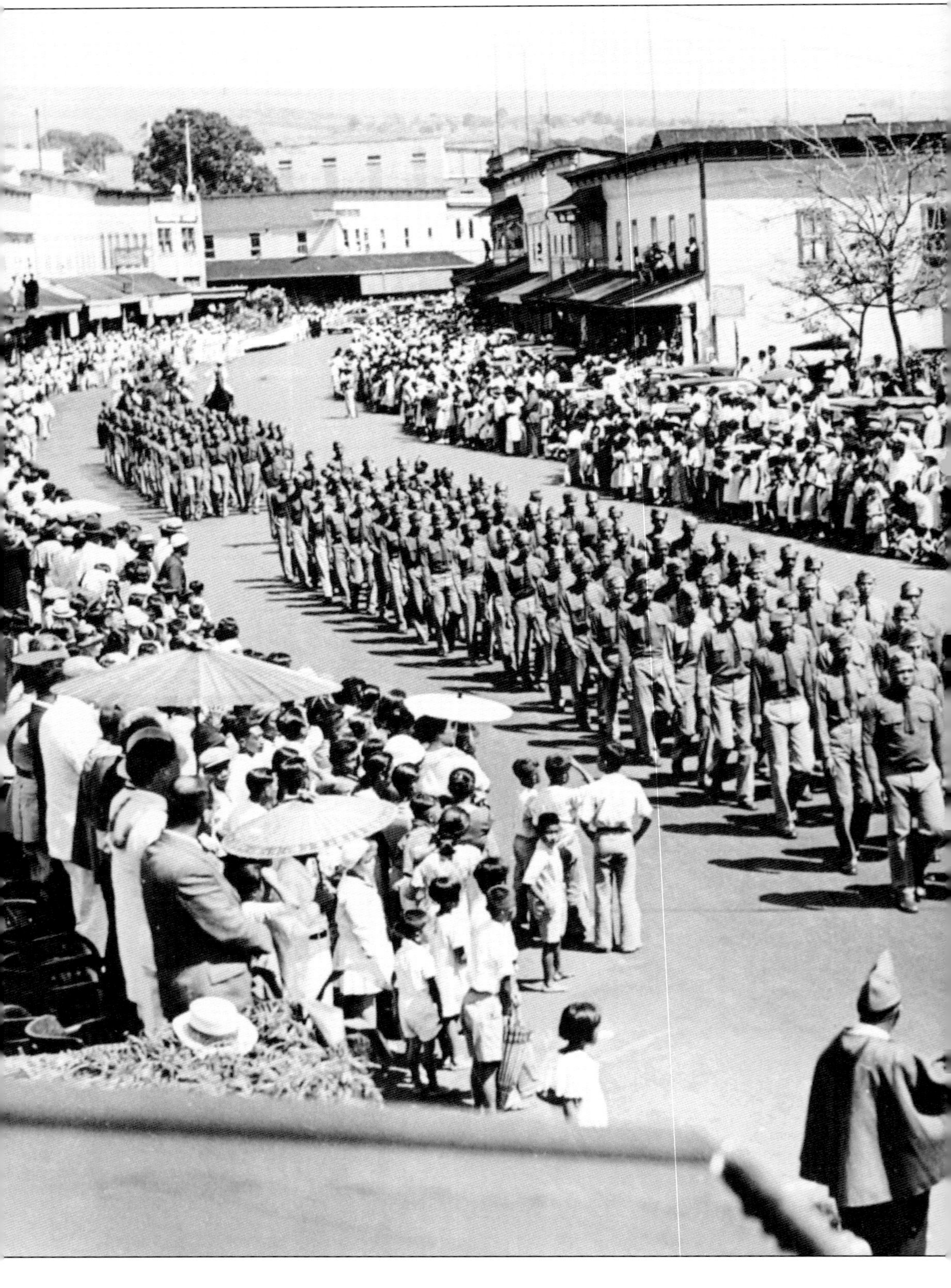

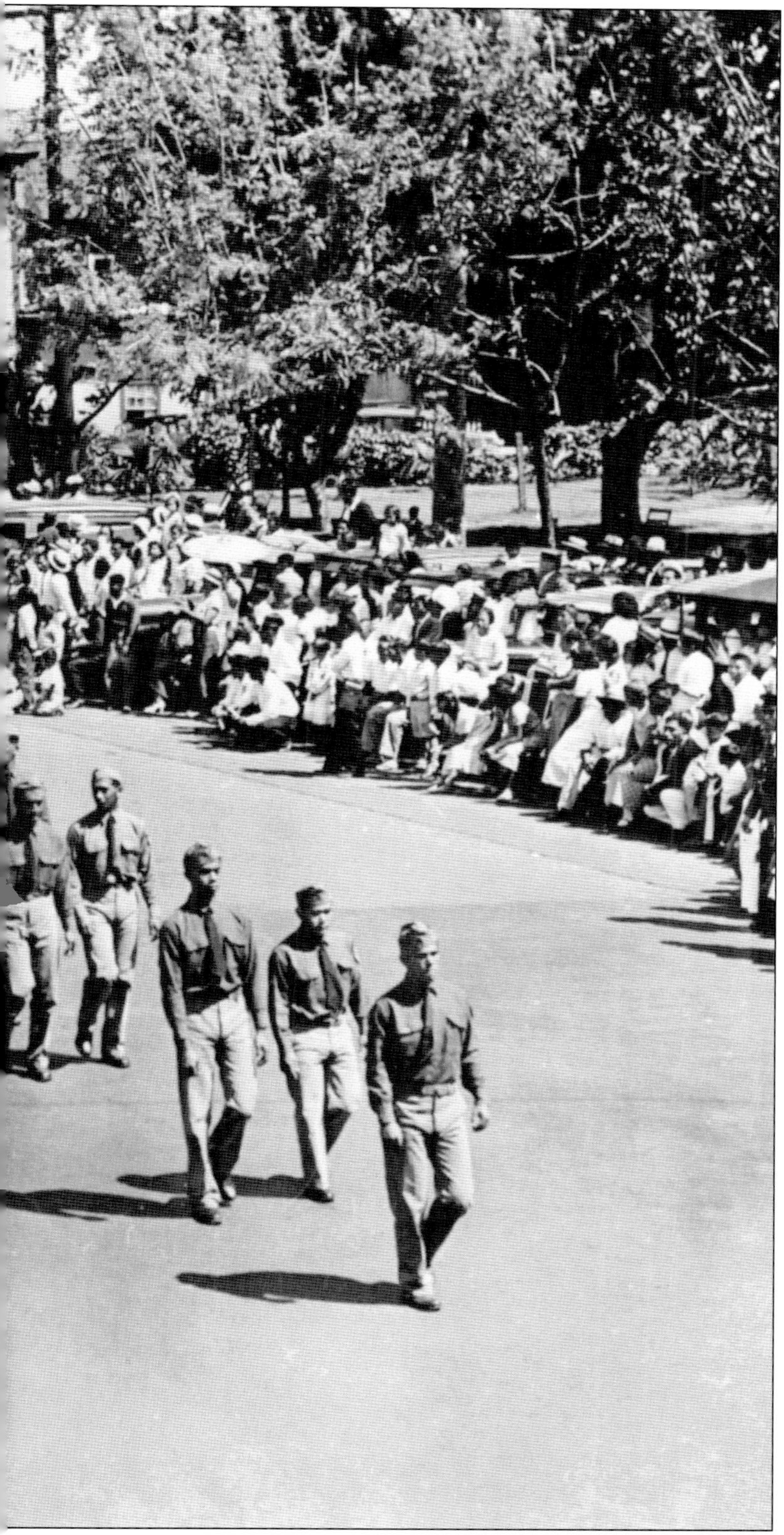

Enrollees for the Civilian Conservation Corps (CCC) march in the Kamehameha Day Parade through downtown Hilo in 1934. The CCC provided jobs for young men during the Great Depression. Construction projects such as roads, bridges, and other infrastructure were accomplished, including trails, walls, and dams at Hawai'i Volcanoes National Park. (Courtesy of Library of Congress.)

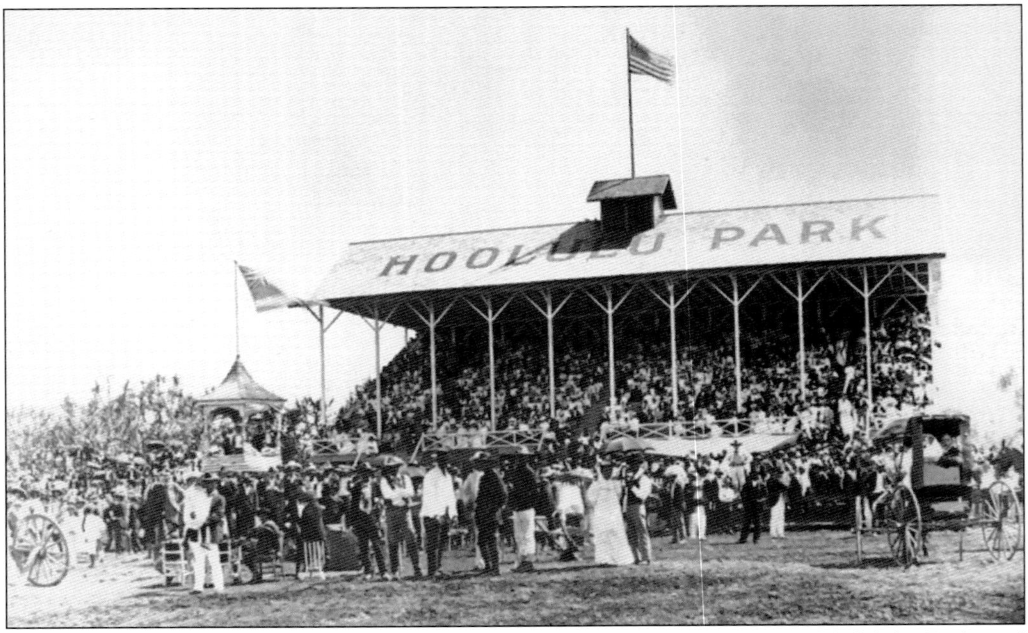

One of the finest recreational facilities in the Territory of Hawai'i was Ho'olulu Park and grandstand, shown here filled with spectators in about 1900. It began in 1900 as a horse track with a unique circular, half-mile loop and a wooden grandstand with a seating capacity of 1,000. It had stables for the horses and a pavilion in the rear for other events. It was demolished in 1913 because of rot and a new grandstand was built in 1925, with nighttime baseball games starting in 1928. In its place today is Edith Kanaka'ole Stadium. (Courtesy of Hawai'i State Archives.)

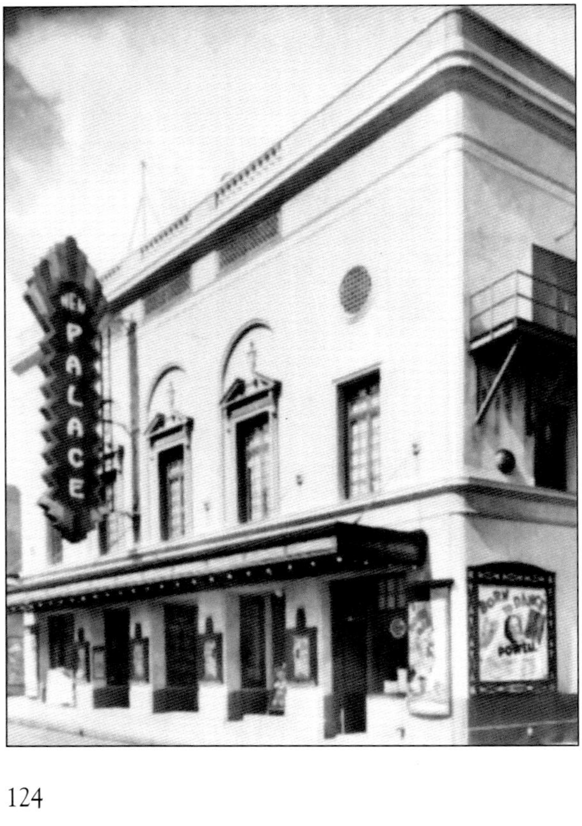

Downtown Hilo's Palace Theater, shown here during the 1930s, was built and opened in 1925 at the peak of the heyday for American movie palaces. The grandest theater in the neighbor islands at the time, the Palace was originally part of a small family of theaters owned and operated by Adam C. Baker, a well-known Hawaiian showman. One famous and popular event lasting from the 1930s to the 1950s was the Saturday morning Mickey Mouse Club, where children enjoyed watching cartoons and wearing mouse ears. It was a gathering place for all, and different nights of the week featured movies from different cultures; there was Chinese night, Japanese night, Filipino night, and so forth. It still shows films (mostly independent), and there are special events there, including concerts and a regular Wednesday morning show called *Hawaiiana Live!* (Courtesy of Palace Theater.)

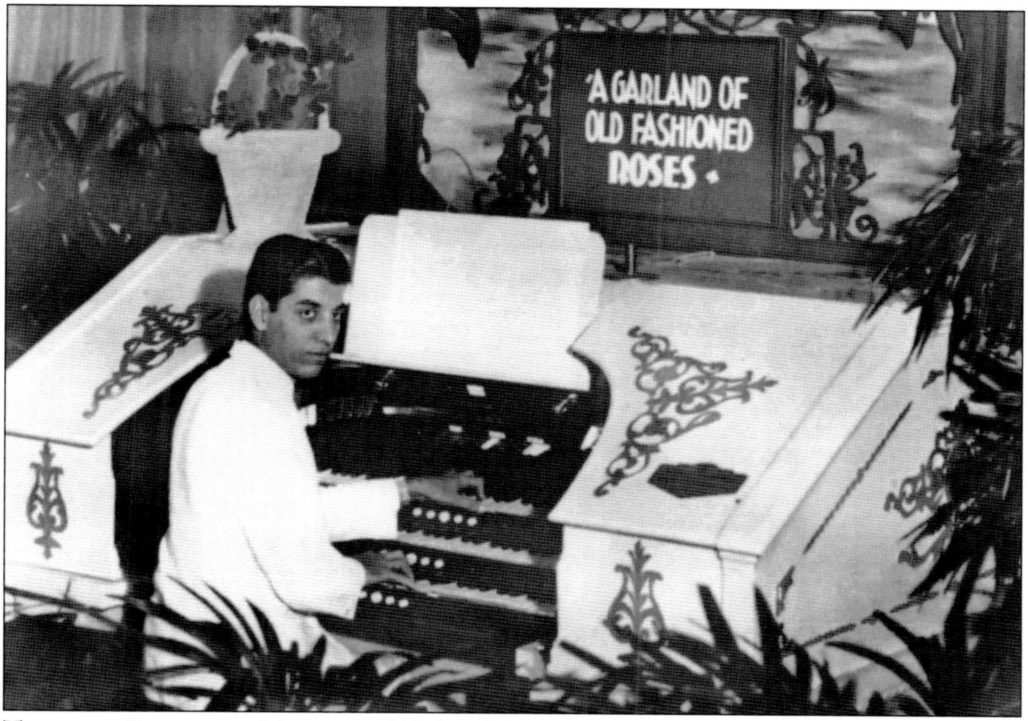

The resounding tones of the original Robert Morton pipe organ, played by organist and emcee Johnny DeMello (seen here in 1933), accompanied movies and concerts at the Palace Theater. The popular personality hosted the Mickey Mouse Club, staged many shows and musical revues, and had a weekly live radio show from the Palace. DeMello also wrote many songs that became popular during the 1930s and 1940s. He is best remembered for "Hilo After Sundown." (Courtesy of Palace Theater.)

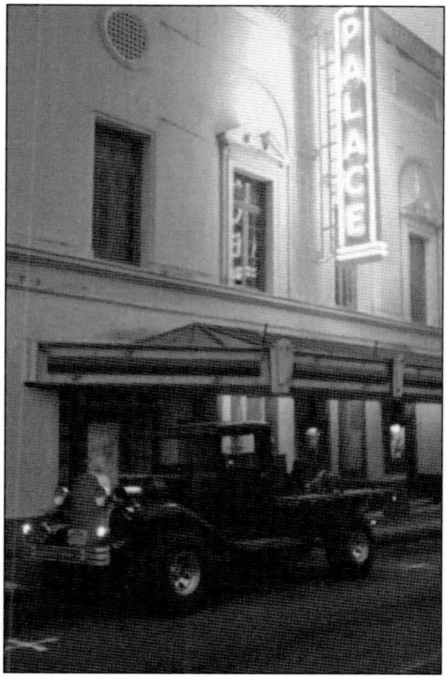

The Palace was built on a scale that had never been seen outside of Honolulu. The building's facade is an elegant, neoclassical design executed in stucco with wood molding accents. The original stadium seating arrangement on a sloped floor, predating stadium seating in modern theaters, accommodated 800 seats. The building was constructed entirely of redwood imported from the Pacific Northwest. It was the last theater to use a carbon-arc film projector, lasting until a major restoration was undertaken in 2003. Consolidated Amusement Company of Honolulu bought the Palace in the 1930s. (Courtesy of Palace Theater.)

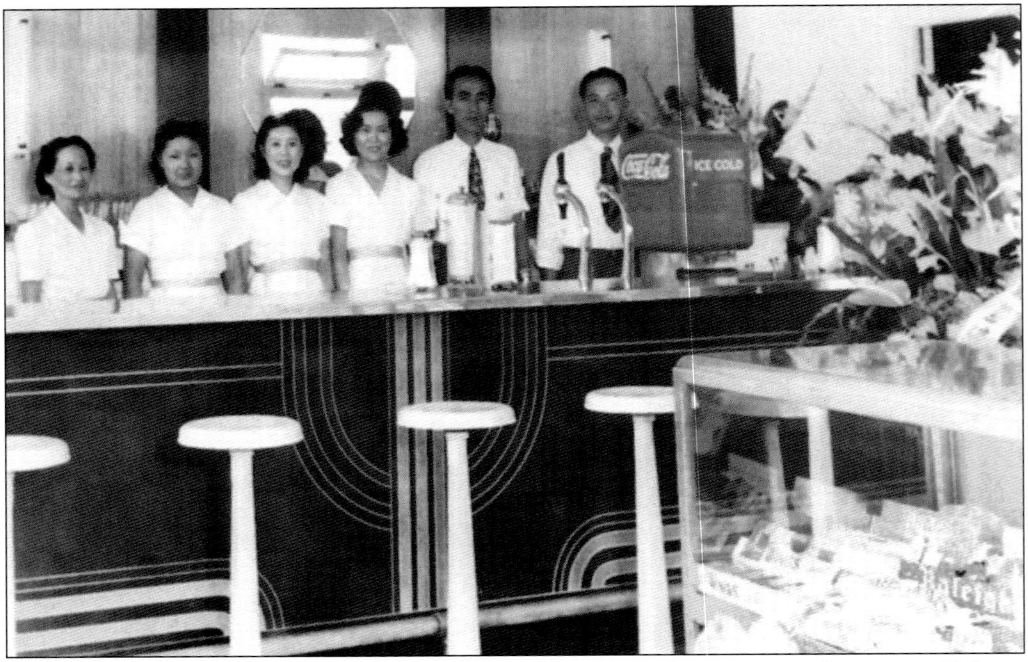

The grand opening of Elsie's Fountain, a famous and popular soda fountain on the corner of Mamo and Keawe Streets in downtown Hilo, was held on October 17, 1940. From left to right are the fountain's namesake Elsie Shinohara, wife of the owner; unidentified; Doris Murakami; Betsy Miyagi; owner James Shinohara; and Robert T. Tanaka. The latter worked for the company that installed the latest in equipment, a modern Bastian Blessing soda fountain. Elsie's served many servicemen during World War II, when Mamo Street was a hub of the entertainment district with several theaters, bars, and restaurants. The soda fountain stayed open until 2:00 or 3:00 a.m. to serve the patrons strolling around during all hours of the night. The store also sold drugs, toiletries, cosmetics, and candies. It operated under the ownership of Shinohara until 1998.

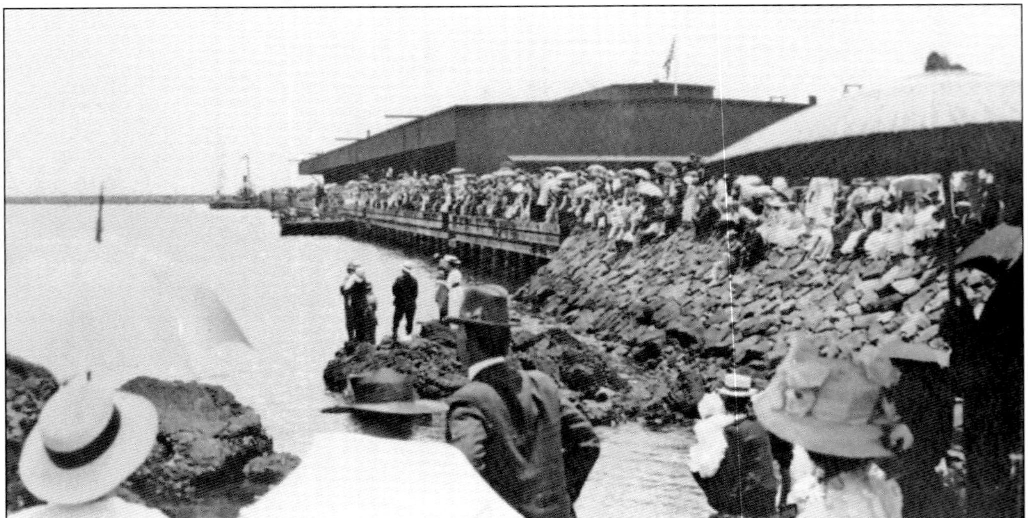

Boat races became popular right after the completion of the new Kūhiō Wharf. Rowing teams from the Hilo Yacht Club and other islands participated. These spectators are gathered here for a race on July 4, 1916. (Courtesy of Lyman Museum.)

Bibliography

Cahill, Emmett. *The Shipmans of East Hawai'i*. Honolulu: University of Hawai'i Press, 1996.

Coan, Titus. *Life in Hawai'i, An Autobiographic Sketch of Mission Life and Labors*. New York: Anson D.F. Randolph & Company, 1882.

Ellis, William. *A Narrative of an 1823 Tour Through Hawai'i*. Honolulu: Mutual Publishing, 2004. First published 1825 by Crocker & Brewster.

Handy, E.S. Craighill, Elizabeth Green Handy, and Mary Kawena Pukui. *Native Planters in Old Hawaii, Their Life, Lore, & Environment*. Rev. ed. Honolulu: Bishop Museum Press, 1991.

Kamakau, S.M. *Ruling Chiefs of Hawaii*. Rev. ed. Honolulu: Kamehameha Schools Press, 1992.

Lili'uokalani. *Hawai'i's Story by Hawai'i's Queen*. Honolulu: Mutual Publishing, 1990. First published 1898 by Lee and Shepard.

Nordyke, Eleanore C. *The Peopling of Hawai'i*. 2nd ed. Honolulu: University of Hawai'i Press, 1989.

Piercy, LaRue W. *Hawaii's Missionary Saga, Sacrifice and Godliness in Paradise*. Honolulu: Mutual Publishing, 1992.

Rogers, Capt. Richard W. *Shipwrecks of Hawai'i, A Maritime History of the Big Island*. Haleiwa, HI: Pilialoha Publishing, 1999.

Subica, Wayne A. *Moms & Pops Before Wal-Marts & K-Marts, Volume I*. Hilo: Memories of Hawai'i Big Island, 2006.

———. *Moms & Pops Before Wal-Marts & K-Marts, Volume II*. Hilo: Memories of Hawai'i Big Island, 2009.

———. *Moms & Pops Before Wal-Marts & K-Marts, Volume III*. Hilo: Memories of Hawai'i Big Island, 2010.

———. *Hawai'i Sugar Days, Working & Growing up with Sugar*. Hilo: Memories of Hawai'i Big Island, 2013.

Warshauer, Kent and Pauline Lilinoe Keliipio-Young. *"Mokuola" Legend & History of Coconut Island, Keliipio Ohana (1909-1960)*. Hilo: Memories of Hawai'i–Big Island, 2011.

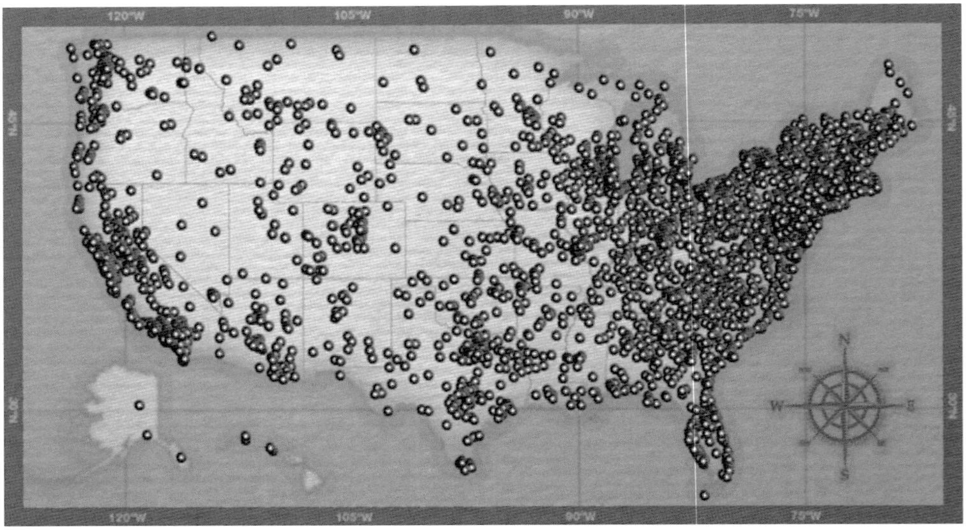